Soul Care

Soul Care

How to Plan and Guide Inspirational Retreats

Compiled and edited
by Rose Mary Stutzman

Herald Press

Scottdale, Pennsylvania
Waterloo, Ontario

Library of Congress Cataloging-in-Publication Data
Soul care : how to plan and guide inspirational retreats / compiled
and edited by Rose Mary Stutzman.
   p. cm.
Includes bibliographical references.
  ISBN 0-8361-9260-5 (pbk. : alk. paper)
  1. Spiritual retreats—Mennonites. I. Stutzman, Rose Mary, 1950-
BV5068.R4S66 2003
269'.6—dc22

                                           2003017892

Scripture quotations are from the *New Revised Standard Version Bible*,
copyright 1989, by the Division of Christian Education of the National
Council of the Churches of Christ in the United States of America. All
right reserved.

Permission is granted to make copies of all pages marked Handout.
You may also make copies of the schedule directly from the book and
of specially marked pages in the appendices. Please follow copyright
regulations on all other material in this book.

*To Mervin, my husband and spiritual companion,
and to my children, Karl, Dan, and Kathy,
through whose creativity and wisdom
I experience God's love.*

Contents

Foreword

In the morning, while it was still very dark,
Jesus got up and went out to a deserted place,
and there he prayed.
Mark 1:35

"Get-away weekends" have become an increasingly popular feature of the American travel scene. Promising peace and quiet and a balm for stressed-out souls, the travel industry lures individuals and families to river or lakeside cottages or to quaint bed-and-breakfasts in unspoiled small towns or countryside for a few days of rest and leisure. Unfortunately, the respite provided by such jaunts is often short-lived. A day or two back into the routine can undo even the most restful get-away weekend.

The retreats Jesus experienced in the midst of his life of ministry had quite a different result. Whether they were early morning solitary encounters with God or nighttime boat rides with his disciples, these times apart became an oasis for the soul. They renewed Jesus' own relationship with God and with his close-knit community. A strengthened and refreshed sense of call supported his return to the arduous, often demanding, ministries of teaching and healing.

The church has always recognized the value of time apart. Caught up in the hectic routines of daily life, Christians can easily lose their vision for God's priorities. Weakened by stress or simply fatigued, once-ebullient Christians can become ineffective servants, unable to share the love of Christ with winsome joy in the world. And though Sunday worship is meant to be a regular "retreat" for Christians, a longer time apart is sometimes necessary to renew and restore the soul. Fortunately for the health of the church, many congregations are seeing the benefits of regularly scheduled retreats and are incorporating such events into the congregation's calendar.

A good retreat, however, is more than "getting away from it all." And that is the purpose of the thoughtfully designed retreats to be found in this guidebook. Little good is served if people simply get away and have a mountaintop spiritual experience but are not equipped for sustaining this vital connection with God upon their return to active life. In other words, the purpose of the retreats found in this book is *formative*. Not only do they guide people into meaningful encounters with God while on retreat, they introduce practices, which, if pursued, will continue to form and transform people in their journey to mature faith.

Sadly, many church retreats fall short of their potential. The commonly planned fellowship retreat typically offers time and space for renewing friendships but may not adequately re-ground those friendships in Christ. A youth adventure retreat may stretch muscles but not provide spiritual exercise. Even a Bible-teaching retreat may inspire participants but fail to equip them for hearing God speak to them in Scripture on an everyday basis. Consequently, Christians do not mature or thrive as they might.

To truly provide soul care, that is, to lead people to the oasis of God's renewing love and care, retreats must create a setting where meeting God is the central objective. All other goals of rest or fun or companionship must serve the main purpose of bringing people—alone or together—into God's presence. When that purpose is accomplished, then the miracle of multiplication occurs: rest and fun and companionship are deeper, more authentic, and more truly exhilarating because God's Spirit is enlivening each moment and each encounter.

Those who are drawn to retreat ministry will find everything they need in this guidebook. A first for Mennonite publishing (and perhaps even for publishing anywhere), this guide provides a comprehensive formation curriculum for every kind of retreat planned by churches. Writers who are knowledgeable in the field of spiritual formation have insured that these retreat designs provide for essentials such as: hospitable space, a leisurely schedule, imaginatively planned worship, thoughtful presentations, guided prayer and silence, opportunities for meaningful interaction with fellow believers, physical exercise, and deliberate preparation for the return to the active world. Offering a well-rounded approach to retreat activities as well as careful integration around a central theme, these designs provide a model or pattern for retreat planning that will spur the imagination of leaders as they develop their own retreat designs in the future.

Finally, congregations who use these retreat designs will find new life sprouting in their midst. When get-away weekends are transformed into spiritual retreats, faith will flourish. Just as Jesus was renewed for ministry by time apart with God, so Christians today can go away for encounters with God that will invigorate them to join God's loving, creative, healing work in the world with compassion and joy.

May this collection of retreats only be the beginning of a fresh moving of God's Spirit to revive and nourish the souls of God's people!

–*Marlene Kropf*, professor of spiritual formation and worship, Associated Mennonite Biblical Seminary

Preface

The word *retreat* was not a part of my vocabulary as a child. But I did indeed take silent retreats back a long lane at the edge of our farm. There I could look across a wide expanse of acreage that had been marsh less than a century before while a hundred shades of green surrounded me. Today, merely hearing the song of a red-winged blackbird brings back both that place and a deep sense of God's love. The two-week summer Bible schools I attended each year had all the markings of a topical retreat. It was a special time and place set apart to meet God. We sang, prayed, studied Scripture, and set beautiful bouquets of peonies in our midst. Both the annual summer Bible schools and my times alone with God on the rich black soils of northern Indiana profoundly shaped my faith in God.

Retreats have long been a part of Christian tradition in some form or another. More recently they have become an important renewal movement. Congregations recognize the important role of retreats in forming faith. Retreats also provide the time and space for transforming faith as believers grow and mature. Now, our teenagers go to youth retreats, many churches have an annual fellowship retreat, and congregational members attend contemplative spiritual retreats. Congregations, retreat centers, and camps plan many retreats every year for a wide variety of purposes.

How can leaders find help in planning retreats that will truly reach the spiritual needs of people? How can we make sure that the energy and time invested does not fall short of the retreat's full potential? This book seeks to answer those questions by bringing together retreat designs from a wide variety of experienced retreat leaders. It also presents templates and guidelines for you to plan your own retreat.

This retreat guide offers a holistic vision of retreat ministry. Its goal is to equip leaders of congregations, camps, and retreat centers to plan and lead spiritually transforming retreats. Each retreat seeks to orient the elements of a retreat around a single focus so there is a satisfying rhythm of quiet and action, individual and group time. The retreat designs are based on the premise that ministry and Sabbath must be kept in balance if we are to be spiritually healthy. It also presumes the necessity of both a personal and a communal encounter with God. It seeks to provide resources and ideas for the entire spectrum of retreats which congregations, church leaders, or camps typically offer.

This book was first envisioned by a group of people who met in November 2000: Brian Burkholder, Joan Yoder Miller, Janice Yordy Sutter, Ken Hawkley, and Marlene Kropf. It was their idea to solicit submissions from a wide variety of sources and invite an editor-compiler to bring those submissions together. Marlene Kropf, who currently heads the Office of Congregational Life for Mennonite Church USA, not only gave birth to the idea of a retreat guide, but has continued to nurture this guide with vision and insight throughout the compiling and editing process.

A special thanks to Rachel Miller Jacobs, who spent many hours contacting experienced retreat leaders. She gathered many of the retreat designs found in this guide and developed the format in which the retreats appear.

The retreat designs come from many leaders scattered throughout Canada and the United States. The contributors to this guide offer the rest of the Christian church a great gift of creativity and deep spiritual insight, which grows out of years of experience.

Retreat Planning Guidelines

This section will help you understand the format of the retreat designs found in this book and will also enable you to effectively plan retreats beyond the designs found here. Please note that each of the six parts of the book also has a template or grid offering specific suggestions for that category.

PURPOSE

Every retreat needs a single focus, a clear purpose.
- What are the needs of the group for whom this is being planned?
- How can we best communicate God's love and desire for wholeness to this particular group?
- What do we hope will happen as a result of this retreat?

MATERIALS NEEDED

Though this section comes near the beginning, you will probably form it last when planning your own retreat. The more complete your list, the more likely that you will be able to give yourself fully to retreat leading without last minute worries.

Note: Many of the retreats suggest using candles at some point. Consider using non-scented candles for those people with scent allergies.

SCHEDULE

Plan the schedule in light of your purpose. This section should be planned in tandem with the Retreat Activities section below. You will find yourself switching back and forth between schedule and detailed activity planning.
- Retreats should include both personal and communal aspects.
- Plan for the spiritual dimensions to flow into all aspects of life. Do not fall into the trap of separating the spiritual (i.e., prayer) from the non-spiritual (i.e., rest and recreation).

- Include even mealtime plans as a part of your focus.
- The amounts of time devoted to various aspects should reflect the purpose of the retreat. Contemplative retreats should have larger blocks of time devoted to solitude. If the goal is teaching and learning together, more time will need to be devoted to discussion. Different age groups have differing needs regarding structured and unstructured time.
- Remember to offer choices and to remain open to the Holy Spirit throughout the retreat. God created us in love and has a special plan for each of us. Sensitive retreat leading means remaining open to the unscripted. Be prepared to change the closing worship as the retreat unfolds.

GATHERING ACTIVITY

Pay attention to the transition from home and work to retreat setting. The gathering time helps with this transition and sets a tone of trust and welcome that will pervade the time together.

- What will help participants feel welcome?
- How do we communicate hospitality in light of our purpose?
- What would help people make a transition from their normal lives to this retreat setting?

RETREAT ACTIVITIES

Retreat activities are the detailed plan that accomplishes your schedule. The resources mentioned throughout this guide will offer you a wealth of materials for prayer activities, readings, and music that will be useful for planning retreats.

- What Scripture texts will meet the needs of this group?
- What visual elements, such as color, image, and symbol, illuminate the purpose of this retreat?
- What songs and hymns capture the heartbeat of this

retreat? And, how much singing is needed to accomplish the purpose of this retreat?

- What rhythms of community and solitude, free time and structured time, quiet and action should mark this particular retreat?
- How does the purpose affect meal plans? Does it call for the formal and beautiful? Something filled with fun and delight?
- How does the size of the group impact its effectiveness? Will you need to break into smaller groups so that participants do not get lost? Will you need to provide more individual time so that people do not feel smothered by the closeness of a very small group?

CLOSING WORSHIP

Create a plan that brings the symbols, thoughts, and experiences to completeness. Remember that people have been transformed by the retreat experience. Be sensitive to the new things that God is shaping in the lives of retreatants and be willing to change your closing worship if necessary.

- What will help people make the transition back into their normal lives?
- What blessing can you offer to mark the transformation brought by the retreat?
- What symbol can participants carry with them to remember and live in keeping with this sacred time?

FINDING BOOKS AND MUSIC MENTIONED IN THIS GUIDE

The retreats in this guide mention resources from a variety of authors and publishers. 1) Many items are available from the publisher of this book. See the list below. 2) All other books and resources are available on Amazon.com unless otherwise indicated. 3) In the few cases where a book or resource is no longer in print, the activity is optional.

Throughout this retreat guide you will find hymns mentioned in this manner: "God loves all his many people,"

HWB 397. *HWB* stands for *Hymnal: A Worship Book* and 397 is the number of the hymn. If you use a different hymnal you will need to locate a similar song that relates to the Scripture, theme, and mood of the retreat session. Many retreats mention playing instrumental music or quiet, meditative music. Choose from the list below.

TO ORDER FROM THE PUBLISHER

Resources mentioned in this guide published by Herald Press, Faith & Life Resources, Faith & Life Press, or Mennonite Publishing House are available via the Faith & Life Resources order line at 1-800-743-2484.

PRINTED MATERIAL

Faith Talk (packets of cards for faith conversations).

Freedom Fences: How to Set Limits That Free You to Enjoy Your Marriage and Family by Gerald W. Kaufman, et. al. Herald Press, 1999.

Jonah and God's Big Love: A Learning Experience for Adults and Children Together by Eleanor Snyder and Allan Rudy-Froese. Faith & Life Press, 2000.

Parents—Passing the Torch of Faith by John M. Drescher. Herald Press, 1996.

Parent Trek: Nurturing Creativity and Care in Our Children by Jeanne Zimmerly Jantzi. Herald Press, 2001.

Praying with the Anabaptists: The Secret of Bearing Fruit by Marlene Kropf and Eddy Hall. Faith & Life Press, 1994.

Teaching a Christian View of Money: Celebrating God's Generosity by Mark Vincent. Herald Press, 1997.

MUSIC AND RECORDINGS (all are available from Faith & Life Resources)

Hymnal: A Worship Book. Brethren Press, Faith & Life Press, and Mennonite Publishing House, 1992.

Abide with Me: More Hymns for Guitar by Tom Harder (Hymnal Masterworks Series)

Classical Guitar by Tom Harder (Hymnal Masterworks Series)

Hymnal Selections, Volumes 1, 2, 3. (Tape recordings only, sold separately or as a set.)

Christmas Sampler (Hymnal Masterworks Series)

Jubilee Songbook and Recording

Let All Who Thirst: Hymns for Piano by Lucia Unrau (Hymnal Masterworks Series)

Organ and Instrument by Shirley Sprunger King (Hymnal Masterworks Series)

Songs to Live By: Passing on Hymns of the Faith (Hymnal Masterworks Series)

Songs to Live By II: Passing on Hymns of the Faith (Hymnal Masterworks Series)

Solo Piano by Marilyn Houser Hamm (Hymnal Masterworks Series)

Note: *Hymnal Subscription Service* is a service available for congregations that have purchased *Hymnal: A Worship Book.* Back issues are generally not available. Any song suggested from this source is optional.

Church Leadership Retreats

The retreats in this section are designed to equip and empower church leaders for their ministries. Some relate specifically to pastoral work and others speak to lay leadership needs. "In our Western society, and in the church, we tend to focus on doing and accomplishing as a means to measure growth and results," says the purpose statement of one retreat. The alternative is "a more fruitful, restful rhythm." Whether the purpose of the retreat is contemplative (Learning to Be with Jesus), or team building (Church Agency Staff Meeting), or equipping for ministry (Come and See and Tending the Center), each of these retreats offers the possibility of deeper listening to the God who loves us and calls us to specific vocations. Each retreat offers rest, refreshment, and joy in the midst of serving God.

RETREATS IN THIS SECTION INCLUDE:
- Learning to Be with Jesus: A Retreat for People in Ministry
- Church Agency Staff Meeting: A Retreat for Dispersed Staff
- Planning Day: A Retreat for Pastoral Teams
- Soul Care for Teachers: A Mini-Retreat for Those Who Teach
- Come and See: A Retreat to Empower Lay Leaders for Christian Witness
- Tending the Center: A Retreat for Pastors, Elders, and Congregational Leaders

WHEN PLANNING A CHURCH LEADERSHIP RETREAT

Aspects of Planning	*Special Suggestions*
PURPOSE	Balancing ministry with Sabbath/rest and renewal Providing focused planning time Doing worshipful-work Building a team
SCHEDULE	Take into account the realities of schedules and responsibilities Give adequate time for solitude
GATHERING ACTIVITY	Build awareness of each other's roles in joint ministry Consider traveling together to the retreat Less get acquainted time needed than in most retreats
RETREAT ACTIVITIES	Include times of solitude before moving into working and planning sections May want to keep a group memory by posting newsprint sheets or writing on an overhead Remember to keep worshipful-work, worshipful
CLOSING WORSHIP	Often includes commitments and designating responsibilities

Learning to Be with Jesus:
A Retreat for People in Ministry

Contributed by Wendy J. Miller

PURPOSE

In society and in the church, we tend to focus on doing and accomplishing as a means to measure growth and results. The purpose of this retreat is to invite participants to enter into the more restful and fruitful rhythm into which Jesus called his disciples, a rhythm of coming to Jesus, spending time with Jesus, and of being sent out to serve.

This one-day retreat is for both those in ministry and for people discerning a possible call to ministry.

MATERIALS NEEDED

- Music: *Hymnal: A Worship Book* or other hymnals; CD player and recorded music
- Food: Sack lunches for the noon meal or provide a simple lunch; coffee, tea, water, juice, and finger foods for closing worship
- Copies: Schedule, Handouts 1 and 2
- Worship center: Table with green or brown/tan cloth, a tall pillar candle to be lit each time you pray to invite God's presence in these sessions; small votive candle for each participant to light during the closing worship

SCHEDULE

8:30 a.m.	Arriving and settling in
9:00	Gathering
9:30	Session 1 – Coming
11:00	Gathering to share one-on-one
11:15	Walk or rest
11:30	Lunch
12:30	Session 2 – Being Named
2:00	Gathering to share one-on-one
2:15	Session 3 – Discerning Gifts and Direction
3:45	Closing worship
4:30	Departure

GATHERING ACTIVITY

Welcome people as they arrive, and invite them to be seated. Explain that the day will include time spent together and in solitude, times for quiet reflection on Scripture, journaling, and prayer. Invite group members to introduce themselves by name, where they are from, and why they desire this day apart.

Distribute schedule. Take a few minutes to explain that each of the sessions will end with a time of silent reflection followed by gathering to share what they are experiencing. After the first two sessions, the sharing will be in pairs. The closing worship will provide a group sharing time for session 3. People may scatter for the silent reflection time. Demonstrate the music signal you will use to mark the gathering times.

Light the candle. Bring the day to God in prayer and invite the help and guidance of the Spirit of Christ throughout the day.

RETREAT ACTIVITIES

Session 1—Coming

Read Mark 3:13-18. Early in his ministry Jesus invited people to come and to be with him as he preached the good news. Those who followed were with him as he confronted evil, as he cast out demons, and as he healed the sick.

Mark's gospel tells us that Jesus formed a rhythm in his relationship with those who followed him, a rhythm of coming to him, of being with him, and of responding to him. He invited them to be with him on the mountain, a place where Jesus regularly went to pray in solitude.

Talk about our lives. We tend to focus immediately on responding to passages like Mark 16 and Matthew 28 that talk about being sent into the world. As followers and servants of Jesus, we are invited into the rhythm for our life and ministry that Jesus had with his disciples—coming, being with him, and then responding as he directs us on our inward and outward journey of ministry. Mark 3:13-18 gives equal attention in the Greek to coming and being sent. For Jesus, both were equally important. Spending time with Jesus puts us in a position to listen. Here, in this time apart, we learn to stop what we are doing, to turn aside, and to come and simply be with Jesus. Here we listen to what Jesus has to say to us. In this passage in Mark we are given some insight into what Jesus draws our attention to in both our inward and outward journey.

Read Matthew 11:28. In the time of solitude, bring your tasks of ministry, your personal needs, and your burdens. Lay them down in Jesus' presence. Notice how he receives what you bring. Then pay attention to how Jesus responds to you. Learn to simply be with Jesus.

Distribute Handout 1 for use during the reflection time. Leave and return in silence.

Gather quietly at the sound of the music and form conversation partners. Take turns listening to each other's experiences. Be sensitive to those who may not be ready to share their experiences.

Session 2—Being Named

Read Mark 3:13-18 together as a group. Note that after Jesus called the disciples he also named them. As Jesus does this naming, he pays attention to two areas. He does an inward naming, inviting attention and change, and an outward naming of gifts and ministry.

In this session we will pay attention to the inward naming. Note verses 16 and 17, "Simon (to whom he gave the name Peter); James son of Zebedee and John the brother of James (to whom he gave the name Boanerges, that is, Sons of Thunder)." Simon needed to know who he really was, hence his renaming. He may have thought he was already a "Peter," a rock, but Jesus knew that Simon needed to discover his own human neediness.

Talk further about Simon's inward naming. When Jesus invited Simon to take his boat out into the deeper waters of Lake Galilee (Luke 5:1-11) and let down his nets, Simon reluctantly agreed because he had worked those waters all night long and caught nothing. However, when he caught so many fish that his nets began to break, he fell at Jesus' knees and said, "Go away from me, Lord, for I am a sinful man!" Suddenly Simon is aware of his own weakness and inability, of his own sinfulness in the presence of this holy one. He reacts by telling Jesus to leave him alone. Then he will not be troubled by his awareness of weakness, inability, and sin. But Jesus stays, and says: "Do not be afraid; from now on you will be catching people." Jesus speaks comfort to Simon's fears, and gives him an invitation to stay with Jesus, to enter into ministry with Jesus. This is the inner work that Jesus does, naming that which is within us, staying with us, and inviting us to stay with him, and to enter into ministry with him.

Talk further about James and John's inward naming. Jesus invited James and John to attend to their anger. This anger could flare up under the cover of religious and prophetic zeal, as we discover in Luke's narrative (Luke 9:51-56). When the Samaritans did not want to offer hospitality, James and John asked Jesus if they should "command fire to come down from heaven and consume them." Again, this inner naming draws our attention to Jesus' concern about our inward journey.

Read Matthew 11:29. In the time of solitude, continue to be with Jesus. Hear his invitation to take his yoke and learn from him.

Distribute Handout 2. Invite participants to use the questions during their time of quiet reflection. Leave and return in silence.

Gather quietly at the appointed time and form conversation partners. Take turns listening to each other's experiences.

Session 3—Discerning Gifts and Direction

Reread Mark 3:13-15. Jesus also named gifts and direction for ministry during the time on the mountain. In Mark 6:7-13 and in Matthew 10:7-8, Jesus also includes the ministry of healing. On our outward journey, our tasks of ministry will always include:

•Communicating the good news of the gospel

•Being empowered to confront evil

•Bringing healing

Note the questions for session 3 on the previous handout. Leave and return in silence.

CLOSING WORSHIP

Light the tall candle and the votive candles. Have refreshments ready to serve to the group.

As the group eats together, invite them to reflect aloud on their experiences during the retreat. Give people permission to remain quiet but allow space for those who wish to speak. Use these questions to lead the sharing time.

In what way did you experience coming to Jesus, being with Jesus, and being named today?

What spoke to you in a personal way today?

Where do you sense this time of retreat is taking you?

At the conclusion of this time invite participants to consider how this time of retreat has reshaped their sense of call and ministry.

Close by inviting people to reflect on the place to which they are returning. Invite them to see Jesus there, greeting them, holding what is heavy for them to carry, and saying to them,

My yoke is easy, and my burden is light. Matthew 11:30

Remember, I am with you always. Matthew 28:20

Allow a few minutes of silence for this concluding meditation.

Sing "I heard the voice of Jesus say," *HWB* 493, or "How clear is our vocation, Lord," *HWB* 541.

Pray this prayer of benediction.

> Jesus Christ, the one who has called you and named you,
>
> now goes with you
>
> and will remain with you always. Amen.

Session 1

He went up the mountain and called to him those whom he wanted, and they came to him.

And he appointed twelve, whom he also named apostles, to be with him, and to be sent out to proclaim the message, and to have authority to cast out demons.

So he appointed the twelve: Simon (to whom he gave the name Peter); James son of Zebedee and John the brother of James (to whom he gave the name Boanerges, that is, Sons of Thunder); and Andrew, and Philip, and Bartholomew, and Matthew, and Thomas, and James son of Alphaeus, and Thaddaeus, and Simon the Cananaean. —Mark 3:13-18

Questions for Session 1

What did you discover yourself bringing to Jesus?

How did you experience being received by Jesus?

How did you sense Jesus responding to you?

Sessions 2 and 3—Reflection

"Come to me, all you that are weary and are carrying heavy burdens, and I will give you rest. Take my yoke upon you, and learn from me; for I am gentle and humble in heart, and you will find rest for your souls. For my yoke is easy, and my burden is light." —Matthew 11:28-30

Questions for Session 2

What do you experience as you agree to receive Jesus' yoke?

In what way is Jesus naming what is within you?

What keeps you from being at rest in your heart and soul?

Questions for Session 3

How has or is God calling you to serve within the church? Beyond the church?

In what ways do you communicate the good news? In your way of being? In your doing?

In what ways do you notice evil and feel led to respond to evil?

How might God wish to bring healing through you in the church and in the world?

Church Agency Staff Meeting:
A Retreat for Dispersed Staff

Contributed by James Waltner

PURPOSE

Denominational agencies and other church organizations often have geographically dispersed staff. Communication among them is often by phone conferences and e-mail exchanges. It is necessary to bring such a staff together at least twice a year. The primary purpose of a staff retreat is team building. Though this face-to-face meeting will also facilitate some program planning, high priority will be placed on staff members learning to know each other, appreciating each other's gifts, and empowering one another. The retreat should be held at a camp or hotel conference setting where meal service is available.

The retreat outlined here can be adapted for special circumstances. Particular attention should be given to welcoming and orienting new team members and to appropriate farewell and blessing of departing staff.

MATERIALS NEEDED

- Furnishings and room arrangement: A comfortable meeting room is needed where all can be seated around a table, but with room to move about and gather in smaller groups if needed.

- •Other: Hymnals; easel, newsprint, pens, whiteboard, or overhead projector
- •Worship center: Cloth and candle; other items as needed by staff members who are planning the worship
- •Prayer resources (choose one or more): *The Oxford Book of Prayer*, George Appleton, ed., Oxford University Press, 1987; *Prayer Book for Earnest Christians*, Leonard Gross, trans. and ed., Herald Press, 1996; *Words for Worship*, Arlene M. Mark, ed., Herald Press, 1995; *Celtic Prayers from Iona*, Phillip J. Newell, Paulist Press, 1997; *Proclaim Praise: Daily Prayer for Parish and Home*, Archdiocese of Chicago, 1995.

SCHEDULE
Day One

1:00 p.m.	Gathering, reconnecting, personal updating
1:15	Worship
1:30	Session 1 – Sharing "The Focus of My Work This Year"
3:00	Break
3:30	Session 2 – Sharing "What Nurtures My Soul and Energizes My Spirit"
4:30	Praying for one another
5:30	Dinner
6:30	Session 3 – Evening Activities

Day Two

7:30 a.m.	Breakfast
8:30	Morning prayers
9:00	Session 4 – Program Issues
10:15	Break
10:45	Affinity group meetings
12:00	Lunch
1:00	Reports from affinity groups
2:45	Break
3:15	Closing worship
3:45	Adjourn

Time adjustments may need to be made to accommodate travel schedules. If this retreat precedes or follows another meeting of the staff, for example with the board, it may need to be shortened to three blocks of time. Retreat participants should receive information about the logistics several weeks in advance. This should include a tentative schedule with invitation for staff review before the final agenda is made. Any assignments for reports or worship should also be received ahead of time.

GATHERING ACTIVITY

Reconnect and update each other. Since the staff is likely a group of people who already know each other, allow 15 minutes for informal interchange of this sort.

Three times of worship are suggested: at the beginning of the retreat, at the start of day two, and at the close of the retreat. *Hymnal: A Worship Book* is an important resource for hymns, readings, and prayers. Ask staff members in advance to lead the worship times.

RETREAT ACTIVITIES

Session 1—Sharing "The Focus of My Work This Year"

Each staff member takes five to seven minutes to share one, two, or three things they hope to accomplish this year as part of their work assignment. Discussion and counsel follow.

Session 2—Sharing "What Nurtures My Soul and Energizes My Spirit"

Invite each staff member to focus on his or her spiritual journey by answering, "What nurtures my soul and energizes my spirit?" This is an opportunity to share with others how we find personal refreshment in life, where we find hope, and how we experience healing.

Session 3—Evening Activities

Dedicate this time to relaxation, recreation, and fellowship. Possibilities include a meal in a nice restaurant, a boat ride, an evening walk, table games for those interested, and seeing a movie or video together.

Shortened schedule evening activity. If the retreat needs to be shortened due to other meetings and schedules, the group can meet from 7:00-8:15 to focus on program planning issues and to identify the most important items for the morning agenda. Hold evening prayers at 8:15.

Session 4—Program Issues

Following morning prayers, the total group can focus on program planning issues. Brief staff reports may be shared about on-going or new program thrusts. Or the group might focus on denominational issues and how their particular area best serves the wider church. Sometimes staff members wish to address denominational leaders or see the need for networking with other agencies on a program. At the beginning of day two it is also important to check what adjustments need to be made in regard to the schedule and agenda.

Affinity group meetings allow for two, three, or more staff members to work together on a specific area of concern. Some staff members may also choose to work alone during this time period.

Following lunch, the entire group meets for reports from affinity group meetings and to continue work with program issues. As the time for closure nears, it is helpful to summarize major topics of discussion, directions suggested, and assignments identified. Note significant future calendar dates that involve the staff.

The close of this session should reflect the Spirit's movement throughout the retreat. One idea is to close with a brief round of sharing by completing one of the following sentences:

My hope for the church is _____.

My hope for our denomination is _____.

One thing I will carry with me from this staff retreat is

_____.

CLOSING WORSHIP

The closing worship should not be short-changed. Here the group celebrates together God's gift of the church and the gifts that staff bring to the church. Hymns of thanksgiving, affirmation from the Scriptures, and prayers of intercession are appropriate. The closing worship may also be a time when group members bless one another for their work.

Formal minutes are not necessary. However it is very helpful if someone has been designated to take notes and gather up ideas recorded on the whiteboard and newsprint throughout the program planning and sharing sessions. A copy of these can then be shared with each staff member to foster a common memory of the staff retreat.

Planning Day:
A Retreat for Pastoral Teams

Contributed by James Waltner

PURPOSE

Strong and effective pastoral teams do not just happen. They develop when the team relationship is nurtured. A new pastoral team will do well to invite outside resource people for help in team development and for understanding the personalities and work styles of the people who make up the team.

This planning day retreat is designed for a team already in place. Such a retreat can help pastoral team members who already know each other and have worked together to get in touch with and nurture each other at a deeper level. A planning day also provides opportunity to draw apart from the multitude of daily tasks to give creative energy to long range planning together.

MATERIAL NEEDS

- Furnishings and room arrangement: A small meeting room or lounge with comfortable chairs
- Resources: Bibles, hymnals, a list of lectionary readings (lectionary readings are available in various forms on the Internet; search for "Common Lectionary")
- Food: Arrange for a noon meal at the retreat center or for staff members to bring items for the meal; provide water, coffee, tea, juice, and healthful snacks for break
- Other: Newsprint, colored pens, tape, easel, paper

SCHEDULE

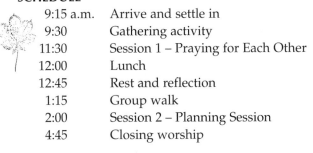

9:15 a.m.	Arrive and settle in
9:30	Gathering activity
11:30	Session 1 – Praying for Each Other
12:00	Lunch
12:45	Rest and reflection
1:15	Group walk
2:00	Session 2 – Planning Session
4:45	Closing worship

Day and Site Selection. If at all possible, a planning day retreat should be held when not only the day but also the evening is free. A work commitment for the evening, such as a committee meeting or counseling session, intrudes into the freedom needed for an effective planning day. Arrangements should be made in advance for emergency pastoral care coverage so the pastoral team is free from interruptions. Let the congregation know about Planning Day and invite their prayer support.

Church camps or retreat centers provide an appropriate setting. The retreat could also be held in the home of a team member where no other family members are present. Such a setting is possible at no cost but is less desirable because of potential interruptions, the familiarity of the setting, and distraction of the host pastor with hospitality tasks. A 30- to 60-minute drive together to the retreat site provides additional opportunity for staff conversation and interaction.

GATHERING ACTIVITY

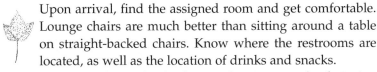

Upon arrival, find the assigned room and get comfortable. Lounge chairs are much better than sitting around a table on straight-backed chairs. Know where the restrooms are located, as well as the location of drinks and snacks.

The pastoral team leader focuses this time together by using Scripture, words of a hymn, and prayer. This does not need to be an extended worship time but should help the team members open themselves to the promise of the day.

RETREAT ACTIVITIES
Session 1—Praying for Each Other

Sharing with each other. The morning time will be given to connecting with each other's lives. Even though pastoral team members may see one another almost daily, they may not know what is happening in each other's lives because so much of this interaction is task oriented. If the team includes people serving part-time, there is often very little opportunity for sharing at a deeper level.

Depending upon how many people are involved, plan to give 15-30 minutes to each person to tell about their work, their family, what they are reading and thinking about, what gives them joy, and what makes them anxious. Team members need to know in advance that there will be such a time of sharing. When a person has finished speaking, other team members may ask questions or respond. Not everyone will use the same amount of time, nor will the time of interaction afterward be the same.

Pray for each other. Adequate time should be left to pray for each other before noon. This could be conversational prayer in which short prayers are offered specifically on behalf of each team member. Or, there can be assigned prayer. For example, you may want to go around the circle with each person praying for the person to the right. Prayers of thanksgiving for celebrative experiences are as important as intercession for needs. Adequate instruction about how the prayer time will close frees people to pray.

Lunch

Lunch should be a time for relaxation and enjoyment of each other around the table. Alone time for rest, reading, or reflection follows. Take a 45-minute group walk before the afternoon planning session begins. Enjoy nature together. A leisurely walk provides an occasion to be playful. Listen to the birds, skip stones on the water, climb a tree, examine the leaves, play on the swings or teeter-totter as a group. The physical activity and playfulness bond us together and prepare us for creative work in the planning session.

Session 2—Planning Session

Worship planning. From 2:00 to 3:30 focus on the church year and the Sundays for the next six months. Ahead of time, print the list of Sundays for the next six months on newsprint. Block the seasons of the church during that span of time. What special days, what emphases and themes, have already been identified? Does the congregation use a worship theme for the year? If so, what sub-themes or series might be used? Is the lectionary used for worship planning? What topics do the Scriptures and the context of the congregation's life suggest at this particular time? What special activities might become part of each Sunday's service?

While the pastoral team will not have time to plan each service in detail now, an hour and a half of intense brainstorming in such a setting will make weekly worship planning easier for the next several months. Often ideas are generated that become part of future planning. Write down ideas on the newsprint sheets as they are shared. Organization of the ideas can come later.

Address a congregational life issue. Take the last 45- to 60-minute block to address one other issue in congregational life, such as organization, the missional thrust of the congregation, the nurture networks, or a pastoral care issue. Likely not more than one of these areas can be dealt with at the end of the day. However, at any given time in a congregation's life, some issues need attention. Identify the issue and talk together about how it might be addressed rather than trying to resolve it.

CLOSING WORSHIP

Summarize key elements of the planning session. Specific assignments should be identified.

A brief reflection by each person on "One thing helpful to me today . . ." can help focus what people will take home.

End the retreat with a prayer of gratitude. Offer the plans of this day to God.

The team leader or designee will gather the newsprint sheets from the planning sessions and commit to recording and organizing the ideas generated so copies can be shared with the other team members within several days. This draft can become the basis for further planning in regular staff meetings.

Eat a restaurant meal together on the way home, if evening and family schedules permit. This extends the bonding time and celebration of the planning retreat.

Soul Care for Teachers:
A Mini-Retreat for Those Who Teach

Contributed by Marlene Kropf

PURPOSE

Teachers are among the busiest people in the congregation. Creative, conscientious, and continually reaching out to others, they need ongoing refreshment in order to fulfill their call to ministry. This 3½-hour Saturday morning retreat can be offered any other morning, afternoon, or evening time slot at the church or at a camp or retreat center. It provides a time for teachers to, first of all, nurture their own souls with Scripture, prayer, solitude, and beauty. At the same time, it invites them to consider how they care for the souls of their students and offers models of prayer and reflection on Scripture for possible use in the classroom.

If you choose, the retreat can be extended to a full day. Though it has been designed for the autumn season, the retreat could be adapted for other seasons of the year. In order to make this day as nurturing as possible for teachers, do not ask them to bring food or other materials to the retreat. Everything should be prepared for them as simply and beautifully as possible.

MATERIALS NEEDED

Note: Though this retreat requires a lot of advance preparation, part of the purpose is to nurture, even pamper, the teachers for a few hours. Because they do this kind of preparation week after week on behalf of those they teach, it will be important to offer them a well-prepared and nurturing environment.

- Invitations: See below
- Food: A variety of muffins or bread, platters of fresh fruit, coffee, tea, and juice
- Copies: Schedule and handouts
- Music: *Hymnal: A Worship Book*, CD player, and recorded music
- Other: Paper and pens for writing, books, suggestions in retreat plan (Unless otherwise noted these are in print and can be ordered online or from a local bookstore. Prepare early for the list of books to gather is extensive.)
- Room arrangement: Low circular table for worship center around which comfortable chairs are arranged in a circle
- Worship center visuals: <u>Session 1</u>—rough textured tan or light brown cloth, colorful fall leaves, autumn colored candle; <u>Session 2</u>—silky rich brown cloth, several gardening hand tools, a collection of books on spiritual disciplines; <u>Session 3</u>—small spring-green cloth, small clay pots and crocus bulbs (or other bulbs of your choice) for each person, potting soil, plastic tablespoons; <u>Session 4</u>—flowing blue cloth, bright bouquet of autumn flowers in a vase; <u>Closing Worship</u>—filmy or shiny gold cloth, basket of small ornamental gourds (one per person)

Some ideas for meditation centers in four corners of the room: Beautiful candle on a simple cloth; a cross with a votive candle burning; sculpture or wood; an art print that evokes God's presence

SCHEDULE
Saturday

	8:30 a.m.	Gathering – Coffee, tea, juice, muffins, fresh fruit
	9:00	Session 1 – Resting: Let the Soil Lie Fallow
	9:45	Session 2 – Preparing: Amend and Enrich the Soil

10:30	Refreshment break
10:45	Session 3 – Planting: Scatter Good Seed
11:15	Session 4 – Watering: Tend the Growth
11:45	Closing – Harvesting: Gather the Crop
12:00	Close of retreat

Invitations to the retreat might include the above schedule and the following poem.

> Be a gardener.
> Dig a ditch,
> Toil and sweat,
> and turn the earth upside down
> and seek the deepness
> and water the plants in time.
>
> Continue this labor
> and make the sweet floods to run
> and noble and abundant fruits
> to spring.
> Take this food and drink
> and carry it to God
> as your true worship.
> —*Julian of Norwich*

GATHERING ACTIVITY

Welcome participants to a festive table spread with muffins, fresh fruit, and drinks as they arrive. A host greets each one personally and invites teachers to eat and visit with one another. Invite teachers to describe what they would typically be doing on a Saturday morning if they weren't attending a retreat.

When all have had a chance to relax, eat, and greet each other, invite teachers to be seated in a circle with a low, circular table in the center. Note that the worship center items for session 1 will have been arranged on this table ahead of time.

The meditation centers (see ideas above) are arranged on

small tables in the four corners of the room. Several chairs are located in front of each center.

RETREAT ACTIVITIES
Session 1—Resting: Let the Soil Lie Fallow

Just as trees shed their leaves in the fall and enter a dormant season, so those who are faithful, productive servants of God need to pause to rest periodically and be renewed. Talk about the rhythm of Sabbath and ministry and how a fruitful teaching ministry is dependent upon cycles of rest and productivity. See Tilden Edwards's book, *Sabbath Time: Understanding and Practice for Contemporary Christians* (Upper Room, 1992), for a helpful resource on the rhythm of Sabbath and ministry.

Distribute the retreat schedule. Explain that this retreat offers time and space for rest and for listening to God. Though it also offers models for praying and listening to Scripture that might possibly be useful for their classrooms, encourage teachers to focus first of all on their own relationship with God today. Let them know that all the suggested activities are just that, *suggestions*. If they are led in prayer in a different direction than the suggested ways, they should follow where the Spirit leads.

As a way of entering the retreat experience, begin with a few moments of silence, light the candle in the center, and read Psalm 46:10a aloud several times with spaces of silence between. If you choose, sing the song, "Be still and know."

Read the chapter, "Seeing," (pp. 155-158) in *Dakota: A Spiritual Geography* by Kathleen Norris. Then invite teachers to go outdoors and take a 20-minute walk. As they go, ask them to be silent and continue in a spirit of listening to God. They may want to meditate on James 5:7-8. They may also look for signs of rest in nature and come back with a symbol of rest to add to the collection of leaves on the table.

Play soft worshipful music as people return in silence. Invite each one to speak just one word or phrase that came to them in the silence or that describes the quality of their solitude.

Session 2—Preparing: Amend and Enrich the Soil

Visual environment. Carefully remove the worship center collection of leaves to a side table and arrange the items for session 2. Here are some suggestions for the collection of books on spiritual disciplines:

> *Soul Feast: An Invitation to the Christian Spiritual Life* by Marjorie J. Thompson.
>
> *Praying with the Anabaptists: The Secret of Bearing Fruit* (with an accompanying recording) by Marlene Kropf and Eddy Hall, Faith & Life, 1994. (Call the company directly for this product, 1-800-743-2484.)
>
> *Prayer: Finding the Heart's True Home* by Richard J. Foster.
>
> *Celtic Prayers from Iona* by Philip J. Newell.

Talk about the way gardeners pay attention to soil, adding compost, patiently hoeing and spading, amending and enriching the soil, making it fertile and capable of verdant growth. Spiritual practices can be understood as tools for working the soil of our hearts and lives. They prepare our spirits, making it possible for God's Word to take root and flourish. Explain that this session will provide an overview of several spiritual disciplines that can work the soil of our lives, enrich our relationship with God.

Read the poem, "Turn Over Gently," by Kathy Keay from her book, *Laughter, Silence and Shouting*. Introduce the books on the table and encourage teachers to examine them at their leisure. (If your church can afford such a gift, it would be wonderful to give a book to each teacher at the end of the day.) Distribute copies of "Praying the Scripture," "Consciousness Examen," and "Spiritual Friendship" (see Appendices), and explain that these spiritual practices are some ways Christian throughout history have nurtured their relationship with God.

Talk about listening as an essential spiritual discipline, a practice that keeps us in touch with God's voice and guidance in our lives and ministries. Note that listening can happen in a variety of ways: with our ears, our eyes, our bodies, our inner hearts. The following exercises offer ways of paying attention to the soil of our hearts.

Listening with our ears.

> Play a meditative musical selection on a CD and invite retreat participants to listen with both their ears and their hearts. Choose a piece of music without words. (A selection that works remarkably well is "Duet from 'The Pearl Fishers'" by Bizet on the recording, *Solitude*, by Zamfir, PolyGram Classics, 1979.) What is the invitation they hear? To what might God be calling them today? When the music ends, leave another brief space for silence. Then invite them to talk together in pairs about what they have heard.

Listening with our eyes.

> Call attention to the meditation corners, each prepared with a visual invitation to listen to God. Participants may choose one of the corners for a time of listening and prayer. After five to ten minutes, ask them to talk together in groups of two and three about what happened when they listened to God with their eyes.

Session 3—Planting: Scatter Good Seed

Visual environment. On top of the brown cloth place the spring-green cloth and the worship center items suggested for session 3.

Begin this session by singing the song, "We plow the fields and scatter," *HWB* 96. Read Matthew 13:31-32 and James 1:21. Talk about the teacher as a planter of seeds. With their skills, care, love, and guidance, teachers cooperate with God's desire to instill the living Word into students' hearts.

Tell the story of someone who made the stories or themes of Scripture come alive for you. Ask the group to reflect silently for a few moments on the question, "Who shared or shares God's word with me? Who made it come alive?" Emphasize that both formation and information are important goals of teaching.

Distribute Handout 1 and read the poem. Then play instrumental hymns on a CD. Invite participants to reflect silently on what God has planted within, and on their role as co-planters with God. Ask them to come to the table, choose a pot and bulb, fill the pot with soil, plant the bulb, and return with the planted bulb to their seats. Suggest planting the bulb outdoors when they get home.

Session 4—Watering: Tend the Growth

Worship center. Remove any remaining pots and bulbs. Arrange the blue cloth on top of the other cloths. Add the bouquet of flowers.

Read Hosea 14:5-6. Talk about the need for ongoing spiritual enrichment and renewal in our lives and give examples of ways this need can be met. Suggest that central to the teaching ministry is the call to be a spiritual guide in the classroom. As spiritual guide we offer prayer and teach others to pray, we listen to God and respond to God's Word. Discuss ways teachers can enrich the environment of prayer in their classrooms.

Lead participants in a prayer of intercession for those we teach. Teachers may pray together in small groups. Or lead in a guided prayer inviting people to imagine each student standing before Christ receiving a blessing. Ask God to supply what each student needs.

CLOSING WORSHIP—HARVESTING: GATHER THE CROP

Swirl the filmy or shiny gold cloth (or ribbon) around the vase and across the table. Add the basket of gourds.

To begin the concluding session, read Isaiah 55:10-13 responsively. (Distribute handout 2.) The leader reads the first stanza. The group reads the second stanza. Talk about God's faithfulness in bringing forth a harvest. Encourage teachers to trust God's goodness.

Pass the basket of gourds around the circle. Let each teacher choose a gourd that symbolizes hope for a bountiful harvest or some promise God has given today. Take a few minutes for people to speak briefly about what they experienced or received during the retreat. Offer a prayer of thanksgiving and blessing to conclude.

Handout 1

>God stir the soil,
>Run the ploughshare deep,
>Cut the furrow round and round,
>Overturn the hard, dry ground,
>Spare no strength nor toil,
>Even though I weep.
>In the loose, fresh mangled earth
>Sow new seed
>Free of withered vine and weed
>Bring fair flowers to birth.
>>—Prayer from Singapore Church Missionary Society

Handout 2

Harvesting: Celebrate a Bountiful Crop

For as the rain and snow come down from heaven,
>and do not return there until they have watered the earth,
>>making it bring forth and sprout,
>>giving seed to the sower and bread to the eater,
>so shall my word be that goes out from my mouth;
>>it shall not return to me empty,
>>but it shall accomplish that which I purpose,
>>>and succeed in the thing for which I sent it.

For you shall go out in joy, and be led back in peace;
>the mountains and the hills before you shall burst into song,
>and all the trees of the field shall clap their hands.
Instead of the thorn shall come up the cypress;
>instead of the brier shall come up the myrtle;
>and it shall be to the Lord for a memorial,
>>for an everlasting sign that shall not be cut off.
>>>—Isaiah 55:10-13

Come and See: A Retreat to Empower Lay Leaders for Christian Witness

Contributed by Elaine Maust

PURPOSE

The purpose of this retreat is to help participants become more comfortable and effective when talking about God's love with their friends. This one-day retreat will reflect on times we have heard Jesus' words, "come and see," through another person. We will then prayerfully explore who in our lives might be ready for a similar invitation to come and see Jesus.

MATERIALS NEEDED

- Music: CD player and recorded music; *Hymnal: A Worship Book*
- Furnishings and room arrangement: Comfortable chairs arranged in a semi-circle with a worship center table at one end
- Worship center: wispy green fabric, tall white candle, small round green candleholders holding unlit white candles
- Other: Bibles, paper, small slips of paper, pens or pencils
- Invitations: See the page after retreat plan for ideas; give schedules along with the invitation

SCHEDULE

8:45 a.m.	Arrive, visit, enjoy coffee and donuts
9:15	Gathering Worship – The God Who Goes Looking: Psalm 139:1-6, 13-18
9:45	Rest and reflection
10:30	Session 1 – Come and See: John 1:35-39
11:30	Free time
12:00	Lunch
1:30	Session 2 – We Have Found Him: John 1:40-42
2:30	Rest and reflection
3:00	Session 3 – Come and See: John 1:43-51
4:00	Rest and reflection
4:30	Closing Worship – The God Who Sends
5:00	Return home

GATHERING ACTIVITY

Welcome retreatants as they arrive. Point them to the coffee, juice, and donuts. Have the worship center prepared and the tall white candle lit. Play music or nature sounds softly in the background.

Thank people for coming. Assure them that God will meet them, though not necessarily with a dramatic experience. It may be in quiet ways. Take time to acknowledge the hassles they may have had in getting away from home. "You may feel like saying, 'God, you better do something impressive here today. You do realize, don't you, that I took off work, found a babysitter, studied my Sunday school lesson early, did not get the laundry done, negotiated with my spouse, gave up football. . . .' But whatever you brought with you today and whatever you left at home, God welcomes you here."

Describe the day. Give schedules again in case someone left it at home. Orient people to the retreat center, pointing out restrooms, trails, indoor rooms that will be open during the times of rest and reflection.

Pray for the group and this day of retreat. Express thanks for God's presence and for calling each person who came.

Read Psalm 139:1-6. God made us, knows us completely, and is always with us. Repeat verse six. Take a few quiet moments to remember how God has searched out our paths. Remember a time when God searched you out. Where were you? What were you doing? How did you need God to be looking for you? How did God lay his hand on you? Give time for silence, then read Psalm 139:5-6 again.

Prepare for the time of rest and silent reflection. Invite participants to think about a time when God searched for them: How did they know that it was God who spoke? At 10:30 we will meet again. The retreat leader can be available in the gathering room during each of these silent reflection times for anyone who needs spiritual direction.

Leave for the time of solitude and rest with this blessing, "May God touch you. May you remember God's kindness in your past. May God give you rest and peace. Go quietly now. Go in peace."

RETREAT ACTIVITIES
Session 1—Come and See: John 1:35-39

Light the candle again. We will be listening to a story about some people who were drawn to Jesus. Amazingly, the God who knows us also loves us, and wants to have a relationship with us. The Bible says, "the Holy Spirit draws us."

Read John 1:35-39. Ask five readers to take the parts of narrator, John, Jesus, and two disciples.

In groups of two or three, share one time when God called you into relationship in a new way. How did that happen? How did you know it was God calling you? What were you looking for? What were the questions and struggles?

Light the candles. Invite each person to take one of the small candles and light it from the large candle. As they hold their lighted candles, talk about how we grow to know God's voice. How do we listen so that it becomes like the familiar and beloved voice of a dear friend or family member whom we recognize immediately when they call us on the telephone? Psalm

103:7 tells us that God let Moses know his ways. Read John 1:39 again and note that the "disciples stayed with him."

Sing or read the words of "O Love that will not let me go," *HWB* 577. Invite group members to remember times when someone invited us to come and see Jesus by their lives and words. Who were the special people who helped you understand that God was speaking to you? Calling you? Quietly return the candles to the table and blow them out.

Session 2—We Have Found Him: John 1:40-42

Light the large candle and begin by singing one verse of "O Love that will not let me go."

Read John 1:40-42 with readers assigned to be narrator, Andrew, and Jesus. Who served as Andrew in your life? What did you appreciate or not appreciate about the way the invitation was given? Pray sentence prayers of gratitude for those who became God's messengers in our lives. As each person prays, they light a candle from the larger candle. Set all the candles on the worship center and leave them burning as you talk about evangelism.

Share perspectives about evangelism by comparing to the experiences people have just described. Some concepts and facts include:

- •Only 2 percent of North Americans are comfortable talking about their faith with their best friends.
- •Most people come to faith or start attending church because of an invitation from a friend.
- •"To help a person become conscious of Christ and to respond to that person is, after all, what evangelism is all about." (Ben Campbell Johnson)
- •"I think we do a disservice to God and others if we begin our evangelism conversations by quoting Scripture or by trying to raise someone's awareness of sin. Why not listen to how God is acting in the other person's life?" (John Ackerman)
- •Evangelism is focusing on what God is already doing versus what we think we ought to tell the person.

- We can trust the God who knows each of us from the beginning to be at work in people's lives. God is working in the lives of every person, from the fellow who changes our oil, to the elderly lady who lives next door. God is working in the life of my child's teacher, and my sister-in-law.
- Just as jazz bands listen to each other to make vibrant music, we listen to God when calling others to deeper faith and trust.
- Many women have a partner and coach when they give birth to a child. An evangelist is like a labor room coach who is paying attention to God's birthing process in a person's heart.

Prayer. After Andrew had been with Jesus for a while, he went and found his somewhat irascible brother Peter, and brought him to Jesus. Pray a prayer of thanks for those who, like Andrew, have invited us. Ask God to guide us to see who it is that needs our invitation, our coaching.

Leave for the time of rest and reflection. Ask people to use their watches to pay attention to the return time. Go listening. Go quietly. Go in peace.

Session 3—Come and See: John 1:43-51

Relight the large candle. Note that it represents Christ, the light of the world.

Read John 1:43-51. This time the roles are narrator, Philip, Jesus, and Nathanael. In the gospel story, Nathanael has also been invited to get to know Jesus better. The heart of evangelism is inviting people into a vital relationship with Jesus Christ. Who in your circle of relationships did God bring to your mind? If you do not have a clear sense of direction, allow it to come as you remain open in the coming weeks. Our focus now will be on learning to listen for God's work in another person's life.

Learn how to ask questions that open a space for God. Discuss the difference between questions that create an open space and questions that impose an answer. An "asking" question allows the other person to express longings and desires. A "telling" question presumes an answer or lays blame. Here are some examples.

Ted is just finishing high school.

Telling Question: What are you going to do now? (Everybody knows you ought to be doing something.)

Asking Question: What do you love to do?

Teresa has just told you about her husband's illness.

Telling Question: What do the doctors say caused this? (Every illness has a cause and you ought to be figuring it out.)

Asking Question: Does God seem closer or farther away because of this illness?

Empower people to share faith in natural ways with those God is calling them toward. Think about these steps together. Do these steps help you pay attention to what God is already doing? Will they empower you to share your faith?

Engage: Ask questions that help you know the story of another person's life. Inquire about past experiences with God.

Explore: Look for ways God is currently at work. Respect the slow unfolding of confidence. It takes time to know you truly care.

Connect: Bring God into the conversation. Share personal stories of God's faithfulness.

Invite: Discern next steps toward God for this person. Present an invitation to respond to God's love.

Gather in groups of two and three to talk about response to God's leading. Who has God brought to your mind? How do you see God already at work in that person's life? What questions might you ask as their faith coach? Do you feel joy and wonder at being a part of God's work in another person's life?

Lead in a guided prayer:

Imagine yourself back in Jesus's time. You have just started to get to know Jesus. You've seen him walk along the road. You went to his house to see where he stays. You are captivated. Even though you don't know exactly what is going on, you have to tell somebody what you are discovering.

And so you go to your friend. You go to his house, or to the place where she hangs out. You say, "We have found the Messiah. Come and see." And . . . you take your friend to Jesus.

Do you see the expression on Jesus' face? Do you notice the look of delight and the love in his eyes? And do you see what it means for your friend? How does it make you feel to have been a part of this moment when your friend met Jesus?

Allow for a time of silence. Then have participants light their small candles from the larger Christ candle. Pray quietly for the person you would invite to meet Jesus. Pray for discernment as you lead this person to God, the One who knows, seeks, and loves.

Spend the time in reflection seeking God's direction and interceding for your friends who are not yet aware of God's love. Return at the appointed time for the closing worship.

CLOSING WORSHIP

As people gather, light the candle again. Open with a prayer of thanksgiving for God's presence during this retreat and for God's steadfast love.

Read Psalm 139:7-12. Sing, "I sought the Lord," *HWB* 506. Then ask someone in the group to read Luke 15:3-7. We are now about to go from this place. We go out with Jesus to join the search. We hear Jesus calling and we call the same name. We will go with him, our voices and hearts joined in the search.

Offering. This is not the usual offering that asks you to take something from your wallet. Give each person a slip of paper. On it write: 1) One way you would like to listen to the Holy Spirit. 2) The name of one person you would like to join Jesus in searching for. When all have finished writing, hold the slips up as an offering to God. Place the slips of paper in your pockets or into your Bibles.

Benediction: "Go in God's love; go listening to God's voice. Amen."

EVANGELISM RESOURCES

Listening to God: Spiritual Formation in Congregations by John Ackerman. Alban Institute. 2001.

A Christian View of Hospitality: Expecting Surprises by Michele Hershberger. Herald Press, 1999.

Speaking of God: Evangelism as Initial Spiritual Guidance. Westminster/John Knox, 1991.

INVITATION

You are warmly invited to
Come and See

A Spiritual Retreat designed to
- Connect you with God.
- Help you become more comfortable talking with your friends about faith.
- Give you a chance to rest.

> We can talk to our friends about the weather.
> "It's so hot you could have . . ."
>
> We can talk to our co-workers about sports.
> "Man! Did you see that shot that . . ."
>
> We can talk to our families about our neighbors.
> "I'm telling you he's so crazy that . . ."
>
> We can even talk to folks about ourselves.
> "Want to know the truth? I'm . . ."
>
> So why can't we talk about God.
> ". . . . ."

Place:

Date:

Time:

Please bring: A Bible, paper, pen, a watch, and an open heart

To prepare:
> Read and reflect on the passages listed on the schedule.
> Remember times when God invited you to follow Jesus.
> Recall specific people who put God's invitation into words for you.
> Come rested and wear comfortable clothes.

Tending the Center:
A Retreat for Pastors, Elders,
and Congregational Leaders

Contributed by Marlene Kropf

PURPOSE

Tending the flame of spiritual vitality at the center of congregational life is a central call of leaders. In this retreat, congregational leaders will step back from business as usual and re-examine assumptions and procedures with regard to the spiritual oversight ministries of church boards and committees. Participants will give special attention to:

- Listening and responding to God in their personal lives;
- Listening and responding to God in the midst of congregational life;
- Guiding the congregation's listening, responding and discernment for ministry and mission.

Gathering around the flame of the Spirit's presence, retreat participants will worship together, reflect on biblical passages, explore a variety of tools and practices, engage in exercises and role plays, and make decisions regarding ways to tend the spiritual health of their congregations.

Planned for four sessions, this retreat could take place on a Friday evening through Saturday afternoon. Though it could also be scheduled over a month's time as four sessions (one per week), it will likely not be as effective in this format. Opportunities for conversation over mealtime and at breaks greatly expand the potential for learning and fellowship and create additional energy for transformation.

Because this retreat design is a teaching retreat, it requires that the leader be comfortable in a teaching role and be well-acquainted with a variety of tools and practices for prayer and discernment. Even though much information for the leader has been included, it will not be used effectively if the leader does not have personal experience with the practices.

MATERIALS NEEDED

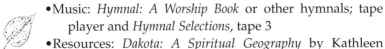

- Music: *Hymnal: A Worship Book* or other hymnals; tape player and *Hymnal Selections*, tape 3
- Resources: *Dakota: A Spiritual Geography* by Kathleen Norris (Ticknor & Fields, 1993); two recommended books for background reading are *Transforming Church Boards into Communities of Spiritual Leaders* by Charles M. Olsen (Alban Institute, 1995) and *Grounded in God: Listening Hearts Discernment for Group Deliberations* by Suzanne G. Farnham, Stephanie A. Hull, and R. Taylor McLean (Morehouse Publishing, 1996). Also useful are two pamphlets available from the Mennonite Church USA Office of Congregational Life, "Discernment: Grounded in God" and "Discernment: A River Runs Through It," by Marlene Kropf (call toll-free 1-866-883-5158) or write CongregationalLife@MennoniteUSA.org Food: hearty soup, good bread, an assortment of cheeses, hot drinks, dessert. Saturday breakfast and lunch will also need to be provided.
- Worship center: A small low table; <u>Session 1</u>—a red or burgundy cloth, sprigs of ivy or green pine or fir boughs, a single light (a large white pillar candle, a large lantern, or an oil lamp with a dancing flame which can be ordered from Wild Thyme Pottery; for information, e-mail June Keener Wink at jkwthyme@bc.net); <u>Session 2</u>

—orange or russet-colored cloth, Bible; <u>Session 3</u>
—yellow or gold cloth; <u>Session 4</u>—basket of small white
candles (with papers for catching wax drips)
•Copies: Schedule, Handout 1

SCHEDULE

Friday evening, 6:30 – 9 p.m.
   Simple supper
   Opening worship
   Session 1 – Dwelling in the Light of God's Spirit
   Closing prayer
   Dessert and fellowship

Saturday morning, 9 a.m. – 12 noon
   Morning worship
   Session 2 – Dwelling in the Light of God's Word
   Morning break
   Session 3 – Dwelling in the Light of God's People

Lunch break, 12 – 1 p.m.

Saturday afternoon, 1-3 p.m.
   Session 4 – Moving with the Light
   Closing worship

GATHERING ACTIVITY

Begin with a simple supper—hearty soup, good bread, an
assortment of cheeses, and hot drinks. (Dessert may be
served later during an informal fellowship hour after the
evening session.) Whether or not those who attend the
retreat know each other well, you can stimulate the opening
conversation by inviting each one to tell of some recent experience when they were especially aware of God's presence
—either personally or in the life of the congregation.

Take a brief break after supper and then gather in the area
where you will meet for the retreat sessions.

RETREAT ACTIVITIES

Friday Evening Worship

Visual environment. The central symbol for this retreat is light —the flame of the Spirit's presence in our midst. A table is covered with a red or burgundy cloth; on it is placed a single light (a large white pillar candle, or a large lantern, or an oil lamp with a dancing flame surrounded by sprigs of ivy or green pine or fir boughs).

Opening worship. Use Call to Worship (Handout 1) and the following hymns chosen in keeping with the central symbol, "Blessed Jesus, at your word," *HWB* 13, and "Immortal, invisible, God only wise," *HWB* 70. (If you subscribe to *Hymnal Subscription Service*, also use "Joyous light of glory," *HSS* 980.)

Read Psalm 36:5-10 and John 8:12 followed by silent meditation.

End with the following prayer and sing "The Lord is my light," (found at end of this retreat.)

> Light of the world
> enter into the depths of our lives
> Come into the dark
> and hidden places
> Walk in the storehouse
> of our memories
> Hear the hidden secrets
> of the past
> Plumb the very depth
> of our being
> Be persistent through
> the silent hours
> And bring us safely
> to your glorious light.

—David Adam, *Landscapes of Light: An Illustrated Anthology of Prayer.* SPCK, 2001. Used by permission

Session 1—Dwelling in the Light of the Spirit

Teaching purpose. This session lays a foundation for understanding the ministry of spiritual oversight as tending the flame of spiritual vitality at the center of congregational life. It introduces the *consciousness examen*, a prayer practice that invites intentional reflection upon lived experience, thereby developing and increasing the group's capacity for recognizing the Spirit's movements

—both in personal life and in the work of committees and boards.

Leader's presentation. If everything the church does should deepen and nourish faith and should also connect with and support God's larger mission in the world, then the spiritual oversight ministries of boards and committees must be part of that life-giving process. In this regard, leaders are presented with a triple challenge: 1) they are called, first of all, to tend their own spiritual health (for congregations cannot be more healthy than their leaders); 2) they are called to tend the spiritual health of their congregations; and 3) they are called to develop spiritual practices in boards and committees that will nurture the faith of leaders as well as empower them for ministry in the church and in the world. To meet this challenge, leaders themselves need to be well-grounded in spiritual disciplines and practices and also have access to a variety of tools for teaching these disciplines to others.

In the past 40 or 50 years, many congregations have become more organizationally sophisticated. As leaders developed more business and professional skills, they put these valuable tools to work in church business meetings and in the work of boards and committees. One result has been better organized, more efficient, and often more productive meetings.

While these organizational skills were being developed, the church may have let another set of skills or capacities deteriorate. While the left hand with its linear processes, parliamentary procedure, strategic goals, and mission statements has been exercised vigorously, the right hand with its prayer, silence, worship, gathering around Scripture, and discernment has been atrophying. Since both sets of skills or practices are essential to the church and its mission, it is necessary to keep both well-exercised.

This retreat gives special attention to the neglected right hand, providing practice at both personal and corporate levels for tending the spiritual center. Central questions to be considered are:

- How can worship and prayer become a more lively part of the work of church boards and committees?
- How can our planning and spiritual oversight be illuminated by the Spirit's energy and vision?

•How can leaders and congregations discern God's call to ministry and mission?

Though many people have developed such spiritual attentiveness in their personal lives, fewer have developed or exercised such skills proficiently in a group context. Yet the ministry of spiritual oversight requires being able to see and sense where God is at work in the congregation and in the world. Those who provide spiritual oversight must be able to see the broad picture —as God sees it; they must also see inside of things and recognize what is hidden or less overt. They must be able to guide others in such discernment.

The basic skill required for discernment (seeing where God is at work) is *paying attention* or *noticing*—something everyone does every day. Yet much of the time people do not really see clearly what is at hand. In an eye-opening chapter called "Seeing" in *Dakota: A Spiritual Geography*, Kathleen Norris writes about how little most people see when they visit the vast, empty expanses of American prairie (read excerpts from pp. 155-158).

Our ability to attend to reality may be more limited than we believe. Lest leaders be too hard on themselves, however, even John the Baptist's disciples had difficulty recognizing God's presence and work when it happened right in front of them. In Luke 7:18-22 they ask Jesus, "Are you the one who is to come, or are we to wait for another?" Though Jesus does not answer the question directly, he asks them to notice what they have just seen: "Go and tell John what you have seen and heard: the blind receive their sight, the lame walk, the lepers are cleansed, the deaf hear, the dead are raised, the poor have good news brought to them." In other words, the irrefutable signs of God's presence and action are healing, release from bondage, and a freedom that is expressed in new life. Those who follow Christ can also come to recognize the unmistakable aroma of Christ (2 Corinthians 2:14-16).

What makes such discernment difficult, of course, is the time and energy required for attentive listening, noticing, and understanding the meaning of what is observed. An evening prayer practice from the Christian tradition called the *consciousness examen* (literally, an examination of consciousness, or paying attention to one's awareness) offers a simple discipline for growing in the capacity to notice and discern God's presence and activity both in personal experience and in the larger context of congregational life. A form of contemplative prayer, it asks people to "pray their day" or to listen to the day just lived, invite the Spirit to shed light on the day, and then respond to what the Spirit brings to mind. Requiring not more than 10-15 minutes and practiced regularly, it is a tried and trusted process for learning discernment (see Appendix C, "The Consciousness Examen—A Traditional Evening Prayer").

Exercise one. Lead the group in praying the *consciousness examen*, reflecting back over the day just lived. What prayers of thanks or confession or intercession are they moved to offer? Guide them to reflect on the gifts of God's presence throughout the day as well as places of struggle or resistance to God. Leave ample space for silence in each movement of the prayer so people can listen and reflect in depth on what the Spirit shows them.

At the end of the prayer, invite people to speak to one another in pairs about what they noticed during the prayer. How was God present to them in their day? Were they surprised at anything the Spirit brought to their attention? After several minutes of discussion in pairs, call the group together and reflect on this experience. What potential might this prayer practice offer for becoming more alert and attentive to God's presence in daily life?

Exercise two. The consciousness examen can also be used to "pray a meeting." Ask participants to choose a recent board or committee meeting as the context for the prayer. Invite them to remember the discussion and interactions as clearly as possible. Then, using the same steps as in exercise one, guide them to reflect on the gifts of God in the midst of the meeting as well as barriers or obstacles that may have obscured God's presence. What prayers of thanks or confession or intercession are they moved to offer? Again, leave ample space for silence in each movement of the prayer.

At the end of the prayer, invite people to speak to one another in pairs about what they noticed during the prayer. After several minutes of such discussion, call the group together and reflect on this experience of prayer. What potential might this prayer practice offer for becoming more alert and attentive to God's presence in the midst of board or committee meetings? Might this prayer be used at the end of meetings to discern what God has been saying and doing? Where/when else might this prayer be used? What might be the outcomes? The obstacles? What questions do they have?

Conclude the evening session by asking participants to identify other tools they have found helpful for developing attentiveness to God's presence in their own lives or in the congregation. Some additional possibilities to mention:

- •Silence and solitude (spending some time in silence periodically can open up a new space for listening and responding to God);
- •Spiritual friendship (expanding one's awareness of the Spirit's movements in one's life by regularly reflecting with a friend committed to the same discipline); see Appendix B, "Spiritual Friendship"
- •Spiritual direction (meeting with a trained guide who helps one notice the presence and activity of God); see Appendix F, "Seeking Spiritual Direction: A Practical Guide"
- •Sunday school classes or small groups or seminary courses focusing on spiritual disciplines
- •Spiritual check-in (a systematic way of inviting congregational members to reflect on the presence of God in their lives); see Appendix D, "Spiritual Check-In"

After a few moments of silence, offer the following prayer:

Thanks be to you, O God,
for the night and its light,
for stars that emerge out of evening skies

and the white moon's radiance.
Thanks be to you
for the earth's unfolding of color
and the bright sheen of creatures from ocean depths.
In the darkness of the world
and in the night of my own soul
let me be looking with longing for light
let me be looking in hope.

—J. Philip Newell, *Celtic Benediction: Morning and Night Prayer*,
© 2000 J. Philip Newell, published by Wm. B. Eerdmans
Publishing Co., Grand Rapids, MI. Used by permission.

Sing "The Lord is my light" again. Dismiss the group for dessert and fellowship.

Saturday Morning Worship

Visual environment. Add an orange or russet-colored cloth to the red cloth already on the table. If you choose, add an open Bible as well. Light the candle or lamp.

Opening words and songs. Read Psalm 130:5-6. Sing "Morning has broken" and "I owe the Lord a morning song," *HWB* 648 and 651, followed by this prayer:

I watch this morning
for the light that the darkness has not overcome.
I watch for the fire that was in the beginning
and that burns still in the brilliance of the rising sun.
I watch for the glow of life that gleams in the growing earth
and glistens in sea and sky.
I watch for your light, O God,
in the eyes of every living creature
and in the ever-living flame of my own soul.
If the grace of seeing were mine this day
I would glimpse you in all that lives.
Grant me the grace of seeing this day.
Grant me the grace of seeing. AMEN

—J. Philip Newell, *Celtic Benediction: Morning and Night Prayer*, © 2000 J. Philip Newell,
published by Wm. B. Eerdmans Publishing Co., Grand Rapids, MI. Used by permission.

Scripture reading. Genesis 1:1-5; John 1:1-5, 14
Silent meditation. People may be invited to respond after the

silence, offering reflections on the Scripture or thoughts that have come during the night.

Prayers for the day. Invite participants to offer spontaneous prayers of thanks and petition for the day ahead.

Closing song. "The Lord is my light" (see words and music on pages 76-77).

Session 2—Dwelling in the Light of God's Word

Teaching purpose. This session builds on the foundation of the previous session by expanding the understanding of the ministry of spiritual oversight as giving leadership to a community of faith, led by God's spirit. It offers another prayer practice, *Lectio Divina*, for tending the flame of spiritual vitality at the center of congregational life. In Lectio Divina, or praying Scripture, the capacity for recognizing God's voice speaking through the words of Scripture is developed personally and corporately.

Leader's presentation. The faithful body of believers is called to listen to and interpret God's Word in their particular time and place. Three sources of illumination are critical for such interpretation:

- the Word of God in Scripture
- the Word of God as spoken by God's living Holy Spirit
- and the Word of God as known and understood by the community (including historical sources) in a particular time and place.

This full-fledged practice of discerning and interpreting God's Word is not some esoteric task unrelated to daily life. Rather, it is understood as essential for participating in God's work in the church and in the world. If the church does not understand God's ways and God's call, then it cannot join with what God is doing.

When a priority of the church is to actively cooperate with God's mission—both within the body of Christ and in the world, it becomes critical that congregational leaders further develop their capacity and skills to interpret and discern God's call. Without such skills and tools, it is easy for the church to misinterpret what God may be saying. For example, many churches who hear a call to become more "missional" may interpret that call as encouragement to become more active, to become busier about the Lord's work. While some congregations may indeed be called to become more active, many others are already too busy—doing good things but perhaps not the one thing needed. When leaders commit themselves to the communal task of interpreting and discerning God's call, they may be surprised to discover that God is asking for a different response. God may, in fact, be inviting them to do less. God may be asking them to develop deeper relationships with God and with one another or to focus on healing broken relationships. Or God may be asking them to notice where and how God's Spirit is already at work in their community and to join with that energy and momentum rather than following their own vision of what needs to be done.

A rich and reliable resource for understanding and discerning God's voice is, of course, Scripture—the Word of God passed on from the past to the church. And again, though many Christians have learned to listen to God speak to them personally in Scripture, fewer have learned how to do so in a group context. A hymn text that describes in a moving way how God speaks, especially in Scripture, is "Lord, you sometimes speak," *HWB* 594. Take time to listen to the song on *Hymnal Selections, Tape No. 3*, or sing it together as an introduction to the prayer exercises to follow.

Introduce the practice of Lectio Divina, a way of praying the Scripture that invites those who pray to become willing listeners, relinquishing the initiative to God's Spirit (Appendix A, "Praying the Scripture"). Explain that the first time the passage is read, participants should be listening for a personal word from God.

Exercise one. Lead the group in Lectio Divina with a passage such as John 15:4-5, 11-16 or Ephesians 3:14-21. Leave ample space for silence in each movement of the prayer so people can listen and attend to the words or phrases the Spirit draws to their attention.

At the end of the prayer, invite people to speak in pairs about what drew their attention during the prayer. What words or phrases did they meditate on? As best as they can understand, what is God's Spirit saying to them?

Exercise two. Not only a personal prayer, this way of praying can also be a way to pray corporately. Repeat the exercise, this time asking participants to listen to the text on behalf of the congregation. Again, leave ample space for silence in each movement of the prayer.

At the end of the prayer, invite the entire group to reflect together on what they heard as they prayed the Scripture, listening on behalf of the congregation. What words or phrases did they meditate on? What might God's Spirit be saying to the congregation? What potential might this practice offer for becoming more tuned to God's voice in the work of boards and committees? What might be the outcomes? The obstacles? What questions do they have?

Conclude this session by discussing other ways to incorporate Scripture in prayerful ways into meetings. Refer to Charles Olsen's book, *Transforming Church Boards*, and explain the idea of using a biblical story as a master story in church meetings. Another effective way to use Scripture is to choose a common text for all the boards and committees or the entire congregation to gather around whenever meetings are held. The following example describes a fruitful Scripture-practice in one congregation:

> "We have discovered two worshipful practices in our church board meetings: Dwelling in the Word and Calling for the Gospel. The board selects a single Gospel text to use for the year. Last year it was the vine-and-branches passage in John 15. This year it is the Lord's Prayer. Each meeting begins and ends with a reading of the Gospel. We listen reflectively, then "dwell in the Word" for several moments. Sometimes one person offers a reflection. Sometimes we all share a thought. Then, during the meeting, at any time, for any reason, anyone may call for the Gospel to be read. We have

"called for the Gospel" several times during the past months, and we're still learning to do it regularly. But we know that something shifts in the tenor of the meeting when we all pause again to return to the Word together."

—Jane T. Roeschley, pastor of Mennonite Church of Normal (Illinois). Used with permission.

Session 3—Dwelling in the Light of God's People

Visual environment. Add a yellow or gold cloth to the red and orange cloths already on the table.

Teaching purpose. This session adds yet another layer to the exploration of the ministry of spiritual oversight by focusing on the corporate practice of discernment, and on the role of leaders in discerning communities.

Leader's presentation. Sing together, "Heart with loving heart united," *HWB* 420, and offer prayer (*HWB* 725) together.

Christians have always understood that it is possible to know and do God's will—both personally and corporately. By listening to the Spirit's promptings and by meditating on Scripture, individual Christians as well as the church come to recognize God's voice and God's ways. Read Deuteronomy 30:11-20 aloud. Ask the group to respond to the following questions (you may choose to divide the group into smaller sections for this exercise):

Who is God in this text? What is God's character or posture toward the people of God?

How are human beings portrayed in this text? What is their potential? What are their capabilities?

Based on this text, what is discernment? What is its purpose? What is the outcome of good discernment? Of faulty discernment?

At the heart of the matter, spiritual discernment means distinguishing the way of life from the way of death. It is the capacity to recognize *where God is* and *where God is not* in the midst of human experience. Consequently, the focus of discernment is not so much on what is right or wrong but rather on the dynamic, moving presence of God's Spirit. When Christians pay close attention to the Spirit's guidance and stay close to God, they choose good paths, not harmful ones. Or when Christians ask themselves, "What would Jesus be or do in this situation?" they gain important clues for discerning God's will.

Ernest Larkin, in the book *Silent Presence: Discernment as Process and Problem*, suggests that contemplation and discernment are two sides of the same coin. In other words, discernment is where prayer meets action. As Christians are able to read God's face, feel God's heart, sense what God desires, they become discerning people who are able to join with God's loving, creative work in the world.

Further, as the church aspires to be discerning, a comforting truth is that God's presence and guidance are near at hand. God wants to be made known, wants to become an ever-present companion on the journey. God's people are not left alone to face the challenging task of discerning God's voice and God's ways.

Yet another comforting truth is that God does not intend for Christians to do this work alone. Christians are given one another as companions on the journey of discernment. They love and trust one another as sisters and brothers and desire to live out the unity of the trinity in their common life.

In such communities, pastors and congregational leaders are called to lead the work of discernment, equipped with skills and tools for guiding this process in fruitful and faith-building ways. The following suggestions offer a starting place for further discussion.

- When a group comes together to do the work of discernment, pay attention to the space in which the meeting is held. Chairs are best arranged in a circle so each person can see others. A worship center that invites prayerfulness provides a visual reminder of God's presence. It is a way of saying, "This is not just business as usual. It is God's business."

- Provide ample time for prayer—not just "book-end prayers" at the beginning and end of the meeting. Sometimes a whole session may be devoted to prayer. The prayer practices explored earlier in the retreat may be used in such settings.
- Learn from the tried-and-true discernment practices that have been handed down in the Christian community. Of what additional examples or processes is the group aware? What are the strengths of each? The limitations?
    a. From the book *Transforming Church Boards* comes the concept of "worshipful-work" and the practice of choosing a group spiritual guide for meetings. This person does not actively participate in the group's work but instead takes responsibility for providing spiritual direction for the entire group by interjecting moments of listening, prayer, singing, and scripture. (Appendix E, "A Liturgist for Presbytery Meetings?")
    b. From the Quakers comes the practice called a Clearness Committee, in which a group comes together to listen in depth as a person or group reflects on a decision. Those who are listening refrain from giving advice and instead spend up to three hours asking honest, open questions to help the discerner discover the movement of God's Spirit in their life. Such intense, prayerful listening and questioning sets people free to become aware of and examine hidden motives, as well as open themselves to fresh, unexplored possibilities. For a delightful account of such a process in action, see pp. 44-46 in Parker Palmer's book, *Let Your Life Speak: Listening for the Voice of Vocation.*
    c. From the Ignatian tradition comes a communal discernment practice which, in a systematic way, separates the pro and con sides of an issue for discussion. The community enters into prayer, and then *all*

members are required to speak—first the arguments *against* a decision, then the arguments *for* a decision. The emphasis in this process is not on forming a consensus but rather on discovering the consensus that is already present. As the discussion develops, the path of life becomes clear.

To conclude this session, invite the group (or a smaller sub-group) to enter into a role play trying out one or more of the following:

1. Ask for one of the committees in attendance to present a 10-minute role play of a recent committee meeting. Invite one retreat participant to practice serving as the group spiritual guide (or the leader may do this), who will interject moments of prayer, silence, singing, or scripture at appropriate points as discussion proceeds.

2. Choose a current issue the congregation is facing (probably not the most difficult issue at hand). Ask someone to present the issue and then invite the rest of the group to ask questions for 10-15 minutes, practicing the Clearness Committee discipline of forming good questions.

3. Choose a current issue the congregation is facing. Ask the group to list all the reasons for or against a particular action. Then invite each participant to speak as convincingly as possible, first against the action and then for the action.

4. Reflect together on the effect of these practices. What is happening in the process? What kind of leadership is required? How might such practices be effectively incorporated into the work of committees and boards?

Lunch time break.

Session 4—Moving with the Light

Teaching purpose. The final session is an integrative session in which the group discerns how they are being called to tend the flame of spiritual vitality at the center of congregational life. It offers an opportunity for exploring and discussing next steps for making worship, prayer, and spiritual discernment a more significant part of the work of boards and committees. It concludes with a brief worship experience in which the light of the Spirit is passed to each one, expressing hope in God's continuing presence and guidance.

Visual environment. Remove the open Bible and place a basket of small white candles (with papers for catching wax drips) on the table.

Leader's presentation. Tending the flame of spiritual vitality at the center of congregational life nourishes and strengthens both the inner life of the congregation and the congregation's engagement in God's mission in the world. When the people of God are united with God's purposes and with one another, they are a powerful sign of God's life and love in the world. Not only does the church thrive but the church guides other seekers to a spacious, light-filled place of freedom and joy.

Because the mission of God is immense, individuals or churches can be tempted to try to accomplish God's agenda with their own limited vision and energy. But God's desire is to provide all the vision and energy that are needed through the entire body of Christ, not through any single person or congregation. Parker Palmer says,

> In the human world, abundance does not happen automatically. It is created when we have the sense to choose community, to come together to celebrate and share our common store. Whether the scarce resource is money or love or power or words, the true law of life is that we generate more of whatever seems scarce by trusting its supply and passing it around....
>
> Abundance is a communal act, the joint creation of an incredibly complex ecology in which each part functions on behalf of the whole and, in return, is sustained by the whole. Community doesn't just create abundance—community is abundance.
>
> —Parker J. Palmer, *Let Your Life Speak: Listening for the Voice of Vocation*. Jossey-Bass, 2000, pp. 107-108

With such an understanding, invite the group to sub-divide into working groups (along committee lines or whatever lines will best serve the future work of the group). Ask each person to respond to the question: "What am I taking with me as I leave today? What will be the most helpful next step in my committee or board's work?" Then ask each group to articulate several long-range goals, as well as more immediate and specific action steps for making use of some of the tools or skills presented or practiced in the retreat. Encourage the groups to pause at appropriate times in their work for silence or prayer. After the groups have completed their work, gather them together for a round of reporting and discussion. As a larger group, decide what the next steps will be. Thank each one for participating in the retreat.

CLOSING WORSHIP

Stand in a circle to sing the theme song, "The Lord is my light." Invite each participant to take a small candle. As leader, light your candle at the large Christ candle. Turn to the next person, light his or her candle, and say, "May the light of Christ shine on your way." Each person repeats it to the next person.

Invite participants to join in prayers of thanks for what has been experienced; ask for the Spirit's continuing light as new steps are taken.

Conclude with this closing dialogue on Handout 1.

The Lord Is My Light

Words by Lillian Bouknight

Music by Lilliam Bouknight
arranged by Paul Gainer

1. The Lord is my light and my____ sal - va - tion, the
3. Wait on the Lord and be of good cour - age, O

Lord is my light and my____ sal - va - tion, the
wait on the Lord and be of good cour - age,

Lord is my light and my____ sal - va - tion;
wait on the Lord and be of good cour - age;

whom____ shall I____ fear?____
he shall strength - en thine heart.____

REFRAIN

Whom shall I fear,____ whom shall I fear?__ The

Lord is the strength of__ my__ life; whom shall I

fear?_____ 2. In the time__ of trou - ble,

he shall hide me, O in the time__ of trou - ble,

he shall hide me, in the time__ of trou - ble,

to Refrain

he shall hide me; whom shall I fear?_____

Call to Worship

Leader: Come, people of God, and worship the Christ.
Once we were separated from Christ,
aliens and strangers who did not belong,
without hope and without God in the world.
Once we loved darkness rather than light.
Once we could not sing the Lord's song.

People: But now we are joined with Christ,
brought near through his blood,
for Christ is our peace.
Now we who lived in darkness
have come into the light.
Now we who could not sing
have been given a new song.

All: *Let us give thanks to God!*
Let us worship the Christ!

—Arlene M. Mark, ed. *Words for Worship* (Herald Press, 1996),
p. 95. Used by permission.

Closing Dialogue

Leader: God is light,
ALL: *and in God there is no darkness at all.*

Leader: God is light;
ALL *let us walk in the light as God himself is in the light.*

Leader: God is light.
ALL: *Let us go to be a light to those who are in darkness.*

—Arlene M. Mark, ed. *Words for Worship* (Herald Press, 1996),
p. 237. Used by permission.

Retreats for Life Passages

God encompasses our whole life journey. Psalm 139:13 reminds us that God has known us even before our birth, "For it was you who formed my inward parts; you knit me together in my mother's womb." This psalm concludes with the words, "Lead me in the way everlasting."

Life passages such as birth, baptism, graduation, and the death of a family member remind us to take a fresh look at God's faithful guiding presence throughout our lives. The retreats in this section capture some of those times. "As a Gift from God" marks the beginning of life with a retreat to prepare for parent-child dedication. "Partners in Nurturing" provides a much-needed forum for including parents in the task of faith formation during preparation for baptism. Other retreats focus on the needs created by change and loss during life passages.

Sometimes retreats fit in more than one category. "Parent-Child Camping" in the Adventure Retreats section would work well to mark a son or daughter's twelfth birthday. "Lead Me to the Rock," though listed under Spirituality Retreats, could easily be adapted for use during one day of a 25th wedding anniversary vacation.

RETREATS IN THIS SECTION INCLUDE:
- As a Gift from God: A Retreat to Prepare for Parent-Child Dedication
- Partners in Nurture: A Retreat During Preparation for Baptism
- The Ache of Autumn in Us: Retreat for an October Morning
- Embracing Pain: Looking to God in the Midst of Loss

WHEN PLANNING A LIFE PASSAGE RETREAT:

Aspects of Planning	*Special Suggestions*
PURPOSE	Inviting God into a significant life passage Marking a life passage such as baptism, graduation, twelfth birthday with a special ritual Finding God's voice in the midst of a life passage such as retirement, death, new responsibilities
SCHEDULE	Pay special attention to a proper balance of structured and unstructured time
GATHERING ACTIVITY	Varies greatly with specific purpose and audience but must always focus on hospitality Ask, what is this group leaving behind? What will help them feel more comfortable? Then, plan accordingly.
RETREAT ACTIVITIES	Allow unstructured time for family needs if children are involved Provide detailed extremely well laid plans for the structured times if it involves groups with children and/or youth Activities should take into account ways the community of faith can support and uphold people during life passages
CLOSING WORSHIP	Symbols work especially well as a closing ritual to mark significant life passages What tangible symbol marks gives hope and courage for the future?

As a Gift from God: A Retreat to Prepare for Parent-Child Dedication

Contributed by Jonathan C. Neufeld

PURPOSE

This retreat is designed to invite reflection on God's love for children, the significance of parenting as faith nurturing, and the place of children in the faith community. Parents will have opportunity to express their hopes for their child's faith journey and find a place of nurture and encouragement for their new responsibilities.

The retreat plan assumes that a parent mentor for each household will also attend the retreat. However, it can easily be adapted if only parents and their children are invited.

MATERIALS NEEDED

- Food: Hot drinks, muffins, snacks, lunch
- Books: *Parents—Passing the Torch of Faith* by John M. Drescher, Herald Press, 1996 (one per household); a selection of books about faith nurture
- Worship center: cloth, flourishing potted plant or tree seedling, small potted plants (one per household)
- Furnishings and room arrangement: comfortable chairs in a circle

*Note: You will need to arrange for a nursery at the place of meeting, hence a nearby church facility or a camp that runs regular family programs would be excellent location choices. Babies are welcome in the sessions at all times, but a nursery should be available when the parents need it. Nursing mothers will want their children in close proximity. The retreat leader will need to arrange for volunteers or paid staff for the nursery. Since families may also have older children, arrange for childcare for all ages represented.

SCHEDULE

8:15 a.m.	Arrive and settle in, hot drinks, muffins
9:00	Gathering
9:30	Session 1 – Babies Change the World
10:30	Break
10:45	Session 2 – Children and Faith
12:00	Lunch
1:00	Session 3 – Parent-Child Dedication Preview
2:15	Closing worship

GATHERING ACTIVITY

Allow for a flexible arrival time in order to take older children to childcare. Drink a cup of hot tea and unwind.

Welcome the group. Have parents introduce themselves and also introduce their new son or daughter. Tell the date of birth, weight, height, and give the name meaning or significance. Parent mentors may introduce themselves first of all in that role, but also feel free to share about their own families.

Sing "In the bulb there is a flower" and "Lord of our growing years," *HWB* 614 and 479. As rain and sunshine fuels the growth of deep roots in tree and flowers, so God preserves and sustains humanity.

Read Psalm 104:1,10-17. Ask people to ponder the images as the passage is read.

Distribute schedule for the day. Assure parents that the babies are always welcome in the group, but that there is a nursery available when they need those services. Talk about the purposes of the retreat:

- •To give new parents opportunity to worship, share, and rest
- •To prepare for the parent-child dedication service
- •To give new parents the opportunity to share with each other and with parent mentors
- •Pray on behalf of the retreat day. Ask God, the creator and sustainer of life, to surround these parents with the physical, emotional, and spiritual strength they need.

RETREAT ACTIVITIES
Session 1—Babies Change the World

Parenting is something we cannot opt out of when it fits our moods and phases of growth. Parents of newborns know that babies have changed their worlds. During this session, invite storytelling from fathers and mothers. Share your own personal story and invite them to tell how their own was the same or different.

Read biblical stories about babies, Genesis 25:19-27 and Luke 1:39-56. Note that the Luke story shows both Elizabeth, who had long-awaited a child, and Mary, whose pregnancy was unanticipated. Allow plenty of time for informal sharing about the experience of total readjustment. Stories from parent mentors can be a source of encouragement for new parents.

Perhaps some parents face issues that move beyond the normal demands. Babies sometimes have unforeseen medical conditions. Sometimes mothers face depression. Perhaps an unplanned pregnancy causes a huge and intimidating barrier to future plans. Talk about what kinds of support parents need from the congregation. Entrust special problems and the more routine demands into God's hands before taking a snack break.

Session 2—Children and Faith

Read Mark 10:13-16. Jesus made children a model of faith. Their dependent and trusting natures make them receptive to God's presence in their lives. In the passage from Mark we are reminded that we can either stand in the way or help children meet Jesus. In the first months, an infant's spiritual nurture includes food, rocking, skin-to-skin contact, and the sound of their parents' voices. We are teaching them about God and about trusting God as we show our love and care.

Show some of the books you have gathered about faith nurture. (See book list.) Some of these pertain more to parents of older children, but it is a good time to become aware of resources. Give a copy of the book, *Parents—Passing the Torch of Faith*, to each household.

Distribute Handout 1. Encourage participants either individually or as couples to find a quiet place to do writing or reflecting in response to one of the quotes, what we have talked about so far, or in regard to their experience as parents. Parent mentors may want to reflect on experiences in the past or their hope for the parents they are supporting. Ask participants to mark the time and return to the group in 30 minutes.

Give time for those who wish to share their reflections with the group.

Session 3—Parent-Child Dedication Preview

Read Luke 2:21-40. Parent-child dedication recalls the Jewish ritual we see in this passage. We say by this service that we seek God's blessing for the child. We recognize, like Simeon and Anna, that this child is a gift from God. We promise, as parents, parent mentors, and congregation, to take seriously the child's faith nurture.

Parent-child dedication is the entranceway to the Christian pilgrimage. Parents and congregation commit themselves to the spiritual and physical well-being of the child. The act of dedication is a declaration that the salvation of Christ includes all who are born. Children remain in a state of grace until the age of accountability when they come to claim their own faith in Christ.

Every child will be introduced briefly during the service. Parents will have the opportunity to present the child, telling his or her name, say what they long for from the congregation, and express their hopes for the child's faith journey. This should take two minutes or less. Give thirty minutes for parents to talk or write about what they want to say.

Review the order of service you plan to use. Distribute Handout 2. Answer any questions about the plan.

CLOSING WORSHIP

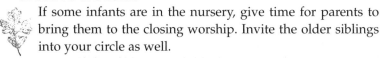

If some infants are in the nursery, give time for parents to bring them to the closing worship. Invite the older siblings into your circle as well.

Sing "Child of blessing, child of promise," *HWB* 620.

Stand in a circle to bless the children in the spirit of Jesus, who embraced children and blessed them. "In the name of God, in the name of Jesus, in the name of the Spirit, we ask that these children be grounded in your love. Keep them secure in your presence. Amen."

Give each household a plant to take home from the worship center.

BOOKS FOR PARENTS

Family: The Forming Center by Marjorie J. Thompson. Upper Room Books, 1989.

Parents—Passing the Torch of Faith by John M. Drescher. Herald Press. 1996.

Parent Trek: Nurturing Creativity and Care in our Children by Jeanne Zimmerly Jantzi. Herald Press, 2001.

Something More: Nurturing your Child's Spiritual Growth by Jean Grasso Fitzpatrick. Penguin Books, 1991.

Why Not Celebrate! by Sara Wenger Shenk. Good Books, 1987.

Children and Faith

"Religious words have value to the child only as the child's experience in the home gives them meaning." Canon Lumb

"The strongest incentives in the development of the character of children often come, not from direct and specific instruction, but from example and unargued assumptions." Elton Trueblood.

"Parents are apostles and pastors to their children." Roland Martinson

"Let the little children come to me; do not stop them; for it is to such as these that the kingdom of God belongs." Jesus

Keep these words that I am commanding you today in your heart. Recite them to your children and talk about them when you are at home and when you are away, when you lie down and when you rise. Deuteronomy 6:6-7

Dedication Service

Leader: (*To the congregation*) When Christian parents present their child to God before the congregation, they come to thank God for the life entrusted to them, to offer their child back to God, and to ask for God's blessing on their life together. We as a congregation come to share their joy, to pray with them for their child's well being, and to receive them into the care of the church. (*To the parents*) Like Mary and Joseph of old, you have brought your children here to consecrate them to God. You have come to offer your children into the strong and tender care of God and the nurture of the church.

Prayer

Questions

Leader: Do you accept your child as a gift from God?
Parents: *We do.*

Leader: Do you dedicate yourselves as parents to bring up your children* in the nurture and teaching of the Lord, preparing them to come to faith in the triune God?
Parents: *We do.*

Leader: Do you promise to gladly surrender your children to the ministry God has in mind for them, even if it might involve going to the ends of the earth?
Parents: *We do.*

Leader: May the God who has entrusted you with these children grant you fullness of love in raising them. May God grant you to live a life of faithfulness to the gospel before your children so that they might know the way of the kingdom.

Leader: (*To parent mentors*) Will you see that these children are nurtured in the faith of the church, and by your prayers and witness guide them into the full stature of Christ?

Parent Mentors: We will.

One by one invite parents to introduce their child, say what they long for from the congregation, and express their hopes for the child's faith journey.

Leader takes the child into his or her arms.

Leader: _____, may the love of God, the gracious Spirit of Christ, and the fellowship of God's people bless your life.

After each child's presentation and blessing, parents turn to the congregation.

Parents: (*To the congregation*) We want to teach our children the way of faith in Christ. We ask for your support and active partnering in our task of parenting. We need your encouragement. We entrust our child to your loving care in this community of faith.

Congregation: You have asked us to participate in the nurture of your child. We humbly accept our partnering responsibility to sustain the spiritual, emotional, and physical well being of your child. We offer the gift of ourselves, as representatives of God's large family, to your child. We offer the strength of our common Christian faith. By our example and our words, we will support your calling as parents.

*Note: If only one child is being dedicated substitute the word "child" for "children" and insert "him" or "her" in place of the word "them."

Partners in Nurture: A Retreat During Preparation for Baptism

Contributed by Marlene Harder Bogard

PURPOSE

This retreat brings together youth and parents to grow in faithfulness to God. The pastor or congregational leader responsible for catechism or baptism preparation class should plan and lead the retreat.

Going on a parent-youth retreat enables families to come face to face with each other in the presence of God. This retreat will allow all participants to connect with God through prayer, meditation, silence, and Scripture reading. As participants experience God in new and creative ways, stronger spiritual bonds within their family will be built and will equip them to take further steps on the path of healthy faith formation.

This retreat brings together several assumptions: 1) that baptism will be upon confession of faith when the youth is old enough to choose a personal commitment to Jesus Christ; 2) that congregations are partners with families in the faith formation responsibility; 3) that we need to equip parents to become the primary faith nurturers.

MATERIALS NEEDED

- Music: CD recording, *Listen* by Michelle Tumes (Sparrow, 1998)
- Visual and worship center items: <u>Session 1</u> – Large clay pot filled with sand, barren branch with plenty of twigs; <u>Session 2</u> – Candles in various sizes; <u>Session 3</u> – Oil lamp, Bible; <u>Session 4</u> – Cross made with branches or scrap wood, basin, pitcher of water, and fluffy white towels; <u>Closing</u> – One white pillar candle per family unit
- Other: Crayons, water-based markers, long strip of newsprint, 3-4 pipe cleaners per person, note cards, basket, matches, small spiral notebook, metal bowl, paper and pencils, extra basins and pitchers of water for foot washing service

SCHEDULE

Friday

6:30 p.m.	Arrive and settle in
7:00	Gathering
7:30	Session 1 – God Is with Us
9:00	Campfire service

Saturday

8:30 a.m.	Breakfast
9:30	Session 2 – God Speaks, Let's Listen
11:00	Free time
12:00	Lunch
1:00	Session 3 – Thy Word Is a Lamp
2:15	Break
2:30	Session 4 – Be Like Christ
3:30	Break
3:45	Closing Worship

GATHERING ACTIVITY

Extend a welcome to all. If people do not know each other, take time for brief introductions. Pray on behalf of the families who have come to this retreat.

Clarify to the group that although there will be free time for recreation and fun, the sessions are designed to be a serious examination of our faith walk. Remind participants that they are invited to share in all discussions and prayers. However, give freedom to participate by remaining silent.

Distribute copies of the schedule. Explain that each session includes *Rendezvous*, the time we spend together as a group; *Family Time*, during which we break into family units and work on projects and options; and *Roundup*, when we reconvene to share what we learned and close with a prayer of blessing. Talk about the goals of the retreat.

- •Transmission of faith. We will provide opportunities for parents and youth to engage in honest conversation and activity around spiritual activities.
- •Sharpen relational skills. We will be working together in an intergenerational setting, expressing appreciation for each other, processing information together, and experiencing God together.
- •Recapture the simplicity of faith. We will approach faith talk in a fresh, simple, and authentic way in order to regain the aspect of wonder and mystery that we often disregard or have forgotten. We will learn how to give spiritual meaning to everyday experiences.

RETREAT ACTIVITIES

Session 1—God Is with Us

Preparation. Prepare a large clay pot filled with sand. In it place a barren branch to hold items brought during *Roundup*. The entire piece should be at least two feet high. Put the pot on the worship center table. For *Rendezvous*, tape a long strip of white paper on the wall. Provide crayons or water-based markers. Have ready three or four pipe cleaners per person. Advise parents that they may wish to prepare a portion of their testimony as a story for sharing during *Family Time*.

Rendezvous. Read all 24 verses of Psalm 139. Ask, "When is God present in our lives?" Wait for responses, then have a brief discussion on Psalm 139. Are there verses in this psalm which give you hope? Contentment? Fear? Other feelings?

On the large piece of paper affixed to the wall, write "Birth" at the far left, "You Are Here" in the center, and "The Future" above the right third of the paper. Invite participants to approach the big paper on the wall and write two or three situations in their lives where they have known God to be present. The comments can be placed at the corresponding time marked on the paper. This can be in phrases, such as, "When I was born" or "When I was in an accident." If the group needs further prompting you may want to ask if there was a time when they had a difficult decision to make, or felt God's protection, or realized God's forgiveness. Several people can be writing at once. Allow time for both thought and writing. If time allows, encourage people to also write how they hope to experience God's presence in the future.

Family Time. Give three or four pipe cleaners to each person and form groups composed of two or three family units.

Listen to each other's stories of specific times when we have realized God's presence. You may continue to use the paper on the wall.

Fashion a design with the pipe cleaners that symbolizes your current relationship with God. If you are currently experiencing faith questions or doubts, these too may be symbolized.

Reconvene the group after 30 to 40 minutes.

Roundup. As people are gathering, play soft music on a CD or ask someone to strum a guitar. "My Constant One" from the Michelle Tumes album *Listen* is one appropriate choice. Invite each person to hang their pipe cleaner creation on the tree branch and describe it and their current relationship to God. Be sensitive to anyone who feels too vulnerable to share in this larger group setting.

Close with this prayer.

When we sing in loud voices, or in whispers;
when we ask questions or have doubts;
when we pray to you on our knees,
or glance at a friend who is hurting;
we acknowledge that you are with us.
In our waking and in our dreaming;
when we are alone or with our family,
with tears, with laughter,
in holding or being held;
may we constantly be aware of your presence among us.
In all things and in all times,
we want to live our faith in you. Amen.

Campfire Service. Invite all participants to walk in silence to the campfire site. At the campfire, sing, share, and listen to the sounds of nature. Invite each person to bring a twig and a slip of paper on which they write something they are turning away from, something they may be asking God to help change. Near the end of the campfire service invite them to gently place their twig or paper into the fire.

Session 2—God Speaks, Let's Listen

Preparation. Gather five to eight white candles of various heights and thickness. Place them in an interesting arrangement on the center table and light them. Have a marker board available. Write the *Family Time* options on note cards and place them in a basket.

Rendezvous. Gather group in a circle. Thank God for the new day. Enjoy the glow of the candles. Read dramatically this excerpt from a Ted Loder poem:

"God . . . are you there?
I've been taught and I've been told I ought to pray.
But the doubt won't go away:
yet neither will my longing to be heard.
My soul sighs too deep for words.
God . . . do you hear me? God . . . are you there?"

Play the song, "Rest My Soul," from the recording *Listen* by Michelle Tumes.

Talk about prayer. Prayer does not change God but rather it changes us. Whatever our age and whatever our faith experience, prayer is about listening for the movement of the Spirit in our lives. Prayer can take a thousand forms and is not limited by time, place, or personal well-being.

Lead the group in a prayer that involves centering our thoughts and listening. Explain centering prayer briefly, if necessary. Give enough information to help people be ready for the periods of silence and the meditative Scripture reading that will come during this prayer. Lead them to relax and become aware of the smells and sounds that are present. Breathe out anxiety and worry. Breathe in God's peace. Read Psalm 25:4-5 slowly and gently. After a minute of silence say, "Listen again," and read it a second time. Read it a third time. Now ask quietly, "Perhaps there are some who would like to tell the word or phrase that became especially meaningful to you." Wait for sharing and close with "Amen."

Explain that this method of Scripture reading while opening our hearts in prayer is an ancient practice called "praying the Scriptures." Ask for response. What was hardest? What surprised you? Write the Four P's of praying the Scripture on the board.

1. Pick a <u>passage</u>. Have it open and ready ahead of time.
2. Assume a <u>posture</u> that is easy and comfortable. Relax, let go, breathe deeply.
3. Become aware of God's <u>presence</u>. Some like to repeat a meaningful praise or phrase such as "Come Holy Spirit" or "Jesus Christ, I worship you."
4. <u>Pray</u> the passage. Read it aloud or whisper it slowly and attentively. If it is a scene, enter into it. Wait for a word or a phrase to strike you with its beauty or truth or new insight.

Take a five-minute stretch break. Get up, get a drink, rub a shoulder.

ACTS. Introduce other kinds of prayer by putting this list on the board.

Adoration—Praising our wonderful and faithful God

Confession—Admitting to God our weaknesses and failures

Thanksgiving—Thanking God for forgiveness, salvation, healing, and hope

Supplication—Asking God's continued presence in our lives and to do mighty works among family and friends. This is the kind of prayer we often excel at.

Brainstorm other ways to pray. Write these on the board.

Family Time. Break into groups of two or three family units. Each group picks a card from the basket with two activity options written on it. They must choose one of the two and return in half an hour to demonstrate it for the group.

1. Sing a Psalm. After looking at several of your favorite psalms, put one to a familiar tune and come back prepared to sing it for us.

2. Prayer with instruments. Go to the kitchen and gather "musical instruments." Tastefully plan a prayer with each person contributing words and adding sounds using the "musical instruments."

3. Psalm with instruments. Choose a psalm that praises God with instruments. Borrow items from the kitchen to add percussion or use a musical instrument that someone brought along.

4. Flea market group. Collect everyday objects such as a shoe or a hat. Arrange yourselves and your objects in such a way that they create a still-life prayer. One member could read a prayer or Scripture while the group is assembling or as the group holds its pose.

5. Pray a hymn. Choose a favorite hymn and illustrate the words by creating hand or body motions.

6. ACTS prayer. Using each of the components of this style of prayer, create a prayer together that incorporates favorite Scriptures or the longings of the group.

Session 3—Thy Word Is a Lamp

Preparation: Create and post the sign on the outside of the meeting room: *Take off your shoes, the place you are entering is holy ground.* Prepare a list of Scripture passages. On the worship table, place an oil lamp and an open Bible. Light the lamp. Dim the room lights. For the beginning activity of *Rendezvous*, assign one parent the role of Jehoiakim, the king who cut up the writing of Jeremiah's scroll and burned it. This person will tear pages from a small spiral notebook, light them on fire, and drop them into a metal bowl. Gather a spiral notebook and some pencils.

Rendezvous. Introduce the theme of loving and learning the Scriptures. Note the sign you posted at the entrance. Ask people in the group to share favorite Scripture verses. Pass around a spiral notebook for people to write the verses, one per page until you have about 8 verses. Then enter the "Jehoiakim" you have chosen beforehand. After he has torn out the pages and burned the verses one by one, he stomps away.

Tell the story of Jeremiah 36. As you do so, people can once again write their verses in the notebook.

Discuss what can be surmised about the value of Scripture from this story. Remind the group of the power of story. How seriously do we take Scripture?

Family Time. Form into groups again. Give each group a list of Bible passages. Each person claims one of the listed Scriptures. Take turns reading your passages. Then read them again silently, praying, meditating, and asking God for direction. Talk about the insights you have gained.

Possible Scriptures: 2 Timothy 3:10-17, 1 Timothy 4:11-16; 2 Peter 1:19-21, John 5:36-40, Acts 17:10-12, Luke 24:36-49, Psalm 119:97-106, Psalm 119:161-168, Psalm 119:169-176, Hebrews 8:7-13, Colossians 3:15-17, Hebrews 4:12-13.

Roundup. Invite people to share one or two sentences of reflection about the Scripture passages they had.

Gather around a plate of honey and dip a cracker into it to represent the sweetness and delight of God's word. This echoes a Jewish practice of putting honey on the tongues of young students learning to read the Hebrew Scriptures.

Session 4—Be Like Christ

Preparation. Construct a crude and humble wooden cross out of tree branches or scrap wood. Place the cross on the worship table along with a large basin, a pitcher of water, and a couple of fluffy white towels. You will need pencils and paper for *Family Time.* Prepare several more basins and pitchers of warm water for foot washing during *Roundup.* Set them on the floor around the worship table.

Rendezvous. Christ is the ultimate model of service and humility. Ask one of the youth in the group to hold up the cross from the worship center while you read Philippians 2:1-11. After about 15 seconds of silence, pass the cross around the circle. Ask participants to share one word that comes to mind when they think of Jesus Christ.

Read the following story based on Jewish folklore. Or read from an illustrated children's book such as *The Two Brothers: A Legend of Jerusalem* by Neil Waldman.

The Tale of Two Brothers

Once there were two brothers who farmed together. They shared the work equally and they shared the harvest equally. In fact they split the produce exactly. Each had his own home and his own granary. One of the brothers was married and had many children; the other brother was single.

One day the single brother thought to himself. "We've been dividing things equally but that hardly seems fair. My brother has all those children to feed and I have grain to spare. I know what I'll do. I'll take a sack of grain each evening and put it into my brother's granary." And he did.

Now one evening after supper, while the married brother held his youngest son on his lap, he thought to himself. "I have many children to love me and care for me in my old age and my brother has none. I know what I'll do. I will take a sack of grain from my granary each evening and put it in my brother's granary." And he did.

Each morning the brothers were amazed to discover

that though they had given grain, just as much remained in their own granary. Though puzzled, they continued their practice of giving grain. One night the married brother was a little later than usual and the single brother a little earlier than usual and so it happened that they met each other halfway between their granaries each carrying a sack of grain. Then they understood the mystery. They embraced and loved each other deeply.

Stand up. Divide into two equal groups and form two lines facing each other. Now form the lines into circles, one circle inside the other and facing the other. This gives each person a conversation partner directly across from where they stand. Discuss the following question with the younger of the two partners answering first, "When was the last time someone asked you to help them?" After two minutes, ask everyone to move one person to the right and discuss the next question. Change conversation partners with each question.

> Who do you know personally that has lived humbly or lived a life of service?
>
> What are barricades to being a Christian who is humble?
>
> What is Christ's expectation of you today, in your family, in your school, or in your community?

Family Time. Invite each family unit to meet separately. In silence and prayer, focus on Christ's call to service and humility. After seeking God's direction, write down a list of ideas that put this call into practice. This can range from offering to do someone's household chores to doing a family service project together. Offer paper and pencils and explain that upon return we will have a footwashing service. After 20 minutes call the group back together.

Roundup. Read John 13:3-17, then lead the group in a foot washing service. This could be done in family units or in a circle. Since this may be new and awkward for some people, set the example before giving specific instructions for the group. Take off your own shoes and socks, go to the worship table and drape the towel over your shoulder saying, "Jesus invites us to wash each others feet as a sign of our willingness to practice service and humility." Invite participants to take off their shoes and socks in silence. Then take the basin and pitcher to one member of the group. Pour some water over that person's feet and pat them dry with the towel. Wash each other's feet at various places around the room. Suggest that parents wash their son or daughter's feet first.

Pray a prayer of blessing when all have finished. This service was adapted from *Prayer Works for Teens, Book 3* by Lisa-Marie Calderon-Steward (Saint Mary's Press, 1997). Announce that after a short stretch break we will gather for a simple and short sending time.

CLOSING WORSHIP

Preparation. Use the break to change items on the worship table. Arrange good quality white pillar candles (one per family unit) on the worship table.

Gather the group. Talk about what will happen during the rest of the baptism exploration or catechism classes. Perhaps yours is a faith exploration class and at some point along the way the youth decide whether or not they feel ready to take the vows of baptism. Include a time line for future topics and activities of the faith exploration class. Give information about the baptism ceremony and ideas for continued family involvement in faith formation.

Sending. Light each of the candles on the worship center table. Stand in a circle. Invite one parent from each family unit to come up and receive a candle then return to the circle. End with this blessing and a final prayer. "As you have experienced the light of the world during this retreat, so I send you bearing the light. Place the candle on your kitchen table and light it each day as you gather to pray with each other, as you read the Scriptures, and as you serve each other."

The Ache of Autumn in Us:
Retreat for an October Morning

Contributed by Bonnie Stutzman

PURPOSE

This retreat plan opens a space for grieving losses and embracing hope for the future. Through time alone with God and meditation on Scripture, we will be led from autumn leaves and dying tree stumps to trust in God's enduring life. In the quietness will be found the grace to let go and welcome the budding that springs forth from God.

MATERIALS NEEDED

- Visual elements: Pressed leaves, acorns, and a candle for worship center
- Journals or other writing paper and pens
- Copies: Schedule, Handouts 1 and 2
- Beverages: tea and coffee

SCHEDULE

9:00 a.m.	Welcome and gathering activities
9:30	Time spent alone out of doors
10:15	Time together in shared reflection
10:30	Time spent alone out of doors
11:15	Time together in shared reflection
11:30	Closing worship and reflection
11:45	Close of retreat

GATHERING ACTIVITY

Invite guests to a hot cup of coffee and tea and a comfortable seat. Introduce each other.

This is your time to spend with God. It is a gift to God and to you. There is no right or wrong spiritual retreat. Present the guidelines of the retreat:

- to find hope in the midst of our good-byes
- to say "no" to the busyness of life and "yes" to the presence of God
- to find time for our spiritual selves and be joyful.

Read the poem, "Leaf Song."

> O Lord of all Autumns
> > you paint
> > > bright
> > > > beautiful
> > > > > colors of dying
> > > > > > On the hills of my spirit
> Give me the leaf grace to let go,
> > to
> > > trust
> > > > in Spring.

—Sr. Lynne Therese, OCD (Eldridge Carmel) Used by permission.

Pray on behalf of the group and their journey into letting go and trusting God.

Distribute the schedule for the morning. Point out the balance of time alone and time spent in shared reflection. If you have a signal for gathering, such as a bell, let them know what it is; if not, ask participants to take responsibility for keeping track of time.

RETREAT ACTIVITIES

Time spent alone out-of-doors. As we begin this morning retreat, find a quiet comfortable place to be alone with God out-of-doors. This is your time to spend with God. Invite the

Holy Spirit to be present to you. Then be still and aware of God's presence within and all around. Distribute Handout 1 along with an autumn leaf from the worship arrangement. Suggest reading the verses slowly and reflectively. Begin to notice what draws your attention. How are you responding? What are you being invited to? Pray your present experience. Focus on the first of the three questions. You may want to journal about what you notice but do not feel compelled to do so.

First group interaction. As people return, light the candle welcoming the Holy Spirit into your midst. Allow time for group reflection. What are the good-byes that are currently happening in your life? What is the hardest for you? What makes it so difficult?

Time spent alone out-of-doors. Read Job 14:7-9 and Jeremiah 17:7-8 aloud. For a second time you will find a place to be alone with God pondering the final two questions. Quietly place an acorn in each person's palm as they leave to find a quiet spot.

Second group interaction. Relight the candle. As the group gathers sing, "In the bulb there is a flower," *HWB* 614. Invite group reflection. What seeds of possibilities are being planted during this autumn time that may bear fruit in some season yet to come? What are the streams that feed you and rebuild you for growth so your leaves stay green?

If anyone becomes overcome with deep sadness during the sharing time, place leaves from the worship center around the person's feet. This serves to validate his or her grief.

CLOSING WORSHIP

Pray for each other and offer respectful silence to each other. Distribute Handout 2 and read the responsive reading together as the closing blessing.

Take leaves and acorns home as a reminder of the retreat morning and as signs of God's grace. You may want to read the poem again at this point.

As you blow out the candle say, "May the Holy Spirit be present to each of us as we leave this place and go forth into the future, trusting, hoping for spring."

The Ache of Autumn in Us

For there is hope for a tree, if it is cut down, that it will sprout
   again,
and that its shoots will not cease.
Though its root grows old in the earth, and its stump dies in the
   ground,
yet at the scent of water it will bud and put forth branches like
   a young plant.
—Job 14:7-9

Blessed are those who trust in the Lord, whose trust is the Lord,
They shall be like a tree planted by water, sending out its roots
   by the stream.
It shall not fear when heat comes, and its leaves shall stay green;
In the year of drought it is not anxious, and it does not cease to
   bear fruit.
—Jeremiah 17:7-8

Questions for reflection:

1. Identify with the autumn leaf. What are the good-byes that are currently happening in your life? Which is hardest for you? What makes it so difficult?

2. What seeds of possibilities are being planted during this autumn time that may bear fruit in some season yet to come?

3. What are the streams that feed you and rebuild you for growth so your leaves stay green?

Responsive Reading

Leader: Blessed are you, for your trust is in the Lord.

All: Our trust is in the Lord.

Leader: Though today you see only the root grown old in
    the earth
Though today you see only the stump dead in the
ground
Yet you will put forth branches of life.

All: We will not fear, we will not be anxious
for we shall be like trees planted by the water

Leader: You whose trust is the Lord.
May you continue to find the leaf grace to let go
and be open to the new budding that springs forth
from God. Amen.

Embracing Pain: Looking to God in the Midst of Loss

Contributed by Sherill Hostetter

PURPOSE

Pain and loss often jolt our theology of God's love and sovereignty. The losses we experience may be in the past or more immediate. Through Scripture and prayer we will be led to express our hurts honestly before God and begin to trust God's healing work in us.

MATERIALS NEEDED

- Worship center: Cloth, smooth stones scattered around on the cloth, candle, grapes, and grape juice
- Food: Hot drinks and muffins upon arrival; lunch provisions
- Music: CD player and recorded music, *Songs to Live By: Passing on Hymns of the Faith*, (Call Faith & Life Resources at 1-800-743-2484 to order.)
- Other: Paper, pens, and colored markers

SCHEDULE

8:30 a.m.	Arrive, settle in, enjoy hot drinks
9:00	Gathering
10:00	Session 1 – Reflecting on My Life
11:00	Reflection – River of Life Time Line
12:00	Lunch
1:00	Session 2 – Praying Our Experience
1:30	Reflection – Writing My Own Psalm of Lament
3:30	Session 3 – God's Presence in the Midst of Pain
4:15	Break
4:30	Closing worship
5:00	Return home

Choose a setting that provides rest and beauty, a place that speaks God's healing and comfort by its ambience.

GATHERING ACTIVITY

As people arrive, greet them at the door and invite them to the table of hot drinks and muffins.

Describe what the day will include. Distribute schedules and indicate both group sessions and reflection times of working on individual exercises. Give directions for places to walk and an orientation to the retreat center facilities.

Guide a time of introductions, giving names and a word about why they were drawn to this retreat. The latter should be shared only by those who wish to do so. Explain that throughout this retreat everyone has the freedom to share only what feels safe and comfortable. Pain and loss should only be shared with others when we are ready and in a place of great caring, safety, and trust.

Lead in a prayer on behalf of the retreatants, a prayer of opening ourselves to what God longs to bring to us during this day.

RETREAT ACTIVITIES
Session 1—Reflecting on My Life

As the facilitator, reflect on your own life story, its pain and joy, gain and loss. We tend to divide our past into the good things to remember with thanksgiving and painful things to forget. Yet, our whole past can become the fertile soil for the future.

Invite group members to reflect on losses in their own journey. These losses may be in the past or more immediate. Others around us may recognize them as significant losses or they may be hidden away. Losses come in varying degrees. Often the losses we bear alone become the most painful. List possible losses:

- •Loss of significant people in our lives due to death, divorce, moving, or mental disorder
- •Loss of a part of ourselves such as a loss of dreams, hopes, job, reputation, or self-esteem
- •Loss of material objects through fire or theft
- •Losses due to normal life changes such as aging, graduation, and children leaving home
- •Loss of what could have been or deprivation due to family dysfunction, abuse, negative choices, or painful unchangeable events
- •Loss of trust in another person through betrayal or moral failure
- •Loss of children due to miscarriage, infertility, abortion, or suicide

Distribute paper, pens, and colored markers for people to use to reflect and record the significant events in their lives. For the painful events, invite them to name the losses and ask God where he was in that event. Ask them to also record who showed God's love to them. Suggest drawing this time line of their lives as a river of life. They should not feel limited to that image and may use any configuration that helps express the story. End with a reassurance that this will not be an exercise to share with others unless they wish to do so. Be available for retreatants who need spiritual direction or a caring listener during the reflection time.

Session 2—Praying Our Experiences

Introduce the session with some thought about David, to whom we attribute many of the psalms. David was a man after God's own heart, not because he was perfect but because he had an intimate relationship with God. He was able to honestly pour out his confessions, feelings, and thoughts. He had learned to trust that God could handle his pain, anguish, anger, and doubts. After expressing the negative and confessing the anguish, he also sat in God's presence and listened.

Read Psalm 77:1-9. Read with real expression of lament and then pause in silence. Explain that these first nine verses could be summarized, as "God is *nowhere.*" After a pause in silence, the psalmist goes on to say, "It is my grief that the right hand of the Most High has changed." Read verse 10, then the rest of the psalm. Ask the group what has taken place. By the end of the chapter the psalmist declares that even though God's way was through the mighty waters, God was there. This last half of the psalm could be summarized with the addition of one space within the word "nowhere" to say, "God is now here."

Explain that praying our experiences is to honestly offer God the reality of my life story and myself. If an experience from the past causes pain and disturbance when it comes to mind we can be certain that it is disturbing us even when we are not aware of it. In acknowledging or naming painful experiences, we open ourselves to God's healing presence.

For the next time of reflection, write laments on any painful experience. Explain that laments are usually structured with:

•an invocation to the Lord
•complaint before God
•a petition for the Lord's intervention
•a vigil of listening
•an expression of certainty that the prayer has been heard.

The letter can be in journal form or follow the more stylized lament form. Offer to be available during the reflection time for anyone who wants further prayer during this time.

Session 3—God's Presence in the Midst of Pain

Invite anyone who would like to share their personal lament with the group. Do not prolong this because it can be perceived as pressure to share. This is especially true if the participants do not know each other well.

Introduce this session with some background on the theology of suffering. Jesus did not promise his disciples safety, but he promised them life. He didn't promise them freedom from pain, but he offered them freedom from fear. Jesus often said to them, "Do not be afraid." Jesus' disciples must have been disillusioned by his death. They thought God would protect the righteous one. Instead Jesus speaks from the very heart of suffering. He was not defeated. He brought a triumph over suffering and opened a way through suffering for us. At the center of our own grief, we find the grace of God.

Christianity is the only faith tradition or religion that confesses a God who suffers. We would prefer a God who prevents all suffering. But God does not prevent us from all pain. God desires to redeem our pain. God comes with love and is present with us. God's power does not force human choices and end all pain but God's power is available to pick up the broken pieces and bring transformation. Sometimes we feel like grapes being crushed and it is difficult to envision the life sustaining wine we become.

Read Romans 8:31b-39 as an exercise in praying the Scriptures. Read the passage three times, each by different readers. Note the pattern of read, reflect, and respond.

1. Read the passage together along with the first reader. (You may want to refer to Appendix A, "Praying the Scriptures.")
2. Listen for a word or phrase that draws your attention in a special way while the second reader is reading. Reflect on that word or phrase in silence.
3. With the third reading, respond to God in whatever way seems appropriate. Then rest in God's presence in silence.

Use the break to stretch, rest, or remain in silent prayer.

CLOSING WORSHIP

Read Psalm 77:19-20 again. This verse recalls the Joshua 3 account of Israelites walking through the Jordan River during its flood season. The priests carried the Ark of the Covenant in front of the people and took their stand in the middle of the river. The people passed through with a high wall of water on the upstream side, held in place by an invisible, miraculous dam. God instructed them to take up stones from the middle of the river to build an altar when they reached the other side. Thus they were to remember God's faithful presence. These stones informed the rest of their journey, shaped the rest of their story.

Invite retreatants to come to the worship table to choose a rock to carry on the rest of their journey and to symbolize God's presence when passing through deep waters. Play recorded music such as "O Healing River" from the recording, *Songs to Live By: Passing on Hymns of the Faith*.

Benediction. Give this blessing based on Isaiah 43:1-5:

Now thus says the Lord,
the one who created you and formed you.
Do not fear, for I have redeemed you.
I have called you by name, and you are mine.
When you pass through the waters,
I will be with you;
and through the rivers, they shall not overwhelm you.
Do not fear, for I am with you. Amen.

Adventure Retreats

The genius of adventure retreats is their ability to disrupt the commonplace and replace it with a transformational experience. Both being in nature and facing physical challenge play significant roles. A retreat in the wilderness releases people from their normal lives and hurried schedules.

Each adventure retreat offers a unique gift. "Bicycle Day Trip" provides a novel way to observe the monastic hours. "Parent-Child Camping" gives an opportunity to strengthen family relationships. "Canoe Trip" provides for a full seven days of retreat and "Mountain Hike" offers a weekend of hiking and solitude.

The retreats in this section contain minimal programming but offer plenty of solitude in God's creation. "For this event, less is better. Let the wilderness speak because God is there," says Lester Lind, in "Mountain Hike."

RETREATS IN THIS SECTION INCLUDE:
- Bicycle Day Trip: A One-Day Personal Retreat
- Parent-Child Camping: Experiencing God's Greatness Together
- Mountain Hike: A Weekend Wilderness Retreat
- Canoe Trip: A Seven-Day Wilderness Adventure

WHEN PLANNING AN ADVENTURE RETREAT

Aspects of Planning	Special Suggestions
PURPOSE	Being with God in nature Disrupting the commonplace in order to attune to God Learning to walk gently through nature
SCHEDULE	No clocks needed
GATHERING ACTIVITY	Involves physical preparations Allow time for acclamation to the wilderness setting
RETREAT ACTIVITIES	Morning meditations, campfire community, and plenty of solitude in between Let the wilderness speak because God is there
CLOSING WORSHIP	Traveling "back" is part of the closing worship An ending meal can provide closure and transition
NOTES	If the adventure retreat involves wilderness camping, you must have an experienced leader

Bicycle Day Trip:
A One-Day Personal Retreat

Contributed by Rod Houser

PURPOSE

This daylong retreat, based on the Benedictine hours of prayer and reflection, provides an opportunity to ponder the seasons of life. This plan may be seen as a pattern for personal retreats rather than as a one-time event. Personal retreats may be held at a retreat center or may involve an activity in nature such as this bicycle day trip.

MATERIALS NEEDED

- Suggested reading: *Music of Silence: A Sacred Journey through the Hours of the Day*, David Steindl-Rast with Sharon Lebell (Seastone Press, 1998)
- Food: Simple lunch, plenty of water
- Other: Journal, copies of Handouts 1 and 2

SCHEDULE

Day Before	Drive several hours to your bike trail location. Stay at a motel or campsite.
Day of Trip	Ride, stopping at intervals to pray, meditate, and journal
End of Day	Shower, eat
Night	Sleep back at motel or campsite

GATHERING ACTIVITY

Group retreats have gathering activities that orient the tone and introduce the retreat. Prepare for this personal retreat by pondering some concepts of time.

The Greeks have two different words for time: *chronos*, from which we get the word chronological, and *kairos*, which can mean opportunity or encounter. In chronological time, "now" can be a very small stretch of time. And indeed, no matter how short a stretch we make it, it can always be cut in half. So the idea of "now" in *chronos* makes little sense. But in *kairos*, "now" is possible.

From the Benedictines of the fifth century come the "hours" observed on this bicycle ride. The Benedictines were people of God who lived a life of prayer and manual labor. They developed an approach that allowed them to remain aware of God throughout each day.

Our Western minds tend to understand time as portrayed by a clock (*chronos*), while the hours observed on this bicycle ride are better understood as opportunity or encounter (*kairos*). The hours used in this retreat are the seasons of the day, but they can just as well fit the seasons of a year, a lifetime, or an event in life. A day of retreat will help us ponder the seasons of our lives as well as become more deeply aware of God's presence in the midst of our daily routine.

RETREAT ACTIVITIES

Drive to a location two to three hours away from home the evening before your ride. Spend the night at a campground or motel.

Relate the prayers and thoughts of the Benedictine hours to the bicycle ride. (See "Benedictine Hours and Meanings.") Celebrate a new day of opportunity at *Lauds* when you are ready to start the day's ride. Note that your energy is at its peak at *Terce*. *Sext* (noon) is decision time when you decide if you'll make it through to the evening. In late afternoon (*None*), acknowledge anxiety, think about death, and forgive yourself for whatever limits and boundaries you discover in yourself.

As these different hours approach, choose an inviting park or coffee shop along your route. Take a break, pull out your journal, and reflect on the particular character of the hour and relate it to the thoughts you have had while riding.

By late afternoon you will want to be back at your campground or motel base. Celebrate *Vespers* with good food. Acknowledge the contradictions of the day and luxuriate in the beauty of the evening.

CLOSING WORSHIP

Conclude the day with *Compline* and approach sleep with trust and joyful anticipation.

Benedictine Hours and Meanings

The Benedictines observe regular times of prayer and reflection. This list gives the Latin name for each hour as well as the particular gift each hour brings.

Vigils, Matins: Night watch hour
- Learn to trust the dark hours.
- This is a symbol of the waking up we may need to do in the midst of our lives.
- We may come out injured like Jacob.
- Ponder the phrase: "Watchman, what of the night? When will it be over?"

Lauds: Dawn
- We have been brought out of darkness into light.
- We find happiness when we realize that all of life is a gift.
- Sunrise comes unbidden.
- Ponder the phrase, "The works of darkness are brought to light."

Prime: Start of day's activity
- We all work together even if we are apart from one another.
- Discover the divine in the material world. Do work for its own sake.
- Set priorities and make right responses.

Terce: Mid-morning break
- Our energy is at its peak.
- This hour is a reminder of outpouring of Holy Spirit.
- Celebrate the thrill of life.

Sext: Noon
- We can either renew fervor or allow the forces of entropy to take over.
- Take time to think thoughts of peace.
- Celebrate the meal even if it is a simple one.

None: The shadows grow longer
- Take time to face anxiety and the reality that we are mortal.
- Connect with something transcendent.
- Forgive yourself and others.
- Give thanks for the limits and boundaries that give life structure.

Vespers: Lighting of lamps
- This is the hour of peace of heart.
- Embrace the inevitable contradictions the day leaves behind.
- Let go of the day and luxuriate in the quiet and beauty of evening.
- Light whatever lights we can in the dark world.

Compline: Conclusion of day
- Confess any failings and make a clean transition into night and sleep.
- Put yourself in the shelter of God's love.
- Rest in the protection of God's love.
- Approach sleep with joyful anticipation.

Bible Passage and Prayers

From *The Book of Common Prayer* (1979) of the Episcopal Church, USA.

In the Morning
From Psalm 51

>Open my lips, O Lord,
>>and my mouth shall proclaim your praise.
>
>Create in me a clean heart, O God,
>>and renew a right spirit within me.
>
>Cast me not away from your presence
>>and take not your Holy Spirit from me.
>
>Give me the joy of your saving help again
>>and sustain me with your bountiful Spirit.
>
>Glory to the Father, and to the Son, and to the Holy Spirit:
>>as it was in the beginning, is now, and will be for ever. Amen.

A Reading

>Blessed be the God and Father of our Lord Jesus Christ!
>By his great mercy we have been born anew to a living hope
>through the resurrection of Jesus Christ from the dead. 1 Peter 1:3

A period of silence may follow. A hymn may be used.
Prayers may be offered for ourselves and others.
The Lord's Prayer

Lord God, you have brought us in safety to this new day: Preserve us with your mighty power, that we may not fall into sin, nor be overcome by adversity; and in all we do, direct us to the fulfilling of your purpose. Amen.

At Noon
From Psalm 1:1-3

>Give praise, you servants of the Lord;
>>praise the name of the Lord.
>
>Let the name of the Lord be blessed,
>>from this time forth for evermore.
>
>From the rising of the sun to its going down
>>let the name of the Lord be praised.
>
>The Lord is high above all nations,
>>and his glory above the heavens.

A Reading

>O God, you will keep in perfect peace those whose minds are fixed on you; for in returning and rest we shall be saved, in quietness and trust shall be our strength. Isaiah 26:3; 30:15

Prayers may be offered for ourselves and others.
The Lord's Prayer

Blessed Savior, at this hour you hung upon the cross, stretching out your loving arms: Grant that all the peoples of the earth may look to you and be saved; for your mercies' sake. Amen.

In the Early Evening

O gracious Light,
pure brightness of the ever living Father in heaven,
O Jesus Christ, holy and blessed!
Now as we come to the setting of the sun,
and our eyes behold the vesper light,
we sing your praises O God: Father, Son, and Holy Spirit.
You are worthy at all times to be praised by happy voices,
O Son of God, O Giver of life,
and to be glorified through all the worlds.

A Reading

It is not ourselves that we proclaim; we proclaim Christ Jesus as Lord, and ourselves as your servants, for Jesus' sake. For the same God who said, "Out of darkness let light shine," has caused his light to shine within us, to give the light of revelation—the revelation of the glory of God in the face of Jesus Christ. 2 Corinthians 4:5-6

Prayers may be offered for ourselves and others.
The Lord's Prayer

Lord Jesus, stay with us, for evening is at hand and the day is past; be our companion in the way, kindle our hearts, and awaken hope, that we may know you as you are revealed in Scripture and the breaking of bread. Grant this for the sake of your love. Amen.

At the Close of Day

Psalm 134

Behold now, bless the Lord, all you servants of the Lord,
 you that stand by night in the house of the Lord
Lift up your hands in the holy place and bless the Lord;
 the Lord who made heaven and earth bless you out of Zion.

A Reading

Lord, you are in the midst of us and we are called by your name:
Do not forsake us, O Lord our God.

Lord, you now have set your servant free
 to go in peace as you have promised;
For these eyes of mine have seen the Savior,
 whom you have prepared for all the world to see:
A light to enlighten the nations,
 and the glory of your people Israel.

Prayers may be offered for ourselves and others. It is appropriate that prayers of thanksgiving for the blessings of the day, and repentance for our sins, be included.
The Lord's Prayer

Visit this place, O Lord, and drive far from it all snares of the enemy; let your holy angels dwell with us to preserve us in peace; and let your blessing be upon us always; through Jesus Christ our Lord. Amen.

Parent-Child Camping:
Experiencing God's Greatness
Together

Contributed by Rose Mary Stutzman

PURPOSE

This retreat will focus on strengthening your relationship with your son or daughter. Quality one-on-one time spent in the outdoors can build love, encourage deeper sharing, and create lasting memories. Spend your days hiking or in some other outdoor activity. Morning devotion times and evening fireside singing will be natural reminders that God's presence is with you as you walk and experience nature.

This retreat can be adapted to include outdoor activities of many kinds, such as canoeing, biking, horseback riding, fishing, exploring, or whitewater rafting. You may want to do this at a special transition age or you may want to make it an annual event.

Note: This retreat can work with any combination of people: uncles and aunts with their nieces and nephews, or grandparents and grandchildren, etc.

MATERIALS NEEDED

- Resources: Trail or hiking maps of the park or area you have chosen
- Camping equipment: Backpacking supplies for the brave and experienced who plan to do wilderness camping,

camping supplies for campground excursions, include such items as sleeping bags, rain suits or ponchos, clothing in layers (wool and fleece is best for the outer layers), flashlight, extra-light rope, water bottles, fishing gear, knife, sunglasses, tent, sleeping bags, matches, plastic bags to protect items from dampness

•Food: Pita pockets, peanut butter, bagels, trail mix, cheese, dried fruits, and nuts travel well in backpacks; bring ingredients for campfire meals such as beans and hot dogs or tinfoil dinners

•Other: Small pocket Bible or copies of Psalms to read, Field Guides for tree, plant, bird, and animal identification, a paperback book to read aloud, camera in a plastic bag

SCHEDULE

7:00 a.m.	Breakfast, devotion time, gather supplies for the day
Morning	Hiking or other outdoor activity
Lunch	Eat healthy foods and drink plenty of water
Afternoon	Hiking or other outdoor activity
4:00	Stop for the day, prepare supper
Evening	Supper, campfire activities, star gaze, plan for tomorrow

GATHERING ACTIVITY

Plan the trip together, read about camping and gather supplies. Dreaming, buying the food, and preparing in other ways are part of the pleasure, an important aspect of this adventure.

After you have loaded your equipment and are ready to start the trip to your camping location, pause to thank God for the time you will spend together. Invite God's presence and ask for God's protection.

RETREAT ACTIVITIES

Days spent camping and out-of-doors develop a certain rhythm. Early morning rising, making fires, keeping things dry, preparing food, early bedtimes. Spend the day hiking or in some other outdoor activity. This is a wonderful opportunity to be playful and have fun. Swing from a vine, wear your hat backwards, whistle, and skip stones.

Take turns reading a psalm each morning. Psalms 1, 8, 23, 24, 42, and 139 all use outdoor imagery.

Sing around the campfire if your son or daughter is comfortable singing. Many pre-teens and teenagers go through a stage of being mortified about parents' singing. If so, talk or tell stories instead. You may want to read aloud a quality children's book such as *The Wind in the Willows*, *Sounder*, *Number the Stars*, or *Rascal*. There are many other choices, of course, for books that inspire and help us care about each other and the world. Take an old paperback copy that you do not mind losing or ruining or using pages from in case you need it for starting a fire when everything else is damp.

Take time to identify birds, trees, and animals. Name the stars and constellations. Express wonder at God's creation by noticing what is there, by hearing what is there, by caring for creation.

Talk and listen. Surprising opportunities will arise to learn from your son or daughter, to experience God's love through your son or daughter. There will be times and ways to express what really matters in your life, times to tell stories of your experiences and faith. Remember that God is present and working in both of your lives, and has known and loved us even before we were born.

If this is a trip to celebrate a special year such as turning ten or twelve or leaving for college, talk about the next stage of life. What was life like for you as a parent at that age? How might your relationship change as a result of growing up and increased independence? What are your hopes for your son or daughter during these next years? What exciting opportunities or anxieties does this time bring for your son or daughter?

Pray and remember verses during the night if you wake up feeling frightened and vulnerable. Whisper as much of Psalm 23 as you can remember together.

Resolve the times of tension. Family adventures often bring irritations and hurts. Did you yell at each other when you felt endangered? Did you get hungry and grumpy? Did you whine excessively when you had to huddle in the rain? These are the times to practice peacemaking and forgiveness. Times for parents to genuinely repent of any ways they have misused their power. Times for children to learn responsibility for their own behavior.

CLOSING WORSHIP

On the last evening, talk about going back home. What do you look forward to at home? What stories and adventures will you tell your friends and family?

Remember this time. Gather a stone, acorn, or pinecone of remembrance. The general rule is to leave nature the way it was so be careful what you decide to take. Make up a crazy song about your camping trip to the tune of some well-known folk song. Thank God for specific experiences, the rare bird you saw or the skunk that waddled across the campground.

Mountain Hike: A Weekend Wilderness Retreat

Contributed by Lester Lind

PURPOSE

This entire event helps participants draw close to God. Carrying packs, safety issues, the beauty of the wilderness, solitude, and the small community of fellow hikers all strengthen our awareness of God.

MATERIALS NEEDED

- Ask participants to bring packs, mess kits, water bottles, and personal items.
- Food and cooking supplies (these are divided among the hikers)
- Advance preparation: The leader will need expertise in backpacking and wilderness camping, as well as familiarity with hiking trails. You will need a carefully laid plan for which hiking trails you will use, as well as where you will camp.

SCHEDULE

Friday afternoon	Gather, load packs, travel to trailhead, begin hiking
Late afternoon	Arrive at campsite, set up camp, prepare supper
Friday evening	Get acquainted, early bedtime
Saturday morning	Solitude before breakfast, eat, meditation, break camp
Noon	Cold lunch along trail
Late afternoon	Set up camp, prepare supper, eat together, personal time
Saturday evening	Campfire reflections
Sunday	Repeats rhythm of previous day
Shortly after noon	Arrive back at trailhead, travel to lodge to eat lunch, reflect on weekend, say farewells

GATHERING ACTIVITY

The gathering activity happens at two distinct points. The first gathering activity involves dividing the food and cooking supplies among the various hikers, loading and traveling to the trailhead.

The second gathering time takes place at the first campsite. Talk about listening and awareness as we walk in solitude. This encompasses both our inner world and our physical bodies. It includes respecting nature, and awareness while being in nature.

Get acquainted with each other at this first campsite. Tell what you are expecting, seeking, or hoping for. Or, you may want to introduce yourselves with something you found along the trail.

RETREAT ACTIVITIES

For this event, less is better. Let the wilderness speak, because God is there. Hike in solitude. Begin each day with a meditation from a psalm of nature.

To prepare people for the day of solitude, talk about ways the entire experience can point us to God. We spend time loading and adjusting our packs. We have all the essentials we need for several days. We are carrying it all with us. But more than what we are carrying in our packs we must also ask, "What are we carrying in our head, our hearts? Is it necessary? Useful?" We treat our packs with care. They provide for our survival. We need to treat ourselves with care as well. Let all of your surroundings treat you with the presence of God. Pay close attention to the trail, the weather, the weight of the pack.

During the afternoon of hiking, stop at some beautiful place and spend time in solitude. A whistle calls everyone back together to continue hiking.

For the campfire reflections, use questions related to awareness of one's body such as, "What was happening in your shoulders? What birds did you hear?" Also, "Where was your inner spirit leading during the silent hiking?"

CLOSING WORSHIP

The shared meal at the end of the retreat provides a time for evaluation and reflection. Use this time to help people ease gently back into their normal lives, taking something of the weekend with them.

You may want to close with a Christian adaptation of the Native American prayer of six directions. Here is the beginning and end of that prayer:

To the Great Spirit
First in all things, Creator of all Life,
Who was, and is, and will always be;
Who, within the immensity of all creation,
Is uniquely present here and now, in this moment.

We offer praise and thanksgiving,
We ask these things:
A heart open and made strong with love,
A mind clear and made wise with understanding,
A life lived with courage and compassion
in the fulfillment of divine purpose.

Canoe Trip: A Seven-Day Wilderness Adventure

Contributed by Perry Yoder and Tim Lehman

PURPOSE

Life in a wilderness setting for an extended period of time detaches us from our normal everyday lives and helps us recognize what is truly important. Being in nature becomes an experience of deep healing as we sense the presence of God more clearly. It also provides an experience of authentic community. The group bonds closely during the daily rhythm of reflection, hard work, meals, and fireside sharing.

For the full impact, this retreat needs to be for the full seven days. It takes most people three days to unwind, to detoxify from their hurried world and truly experience God's presence. It is at that point that the value of the retreat really takes hold.

This retreat plan grows out of a specific setting and experience. For many years, the contributors have led canoe trips that take groups of six to eight people into the Boundary Waters Canoe Area Wilderness in the arrowhead of Minnesota. Other wilderness trips can be patterned on this plan. It is very important that the leaders be experienced, comfortable, and confident in the wilderness. Leaders must do the trip enough times to become competent and confident guides of others. Outfitters in wilderness locations sometimes provide canoes, food, and guides, but even so, wilderness retreats require expert and experienced leaders.

"A paddle dipping into the water ...
The splash of a beaver tail ...
The echoing call of a loon ...
A northern sun setting on a glassy lake ...
Tall pines whispering in the wind ..."
—From Boundary Waters Canoe Area Wilderness website

MATERIALS NEEDED

- Advance information packet for all participants containing instructions, weight limits on personal items (15 pounds or less), and wilderness orientation. This information should include adequate information about sound ecological practices in a wilderness setting, instructions about what and what not to bring, and a list of practices for safety in the wilderness.
- Suggested advance reading: (For all group members) *Creation and the Persistence of Evil* by Jon Douglas Levenson (Princeton University Press, 1994); (For leaders and interested group members) *Ecotherapy: Healing Ourselves, Healing the Earth* by Howard John Clinebell (Fortress Press, 1996).
- Food: All food will be carried by backpack in waterproof bags. Purchase food and package it to divide the weight among group members. Leaders must find out about special food requirements and food allergies in advance.
- Equipment: Compasses, whistles, and backpacks for each person. Bear bags and rope to store food at night. Life jackets and canoes are the obvious. Please note that this is not a complete list but rather serves to describe this category.
- Participants are asked to bring Bibles, journals, and limited personal items. They are asked to get in shape beforehand to prepare for this physically challenging experience.

SCHEDULE

Weeklong Overview

Day 1	Afternoon arrival and orientation
Day 2	Begin the trip
Day 3-6	Wilderness experience
Day 4 or 5	Don't break camp (spend two nights at the same camp), eat a pancake breakfast, spend entire morning in silence, do a canoe side trip, hike, fish, rest, or journal
Day 7	Get up at sunrise, return to base camp, take out by early afternoon

Daily Rhythm

> Morning Bible study
> An hour of silence (exactly when varies with the group)
> Canoeing, portaging, setting up camp
> Making and eating meals
> Journaling
> Evening fireside sharing

GATHERING ACTIVITY

This is really an orientation versus one single activity. It is best to have people spend the afternoon and the first night gradually getting adjusted for the wilderness experience. This also allows for time to give safety orientation and provide ecological perspectives.

Give further ecological perspectives that will help people move respectfully through nature. Reiterate rules given in the advance information packet (i.e., no use of soap in the wilderness.)

Repeat safety instructions such as: a) Anything with a smell, such as toothpaste and insect repellent, must go into bear bags at night; b) Always tell someone if you are leaving camp; c) Wear your life jacket at all times while on the water. Add to these as needed.

Teach people how to use compasses and provide other wilderness orientation as needed. Become adjusted to being away from normal schedules. Prepare to leave your watches behind.

Assemble backpacks. Do not assume that men are the better carriers and should have heavier loads. The ability to carry packs and portage canoes is more a matter of determination than a function of gender. Age, however, may make a difference. A 70-year-old person may not be able to carry as heavy a load as a 35-year-old person.

RETREAT ACTIVITIES

Adapt the route and travel tempo to your needs. The goal is not to see how far you can paddle the canoes in a day. Some days you may decide to set up camp at mid-afternoon. On other days it may be later.

Morning Bible study. Base Bible studies on the book of Job, which has a lot of nature imagery without romanticizing nature. (Psalms would be another possibility.) Set daily themes such as Letting Go, Receiving, Simplicity, Integrity, Community, and Healing.

Sometime during the day, take an hour of silence. This can be while canoeing, at a stop along the way, or after arriving at a campsite for the evening. Encourage people to reflect throughout the day and to journal. Being in nature is conducive to feeling God's nearness and being wrapped in God's presence.

On the day that you don't break camp make pancakes as a special treat. It takes longer and won't be possible on other days. After Bible study, spend the rest of the morning in silence.

Evening fireside is the time for people to share their reflections of the day. Leaders are the spiritual guides, aware and attune to God's leading within the group. The group shares from their reflections throughout the day, usually on the particular theme of the day. Group closeness grows as people work, eat, and share with each other on a daily basis. Out of this closeness grow the deep discussions, trust, openness, and community that is the hallmark of this experience.

Special Group Retreats

Retreats planned for specific audiences will meet distinct needs. Women and men's retreats provide forums for discussing issues that concern each group. "Consider the Lilies" offers a schedule and activities uniquely suited for people with developmental disabilities and "Embracing God" provides ample opportunity for a church small group to grow spiritually in a context of sharing and trust.

Each of the retreats in this section offers a deep understanding of specific audiences and a special sensitivity for the soul care of a particular group. In addition, some of these retreats ask us to rethink our normal church programming. Two intergenerational retreats bring together children and adults for dynamic half-day retreats, offering a much-needed corrective to the separation of age groups. Many congregations hold an annual church retreat to promote fellowship. But, "Seeker-Friendly Church Campout" challenges us to include our neighbors and friends who do not attend church.

RETREATS IN THIS SECTION INCLUDE:
- Single and Single Again: A Weekend of Nurture and Friendship
- Jonah and God's Big Love: An Intergenerational Retreat
- Sharing God's Love: An Intergenerational Faith-Sharing Retreat
- And Jesus said, "Come": A Retreat for People Who Are Chronically Ill
- A Well-Watered Garden: A Daylong Retreat for Women

- Prayers for Healing: A Weekend Retreat for Women
- Shaping the Christian Male: A Weekend Retreat for Men
- Seeker-Friendly Church Campout: Including Our Friends and Neighbors
- Consider the Lilies: A Retreat for People with Developmental Disabilities
- Experiencing God: For Sunday School Classes or Small Groups

When Planning a Retreat for a Special Group

Aspects of Planning	*Special Suggestions*
PURPOSE (Varies with group)	Empowering group to give voice to the truth of their experience and God's purpose in their lives Providing in-depth pastoral care Bringing God's family together in new and dynamic ways Forming lasting, supportive communities of hope
SCHEDULE	Vary according to the special needs of the group Avoid over-scheduling group oriented activities
GATHERING ACTIVITY	A creative introduction time is important If the group is large, provide for a small group that will function throughout the weekend Balance individual and group time
RETREAT ACTIVITIES	Focus discussion times so that they empower rather than discourage Both singing and fun times can provide a tone of informality and community
CLOSING WORSHIP	Be especially open to what transformation has happened and be ready to adapt closing worship plans

Single and Single Again: A Weekend of Nurture and Friendship

Contributed by Amigo Centre

PURPOSE

This weekend retreat is designed to empower people who are single to claim their value and worth in the faith community and in the world. Because society and the church are often oriented toward the needs of couples and families, it is especially important for people who are single to find fellowship and encouragement in a nurturing, supportive setting.

Through worship, Bible study, and group discussions, we will be led to claim the wholeness that God intends for us. A candlelight dinner and music concert will provide enjoyment and celebration.

MATERIALS NEEDED

- Special arrangements: Schedule a music group that will have broad appeal. Plan with the retreat center for a beautiful and special candlelight meal.
- Food: Arrange for meals at the retreat center. Provide special late night snacks for those who gather to talk and fellowship after the planned activities.
- Copies: Schedule and handout
- Resources: *Psalms Anew: Inclusive Language (Praying with Hebrew Scriptures)* by Nancy Schreck and Maureen Leach (St. Mary's Press, 1986); other books on singleness
- Music: *Hymnal: A Worship Book* or other hymnals.

SCHEDULE
Friday

7:00	Registration
7:45	Gathering
8:15	Evening worship
9:15	Popcorn campfire

Saturday

7:30	Morning walk
8:30	Breakfast
9:30	Session 1 – Bible Study: An Old Testament Perspective
11:00	Session 2 – Friendship Circles
12:30	Leisurely lunch
2:00	Activity options (ball games, use of camp recreational facilities)
4:00	Free time
5:30	Candlelight dinner
8:30	Coffeehouse and concert

Sunday

8:00	Morning walk
9:00	Big brunch
10:30	Session 2 – Bible Study: A New Testament Perspective
11:30	Closing
12:00	End of retreat

GATHERING ACTIVITY

Welcome the group. Talk about what bring us together. Recognize the differences among us. We are single by design, default, delay, divorce, or death. Describe these briefly as follows.

Design: People choose to be single. Some have chosen careers over marriage. Some may simply like to live alone. Some may not want the burdens of family because they carry other responsibilities and choose to have more space and time for themselves than a family would allow.

Default: Some feel a responsibility to aging parents or some other family members. Others may have physical problems that prevent them from marrying.

Delay: Some people have so much to do, so many places they want to see, and then find out that all their friends are all married.

Divorce: The added dimension is that divorced singles often need to deal with the pain, anger, and grief that accompany broken relationships. In addition, they often have responsibilities for their children.

Death: Grief over the loss of a dear friend and constant companion is often overwhelming. This comes, in addition, to facing the changes brought by living alone.

Introduce yourselves to each other either in the whole group or in smaller groups. In a large group wear name tags and form small groups in which people can relate more easily.

We gather here as people who are unmarried. We want to share good times and develop a kind of extended family. In this kind of gathering we can form a network of people with whom to fellowship and grow. In the book, *A Different Woman*, Jane Howard says, "Only children should be brought up close to other only children so they will not someday have to reminisce alone. We who are unmarried, only children of another sort, must deepen and cultivate our friendships until water acquires the consistency of blood, until we develop new networks as sustaining as orthodox families."

You may want to read a few selected quotations from books about singles. *Single Adult Passages, Uncharted Territories* by Carolyn A. Koons and Michael J. Anthony (Baker Book House, 1995) is one example.

Distribute schedules if people do not already have them. Take care of any logistics or introductions to the retreat center. Sometimes retreat center personnel bring a special group welcome and make announcements.

Evening Worship. Lead a short worship time. Read Isaiah 43:1-7 as a special affirmation of each of us. Sing "God loves all his many people," *HWB* 397. Pray for a weekend that brings wholeness and friendships. Thank God for each person.

Popcorn campfire provides a time of informal fellowship and sharing.

RETREAT ACTIVITIES

Session 1—Bible Study: An Old Testament Perspective

Thank God for the beginning of this new day. Sing hymns that focus on God's love and greatness and wonders. Many have already taken a morning walk in this retreat setting.

Read Psalm 68 from *Psalms Anew* by Nancy Schreck and Maureen Leach.

Lead a Bible study. This look at Old Testament Scripture is divided into two parts: 1) First there is a theological focus on the underlying concern for wholeness presented in the Scriptures; 2) Secondly, there is a list of Old Testament characters whose lives in some way relate to people who are single.

Wholeness:

Not much is said about singleness in the Old Testament. Unmarried people were simply a part of the large extended family. However, we do get a broad picture of wholeness. God's concern about Adam's aloneness (Genesis 2) speaks to our need for human community and interrelatedness, not just love between a man and a woman. Rather than indicating that marriage is for everyone it shows us our need for companionship and emotional intimacy. God's concern about the misery of the Israelite people in Egypt and their dramatic release gives us yet another picture of the importance of wholeness (Exodus 3:7-8, Exodus 12). The Ten Commandments (Exodus 20) give guidelines for living together in wholesome ways. The laws regarding Sabbath Year and the Year of Jubilee offer a picture of communities of wholeness both for humans and the land (Leviticus 25). Being whole means being rooted in God's words and using that power to act in the world in order to bring life to others. We need to create faith communities that help people thrive.

Old Testament characters:

Sarah: We learn from Sarah's experience that we as humans look at things differently than God does. She had made peace with her childless state and so laughed when God told her she would have a child. But new life is always possible with God.

Ruth understood that by following Naomi she might never meet a man with the specific requirements needed for her to remarry. She was willing to forego marriage possibilities because she cared about Naomi.

Elijah was a single adult who heard God's call and was prepared to give the Lord his best regardless of the cost or consequences. He lived a solitary life characterized by travel, adventure, and hardships. His freedom from family responsibilities brought a single-minded approach to the mission God gave him.

Jephthah's daughter knew that because of her father's vow she would die without marrying and having children. Although she had no descendants, her friends made sure that she would not be forgotten. This otherwise troubling story shows her understanding of the need for close friendships and honesty about mourning lost opportunities (see Judges 11).

Session 2—Friendship Circles

Talk about the need to help our congregations and communities bring healthy changes so that people who are not married belong and thrive. As people called to wholeness, we need to become aware of the effect of exclusive practices as well of dream ways to make changes. One example of a small but significant awareness is that many congregations have begun to use phrases like, "every household," rather than "each family." We all, single and married, live in households.

Break into small groups to discuss scenarios that people who are not married often face. Distribute the two pages of the handout. Briefly review the instructions. Ask groups to return at noon to share their best ideas with the whole group.

Group discussion. This is an empowering time where groups share their dreams of a community of wholeness. Write down the dreams and ideas on large sheets of newsprint and post them around the room. This forms a communal memory of ideas generated together.

Outline plans for the rest of the day. Encourage participants to continue their creative discussions and friendship connections during the informal activities of the afternoon. The candlelight dinner should be a truly special celebrative and beautiful event.

Session 3—Bible Study: A New Testament Perspective

Sing gathering hymns, such as "Here in this place" and "Here, O Lord, your servants gather," *HWB* 6 and 7.

Read Psalm 42. Sing hymns of praise, such as "Christ is the world's true light," *HWB* 334, and "In the rifted Rock I'm resting," *HWB* 526.

Lead the Bible study focusing on the New Testament.

Jesus' Practice and Teaching:

Jesus' ministry and circle of disciples included women, presumably some of them single (for example: Mary, Martha, and Mary Magdalene).

Jesus rejected the idea that a woman's worth came from childbearing (see Luke 11:27-28).

Jesus, the fully authentic person, did not marry but rather existed entirely for the sake of his fellow humans. Clearly, Jesus' life and ministry shows that we do not need to believe the larger culture's message that only in marriage can we find completeness.

Wholeness:

Singleness need not be a burden or a punishment. Certainly not all of us are single because we have chosen it. We may continue to desire a spouse. However, singleness can be accepted as a gift from God for a season or for a lifetime. It allows us freedom to have a simple life, the freedom to be more efficient in one's calling without the demands of family, and the freedom to develop deep friendships. The theme running through Scripture is that God desires our best. God's knows us better than we know ourselves. We can thus accept God's unconditional love and accept our need for companionship, and know that we have much to offer others with our friendship and our gifts. We can also accept the gift of expediency that Paul talks about in Ephesians 5:15-16. We can give the best to God and pursue excellence in our daily life.

CLOSING WORSHIP

Sing, "God loves all his many people," *HWB* 397, and "If you but trust in God," *HWB* 576.

Lead in a closing prayer of lament, empowerment and thanksgiving.

O God who loves all your many people, many times we forget that we are all your children—single, married, divorced, or widowed.

We confess that sometimes the church has viewed us as incomplete and less than whole. We know that the church has often seen marriage as a "Win" rather than a gift.

We confess that sometimes loneliness overwhelms and forces us into a narrow world.

We stand with Ruth and Naomi, returning in sadness to Bethlehem.

We long for communities of wholeness.

We affirm that you call a special people to singleness. We stand with Elijah and Paul, with Mary and Martha and with the many saints of the church who have been spiritual and moral guides.

We want to serve you. If our being single or single again can serve that purpose, we long to know that.

Make us vessels that can be used. Mold us into shapes that can honor you and show your love to others.

We thank you for good friends, for times and places of being accepted without question. We thank you for the many opportunities that enrich our lives. Amen.

Sing, "My life flows on," *HWB* 580.

Scenarios

a) Discuss several scenarios in your group. Some scenarios show ways that singles are thoughtlessly excluded. Some deal with the boundary issues and other decisions that singles often face.

b) Dream of a community that truly welcomes and includes people who are single. Choose at least two scenarios and decide what you would like to see happen. What could be done to help raise awareness? How could you contribute toward that awareness?

1. Younger singles often hear the question, "How come a nice young man (or young woman) like you is not married?" Older singles may be asked questions about a spouse, with the assumption that they must surely have one.
Have you encountered these questions?
How do you feel about these questions?
What do you reply?

2. You have friends from church who are married. Suppose a friend of the opposite gender says to you, "My husband (wife) is out of town, would you like to go out for a meal?"
Have you ever received an invitation like this?
How would you feel being asked this question?
Would you go to lunch or dinner with this friend?
Does this raise boundary issues for you?

3. Sometimes finding a friend to do things with is difficult. You end up going alone. Do you ever hear other singles say, "I'd never go to a concert or dinner without an escort"?
If an acquaintance said this to you, how would you reply?
Do you go to events by yourself?
How do you feel about that?

4. The youth sponsored a Valentine's Dinner to raise funds to go on a mission trip. You went because you wanted to support their cause. When you arrived, you realized you were the only one without a partner and you upset the couples-oriented seating arrangement.
How did you feel?
Would you have gone if you had known?
How could you or the youth have handled the situation differently?

5. A common assumption is that singles have lots of time. You may hear remarks like, "Gloria can do it, after all she's single and has no responsibilities."
When you hear this kind of remark, what do you say?
What do you think about this assumption?
Do you perceive that most married people believe this?

6. You've been taught to pray about pain and joy. You prayed for a long time for God to direct you to a partner.

How do you feel about this?
Do you blame God? Are you angry at God?
Do you accept the situation? How?

7. My friend had a "maiden aunt" who was teased unmercifully at family gatherings. One Christmas all her siblings seemed to be bickering with their spouses. Finally she had had enough and responded, "I'd rather be single than wish I were single."
Do you think this could actually have happened?
How would you have replied to the situation?
Would you accept the teasing as a sign of affection?
How do you deal with hidden barbs?

8. First Christian Church, your home congregation, is having their annual New Year's party. Only couples are invited.
What is your response?
Would you go if you were invited?
Would you make a comment to anyone about it?

9. A nearby church college is having a fundraising dinner. You and a friend of the same gender decide to go to give support to the college. The tickets state $25 a couple; $15 a single ticket. You expect to get in for the couple price because there are two of you. However, the reservations attendant tells you that you don't qualify as a couple.
Have you experienced something similar? How did you feel?
How do you respond?

10. A friend turned fifty last year. You were not invited to the party. In fact, you didn't know about the party until the friend's spouse showed you photos of the party. All your couple friends were invited.
How do you feel?
Would it make a difference if the birthday person was of the opposite gender?
Would you have gone or would you have felt out of place?

11. Statistics show that in the past most marriages were "made in church," that is, people met their spouses in church.
Do these marriages work out better than other marriages?
Are mates still found in the church?
Would you marry outside the church? Why or why not?

12. The rituals of the church often seem exclusive. Child dedications or baptisms, weddings, Mother's Day, and Father's Day celebrations often speak only to a certain segment of the church.
Do these occasions bother you? Do you choose not to attend?
Do you feel excluded? By the occasion or by what is said?
What issues does it raise for you?

13. Write a scenario of your own.

Jonah and God's Big Love:
An Intergenerational Retreat

Contributed by Eleanor Snyder

PURPOSE

This half-day retreat is designed to create a setting that bring adults and children together. Through songs, a Bible story, and a choice of activities, we will experience and respond to God's never-ending love.

The schedule here is arranged as a morning retreat but could also begin with lunch and be an afternoon retreat. This could be planned as a part of an informal Sunday school fellowship retreat or extended to an overnight retreat using other sessions from the resource mentioned below. It could also be extended to an all-day retreat by adding the Sharing God's Love retreat plan for the afternoon.

This retreat borrows from the book, *Jonah and God's Big Love* by Eleanor Snyder and Allan Rudy-Froese (Faith & Life Press, 2000). This is a four-session book for adults and children based on the book of Jonah. The retreat could be expanded to a weekend parent-child retreat using more ideas from the book.

MATERIALS NEEDED
- Music: Drums, shakers, rain sticks or xylophone, *Hymnal: A Worship Book* (for the leader)
- Memory text: Poster board with Jonah 4:2b written out in large letters

- Activity center supplies: Music (coffee tins, brown paper, markers, dowels or sticks, pop cans, dried beans, rice, pebbles, duct tape, paper, scissors, glue, memory verse poster); Read, Write, and Pray (Books, paper for journals, writing tools); Art (large sheet of newsprint that says, "His Banner Over Me Is Love," crayons, markers); Game (rope or masking tape)
- Copies: Schedule, Handout 1 for leaders, cut-apart copy of Handout 2 to place at each activity center
- Break: Crackers with tuna spread, or fish-shaped cracker and juice; add net, seashells, and other seashore items as visual reminders of the story

SCHEDULE

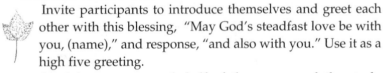

9:00 a.m.	Gathering – Introduction
9:30	Session 1 – Worship and Story
10:00	Break and organize groups
10:15	Session 2 – Jonah Activities
11:00	Closing worship and reflection
11:30	Lunch

GATHERING ACTIVITY

Invite participants to introduce themselves and greet each other with this blessing, "May God's steadfast love be with you, (name)," and response, "and also with you." Use it as a high five greeting.

Lead in a prayer on behalf of the group and the study together about Jonah and God's love. Present the goals of this half-day retreat:

- To give children and adults opportunity to learn about Jonah
- To know God as gracious and loving
- To affirm that God seeks a relationship of love and obedience with each of us

• Distribute schedule and introduce the subject and activities of this intergenerational retreat time.

Form into groups of four to five people. Form a group with children, youth, and adults together so that the ages are mixed within the group. Parents with young children may want to form their own family group so that the young children feel secure in a new setting. Designate a leader for each group.

If you have a signal for the end of the Talk-it-over Time, such as a bell, let them know what it is; if not, ask participants to take responsibility for keeping track of time.

RETREAT ACTIVITIES
Session 1—Worship and Story

Sing three or four songs from the following list. The number after each one indicates its location in *Hymnal: A Worship Book*, if it is found there. The rest are familiar camp songs.

"For God so loved us" 167

"God loves all his many people" 397

"Kumbaya"

"Jesus loves me" 341

"O Lord, hear my prayer" 348

"I'm gonna sing when the Spirit says sing" (add "go when the Spirit says go")

"It's me, it's me, it's me, O Lord"

Introduce the memory verse as a prayer to God. It is best to have it written on poster board or chart paper. Use percussion instruments to help the group learn the words.

"For I knew that you are a gracious God and merciful, slow to anger, and abounding in steadfast love, and ready to relent from punishing" (Jonah 4:2b).

"For I knew" (*three drum beats*)

"that you are" (*three drum beats*)

"a gracious God and merciful" (*shakers*)

"slow to anger" (*drum beat, then say slowly*)

"and abounding in steadfast love" (*say faster, accompany with xylophone or rain sticks*)

"and ready to relent from punishing." (*whisper in awe*)

"Amen!" (*shout and use all instruments*)

Sing "We give thanks unto you," *HWB* 161.

Tell the story of Jonah. Read all of Jonah from an easy to understand version of the Bible or retell, preserving the events of the story, but simplifying and shortening it somewhat. You may want to tell it garbed in burlap (sack cloth).

After the story, think quietly for a moment to let the story settle in. Then discuss the story in family groups. Each group will want to find a spot to talk quietly with each other about the story. Give Handout 1 to family group leaders to guide the discussion.

Break—A mid-morning Jonah snack. Visual and food ideas: Offer crackers with tuna spread, or fish-shaped cracker and juice. Add net, seashells, and other seashore items as visual reminders of the story.

Session 2—Jonah Activities

Quiet and gather the group by dimming the lights and beginning to sing one of the songs sung earlier.

Introduce the activity options. People choose one activity to start. Later, they may add another activity if time permits. The leader will need to present the following options and show where they are located so that people will be able to choose. Directions for set up follow.

- •Music: You will make shakers and drums. Then you will decorate them, review memory verse with rhythm, and create a song using the memory verse.
- •Read, Write, and Pray: Read one or more of the books. Write about ways you experienced God's never-ending love. Or draw a picture that reminds you of God's patient love for you. Books: *Love You Forever* by Robert Munsch (Firefly Books, 1996); *The Runaway Bunny* by Margaret Wise Brown (Harper Trophy, 1942); *Walking with Jesus* by Mary Clemens Meyer (Herald Press, 1992). This last book is a collection of stories. Read "Neighbor Al" and "Beth, Kind Friend."
- •Art: On the large sheet of newsprint that says "His Banner Over Me Is Love," you will draw scenes from the Jonah

story that tell something about your relationship with God, or write slogans and draw how you understand your relationship with God.

• Game: You will go outdoors to play the tag game, "Jonah and the Big Fish." Mark off an area as the "ocean," so that everyone has room to "swim." At both ends of the ocean, mark off a "ship" with a rope or masking tape. The ship should be large enough to hold most of the players. To begin, one person, "the big fish," stands in the middle of the ocean and the other players are on the ship. When the big fish says, "Sailors overboard!" all the players must jump into the ocean area and run to the other ship without getting swallowed by "the big fish." Anyone who is tagged becomes a big fish, too, and joins in the search for more swimming sailors. The game is over when the last sailor is swallowed.

• Drama. This is for the brave and creative. You will create a modern day skit to present to the group. Who would be the prophet today? Where would the prophet be sent? How would the prophet "run away"? What would fulfill God's purpose of love? How would the story end?

CLOSING WORSHIP

Gather in family groups. Allow time for each person to share what they did, what they learned, how they felt, what new thing they will remember about Jonah or God's love.

Allow time for sharing new insights, the drama, and the art with the whole group. Use the drums and shakers to review the memory text.

Closing Song. Sing "Go now in peace," *HWB* 429, as a round and with movements.

Go now in peace, *(extend right arm and open hand in front of you)*
Go now in peace, *(extend left arm and open hand in front of you)*
May the love of God surround you everywhere, *(circle to the right, both arms out stretched)*
Everywhere you may go *(join hands in a large circle).*

Talk-it-Over Time

Thinking

(Don't expect factual answers. Ask the question in a wondering tone of voice and give time to ponder the meaning of the story. With young children, parents may wish to review the story again to avoid or correct any misunderstandings that would hamper their work with the story.)

I wonder why Jonah thought he could run away from God.
I wonder why God sent the big fish.
I wonder why all the people of Nineveh listened to Jonah and wanted to change.

Sharing

(Invite verbal responses to these sentence starters. Add your own.)

One thing I learned about God in this story . . .
One time when I felt or acted like Jonah did . . .
One thing I need to think more about . . .

Praying

Take time to huddle together in the smaller groupings for a short prayer to end this reflection time.

Dear God, I am glad that . . .
Dear God, I am sad about . . .
Dear God, because of your steadfast love for all your people, I . . .
Amen.

Jonah Activities

Cut apart and place instructions at each of the activity locations.

MUSIC

You will make shakers and drums. Then you will decorate them, review memory verse with rhythm, and create a song using memory verse.

Instructions for a pop can shaker:
1. Pour seeds or stones into the can through the opening.
2. Cover the opening with duct tape.
3. Decorate the can with paper shapes or pictures from the Jonah story.

Instructions for a drum:
1. Cover the sides and base of the metal coffee can with brown paper.
2. Decorate the drum with markers.
3. Use sticks for drumsticks.

READ, WRITE, AND PRAY

Read one or more of the books. Use the paper and writing tools to write about ways you experience God's never-ending love. Or draw a picture that reminds you of God's patient love for you.

BOOKS: *Love You Forever* by Robert Munsch (Firefly Books, 1996); *The Runaway Bunny* by Margaret Wise Brown (Harper Trophy, 1942); *Walking with Jesus* by Mary Clemens Meyer (Herald Press, 1992). This last book is a collection of stories. Read "Neighbor Al" and "Beth, Kind Friend."

ART

On the large sheet of newsprint that says "His Banner Over Me Is Love," you will draw scenes from the Jonah story that tell something about your relationship with God. Or, write slogans and draw how you understand your relationship with God.

GAME

You will go outdoors to play the tag game, "Jonah and the Big Fish." Mark off an area as the "ocean," so that everyone has room to "swim." At both ends of the ocean, mark off a "ship" with a rope or masking tape. The ship should be large enough to hold most of the players. To begin, one person, "the big fish," stands in the middle of the ocean and the other players are on the ship. When the big fish says, "Sailors overboard!" all the players must jump into the ocean area and run to the other ship without getting swallowed by "the big fish." Anyone who is tagged becomes a big fish, too, and joins in the search for more swimming sailors. The game is over when the last sailor is swallowed.

DRAMA

This is for the brave and creative. You will create a modern day skit to present to the group. Who would be the prophet today? Where would the prophet be sent? How would the prophet "run away"? What would fulfill God's purpose of love? How would the story end?

Sharing God's Love:
An Intergenerational Faith-Sharing
Retreat

Contributed by Eleanor Snyder

PURPOSE

This half-day retreat is designed to increase our ability to share faith stories and respectfully listen to others' experiences across the generations. Through communication activities, biblical reflection, and a closing blessing we will be introduced to practices that help us talk about our experiences with God. This retreat could be used as a part of a larger church campout event or family reunion.

MATERIALS NEEDED

- Resources: *God Is Like a Mother Hen and Much, Much More* by Carolyn Stahl Bohler or *In God's Name* by Sandy Eisenberg Sasso.
- Emmaus Walk Plan: The stops along the way can be: a picnic table, a ball diamond, blanket near water or under a tree. Fill in the locations on Handout 3. Site 2—Lay several Bibles on a solid blue cloth. Site 4—Arrange crackers, cookies, grapes, and fruit pieces in baskets covered with cloths that blend with the colors of nature. Site 5—Place a container of markers and Post-it Notes and one of the books mentioned as resources above. Anchor a

large sheet of paper with rocks for the chart. Site 7—
Make a nature arrangement with leaves, sticks, rocks,
flowers, bird nests, feathers, and other such items. Or
plan this stop where people can gather items from
nature. Include modeling clay at this site.

• Locate the sites on a map and make copies. Copies of
Handouts 1-3

• Optional site: Place Faith Talk cards and invite participants
to choose a card and share. Faith Talk cards are available
from Faith & Life Resources at Mennonite Publishing
Network. (Call 1-800-743-2484.)

• Furnishings: For the closing worship, place a table for the
altar in a sunlit area or close to the window of the room.
Cover with a green or brown cloth. Arrange chairs in
semi-circle facing the table. Arrange candles (one per
Emmaus Walk group) in wooden candleholders on the
table.

SCHEDULE

1:00 p.m.	Gathering activity – Introduction
1:30	Session 1 – Faith Talk
2:15	Session 2 – Emmaus Walk
3:30	Closing Worship
4:00	Close of retreat

This retreat could also be extended to include a simple
evening meal of bread and cheese, marmalades and other
spreads, fruit, and hot tea. Shorten the Emmaus Walk slightly
and use item four on the Emmaus Walk handout as the plan for
your meal conversation. Move closing worship plan to after the
meal.

GATHERING ACTIVITY

Invite participants to gather in a circle. If they haven't
already done so, ask them to introduce themselves briefly to
one another. Present the goals of this half-day retreat:

- To share faith stories and respectfully listen to others' experiences across the generations.
- To learn practices that help us listen and share as we continue on our faith journey.

As you begin, remind the group that we have set aside time to pay attention to the ways we can share God's love. The journey of faith is not made alone. We walk with others in our families and congregations and we gain from sharing our stories with each other.

Lead in prayer on behalf of the group and the sharing of their faith experiences.

Distribute the schedule and discuss the alternating rhythm of group sessions and gathering. If you have a signal for gathering, such as a bell, let them know what it is; if not, ask participants to take responsibility for keeping track of time.

RETREAT ACTIVITIES

Session 1—Faith Talk

 Practice and review communication skills. Form the participants into groups of four. People in the group should be different decades in ages. Choose one person in each group to be the group leader. Give Handout 1 to each group leader.

Discuss the experience when groups return. Invite responses from the group about how they felt as observer, storytellers, and listeners in each of the three activities.

Talk about good communication skills. A key to good conversation is good communication skills.

Skills involve what we say, how we say it, and how we listen. Active listening involves paying attention to non-verbal language. What types of non-verbal communication did you observe that were positive? What other clues to effective communication did you observe?

EXAMPLES OF NON-VERBAL LANGUAGE

Body language (facial expressions, hand gestures, embracing)

Intonation (voice pitch)

Physical space or distance (how close were you to each other)

Eye contact

Silence or lack of participation (positive or negative)

Sounds (ummmh)

Frequency of contact (or avoidance)

Loudness of voice

Discuss showing respect for what is being said. When we listen we do not interrupt with our own stories, but listen to the speaker. We do not think about a personal story that we can add after the other is finished. We immerse ourselves in the story, let go of our own stories, agenda, and give our full attention to what is being said.

Faith talk. It is sometimes hard to talk about our relationship with God to each other. Sharing faith means telling each other about our memories, our feelings, and our thoughts about God. They are our own thoughts and no one can take them away. Our experiences are our own experiences and no one can take them away. God speaks to each of us in different ways for we are unique and loved by God.

Distribute Handout 2. Gather in the groups used for the communication activity above. Each participant chooses which one of the ideas they wish to share about. Allow two minutes for each one to share while the others listen.

Session 2—Emmaus Walk

Tell the story of the walk to Emmaus from Luke 24:13-35. Point out the aspects of faith sharing that are evident in this story.

Two disciples as companions—Faith needs other people

Walking on the road—Faith is a journey

Making sense of daily life and tragic events—We can share concerns and questions

Welcoming the stranger as he walked with them—We make
    room for others on this journey

Listening to the Scripture—Scripture informs our faith journey

Practicing hospitality—By inviting a stranger they invited
    Jesus

Sharing a meal together—While eating together they recog-
    nized Jesus

Telling the good news—Sharing God's story allows for new
    insight

Instructions for the Emmaus Walk. Set up stations and make
maps showing site locations. If possible, plan to do this walk
outdoors. The stops along the way can be a picnic table, a ball
diamond, a blanket near water or under a tree. Groups of six max-
imum or a family can travel together. You will need as many
groups as stations. If you are working with a large retreat group
you will need to plan for two sets of Emmaus Walk sites. Each
group starts at a different station and rotates in the same direction.
Spend approximately 8-10 minutes at each site. When you arrive at
the site, read the instructions and respond accordingly. When
finished, return to the common area for some singing and sharing.

CLOSING WORSHIP

When people have reassembled, sing songs people learned
in childhood. Comment that music has power beyond
words. Invite children to suggest favorite songs and older
people to share songs that stayed with them from their
childhood. Share stories about songs. While singing bring symbols of God's love (Emmaus Walk, 7) to place on the altar.

Prayer as faith sharing. Invite the participants to form into
the groups used for the Emmaus Walk. Give each group a stick
or candle. Remind them of the gift they gave to each other as
they shared stories. Invite participants to name one thing they
would like others to pray for on their behalf. Each person is
invited to take a turn holding the candle "prayer stick." Others
pray quietly for that person's request. Even if the person has not
mentioned a request, thank God for the person.

Closing Blessing: May God bless you and make you a blessing.

Communication Activities

Group facilitators assign the role of storyteller, listener, and observer to people within the group. **Switch roles for each activity** so that the storyteller has opportunity to be the listener, and the observer becomes the storyteller in Activity B.

Give each one instructions. Allow about two minutes for Storyteller to talk in each activity.

Activity A
Storyteller: Think of a birthday story to tell.
Listener: This person is told privately to listen to the story, but not to make eye contact or appear too interested. (No body language)
Observer: Watch the dynamics between the storyteller and the listener.

Activity B
Storyteller: Tell story of a trip taken when you were a kid.
Listener: This person is told privately to listen to the story, make eye contact, but do not respond or nod. (No supportive body language)
Observer: Watch the dynamics between the storyteller and the listener.

Activity C
Storyteller: Tell a memory from an experience of church.
Listener: This person is told to listen attentively, by keeping eye contact and appropriate body language (nodding, responding, affirming).
Observer: Watch the dynamics between the storyteller and the listener.

Return to the common area to talk about your experience as story-tellers, listeners, and observers.

Faith Talk Questions

You may choose any one of the following areas to talk about. You will have two minutes to share while the rest of the group listens using the skills we discussed.

Tell about your earliest memories of praying . . .

A favorite song/prayer/Bible verse I learned as a child is . . .

The Sunday school teacher I will never forget is . . .

The person who showed me what God is like is . . .

When I think of church, I . . .

Emmaus Walk

Spend approximately 8-10 minutes at each site. When you arrive at the site, read the instructions and respond accordingly. When finished, return to the common area for some singing and sharing.

Talk Points Along the Way (based on Emmaus story)

1. *On the Way*—Located at _____
Tell one thing that happened to you in the last days or weeks that made you think about God. Are there certain times that you are more aware of God than others?

2. *The Bible Speaks*—Located at _____
Tell a favorite Bible story or verse from your childhood. Why do you think you remember it? Why is it still important to you?
Someone read Psalm 148. Each person will give a personal response to this psalm by completing this sentence:
"I praise God for . . ."
All respond with, "Praise God for . . . " (repeating what was just said).

3. *Friends Along the Way*—Located at _____
Tell a story about how someone helped you understand God/ Jesus better. This may be a parent, grandparent, child, youth, mentor, friend, Sunday school teacher. What did they say or do that was helpful to you?

4. *Making Room for God at Home*—Located at _____
Eat a simple snack: crackers, cookies, grapes, fruit pieces.
Talk about the table graces or rituals you have at home now. What are other ways that you welcome God in your homes?
Older people share appropriate stories from your childhood around mealtime graces, family devotions, and other practices.

5. *What Is God Like for You?*—Located at _____
Read the book and think about the images for God that are mentioned. Think of a time that you felt really close to God. What word would best describe what God was like for you? Write it on the paper or draw a picture, then place it on the large sheet of paper provided. Each group will add to this chart of images for God.

6. *Practicing God's Love*—Located at _____
What is one way that you can practice God's love to someone you do not know or like very well (at work, in school, in your neighborhood)?

7. *Personal Quiet Time*—Located at _____
Spend half of this time alone. Think about a symbol or item of nature that reminds you of God's love. Without disrupting nature, bring the symbol back to the common area for Closing Worship. If you cannot easily bring the item back, use modeling clay to resemble it. Tell briefly why you chose the symbol, what it tells you of God/Jesus or your relationship with God.

And Jesus Said, "Come": A Retreat for People Who Are Chronically Ill

Contributed by Cindy Breeze

PURPOSE

This weekend retreat focuses on issues regarding long-term illness and disability. It offers a confidential environment for worship, sharing, and celebration. The participants will find encouragement and support through Scripture reading, prayer, and mutual sharing of struggles in a safe environment.

A retreat such as this one grows out of congregational care and should be done with sensitivity to the invitees. Extend personal invitations rather than a bulletin announcement. Arrange for a retreat center that is fully handicapped accessible. Meal plans may need to take into account special dietary needs. The cost of the retreat might come from a mutual aid fund rather than from participants. Take into consideration any modifications you will need to make due to specific disabilities.

Chronic illness includes three components: Any condition that lasts at least three months; any condition that interferes with daily function; any condition marked by uncertainty, the need for lots of care, and lack of a cure.

MATERIALS NEEDED

- Music: *Hymnal: A Worship Book* or other hymnals; CD player and music recordings; *Abide with Me: More Hymns for Guitar* by Tom Harder (Herald Press)

- Worship centers: <u>Session 1</u>—light blue cloth, darker blue scarf, bouquet of flowers, blue candle; <u>Session 2</u>—dark purple cloth, an upright wooden cross; <u>Session 3</u>—black cloth, tall white candle on a gold pedestal holder, empty candle holders, basket of taper candles (one per person); <u>Session 5</u>—white cloth, smaller gold cloth, grape juice in a pottery pitcher, small paper cups, bread on a plate, flower petals, and two vials of olive oil
- Food: Set a beautiful table with tablecloths and real dishes to communicate God's special love and care. Arrange with the retreat center for any special dietary needs.
- Copies: Schedule, Matthew 11:28-30, Handout 1 cut into strips
- Other: Gift baskets, rocks, markers, newsprint sheets, small notebooks, tray with water in small glasses
- Resources: *Ministry to Persons with Chronic Illnesses: A Guide to Empowerment through Negotiation* by John T. Vanderzee (Augsburg Press, 1993)

SCHEDULE

Friday

7:30 p.m.	Arrival and moving in
8:00	Gathering activity
8:30	Session 1 – Come and Rest Awhile: Mark 6:31
9:00	Snacks and free time

Saturday

8:00 a.m.	Morning prayers for retreat leaders
8:30	Breakfast
9:15	Session 2 – Come, You Who Carry Heavy Burdens: Matthew 11:28-30
9:45	Stories and discussion, part 1
11:00	Free time
12:15	Lunch
1:00	Stories and discussion, part 2
2:15	Free time
5:15	Discussion: What I want my family and close friends to know

6:30	Dinner
7:30	Session 3 – Come to the Light: John 12:46
8:00	Movie and popcorn
10:00	Snacks and free time

Sunday

7:30 a.m.	Morning prayers for retreat leaders
8:00	Breakfast
9:00	Session 4 – What I want my congregation to know
10:30	Personal quiet time
11:30	Session 5 – Come for Everything Is Ready Now: Luke 14:17
12:30	Lunch
1:30	End of retreat

This retreat works best with two or more people leading the retreat as a team. Extra support staff may be needed depending on the needs of the participants. Retreat leaders meet each morning to pray for God's leading. Remember that this is not a strict script to follow but rather a place to begin. Be open to the leading of the Holy Spirit and the needs of the group.

GATHERING ACTIVITY

Place gift baskets and notes of welcome in each of the rooms. Contents may include gift soaps, lotion, fruit, home-made cookies, or other items.

Welcome participants. If the retreatants are from a single con-gregation they will not need formal introductions. Use this time to help people get to know each other better. Ask partici-pants to share three things about themselves. What is your favorite food and why? Tell of a time in your school days when you got in trouble. If you could choose anywhere in the world to be next week at this same time, where would that be and why?

Give an overview of the theme and purpose of the weekend. Recognize that all present have ongoing serious health issues. Acknowledge that some may feel angry with God because of their suffering. Stress that this will be a safe, confidential, and trustworthy place. Give permission to use free time entirely as desired by each participant. Look at the schedule together and briefly identify locations for the sessions and the meals. Locate other important retreat facilities, such as handicapped accessible nature trails and restrooms. Be open to private listening times with retreat leaders and explain how to arrange a time.

RETREAT ACTIVITIES
Session 1—Come and Rest Awhile: Mark 6:31

Visual elements. Cover worship center table with a light blue cloth and a darker blue scarf-like cloth placed flowingly through the middle. Add a large bouquet of flowers and a blue candle. The worship center should communicate rest and peace.

Read Mark 6:31 and play "I heard the voice of Jesus say," *HWB* 493, on the recorder, then sing the first verse. Read Isaiah 40:31. Another possibility is to set a peaceful tone by playing a recording of "Arioso" by J. S. Bach.

In your own words, tell the Bible story surrounding Mark 6:31. After burying John, the disciples had clamored around Jesus, all speaking at once about their experiences, about their hard work, and about their intense grief. Jesus invited them to a quiet place to rest. That invitation is for us, too.

Lead in a prayer for the weekend and the participants. Invite people to put aside the busyness of the week and the hardships of the week, and accept Jesus' invitation to rest.

We hear, O Jesus, your voice saying, "Come to me and rest awhile."

We do come to you, just as we are.

We come to you tired, thirsty, hungry, weary.

We rest in the knowledge that you love us.

We rest in the knowledge that you want to help us carry our loads.

We find in you a resting place, a hiding place, a place where our souls are refreshed by your living water. Amen.

Play "Jesus, Rock of ages," *HWB* 515, on a recorder. Pass around a tray with small glasses of water, indicating that participants should hold the glasses until everyone has water. Sing "Jesus, Rock of ages," again (the words are simple enough to do so without having to open hymnals), then say, "And now, may the one who calls you to rest, grant you a night of peaceful sleep." Drink the water together.

Session 2—Come, You Who Carry Heavy Burdens: Matthew 11:28-30

Visual elements. Cover the worship table with a dark purple cloth. Add only an upright wooden cross. Place two large rocks and a marker under each chair.

Sing "Morning has broken," *HWB* 648, and "Jesus, thou mighty Lord," *HWB* 115. Offer thanks for the night's rest and for the Holy Spirit's leading, then read Matthew 11:28-30.

Distribute copies of Matthew 11:28-30 along with a pencil for each person. Read and reread the verses, letting them soak into our minds and hearts. Underline words in the passage that particularly stand out to you. Read it aloud again, inviting people to join the leader on the words that they underlined. Allow time for sharing thoughts and insights from the group.

Rock burdens. Invite people to take the rocks and markers from under their chairs. Say: "These rocks are symbolic of the burdens you are carrying. Put the rocks in your laps. Pick up one of them to feel its weight. What does that rock symbolize for you? What burden is weighing you down right now? Name the burden silently. If you feel comfortable doing so, write a word or phrase on the rock to name the burden. Now lift the other rock. What additional burden is weighing you down? If you feel like you need to add rocks to your pile, we can bring more rocks to you." Reassure people that if they don't feel comfortable making a public statement by writing on the rock, knowing it in their own minds is enough.

Play recordings of "Come, ye disconsolate" and "Great is thy faithfulness" from *Abide with Me: More Hymns for Guitar* while people are writing on their rocks. Then with the music still playing softly, invite participants to bring their rocks to the table and place them around the bottom of the cross.

Sing the first three verses of "My hope is built on nothing less," *HWB* 343.

Pray this prayer to close the session.

> To the one who takes your burdens,
> who is gentle and humble in heart,
> who gives you rest for your souls,
> and who carries your sorrows:
> All praise and honor and glory. Amen.

Stories and discussion, part one. Begin to hear the stories of the participants' illnesses. Explain that the purpose is for participants to know each other better, to relate their own personal stories to the stories of others, and to begin to see the possibilities for encouragement and support from each other.

Distribute small notebooks. These may be used to jot down notes about what they want to share, as well as questions while someone else is sharing. Emphasize that it is fine if someone does not want to share their illness story.

Stress that each storyteller will be given our undivided attention and that each story will stand alone. We will take plenty of time to hear each other; that is why we have set aside two times for these stories. We will not ask questions during or immediately following the story, but questions may be written down to ask later. Give people about 10 minutes to prepare, then let people volunteer to begin or be next. After the telling of each story, allow a minute of quiet reflection time. After the silence say, "We hear your story. Jesus hears your story." Around 11:00 leave quietly and respectfully for the free time, knowing that the rest of the stories will be shared after lunch.

Stories and discussion, part two, follows the same plan as outlined above. After all have finished, allow time for the questions people have jotted down. Before breaking for the afternoon free time, briefly introduce the next discussion topic so that people can be thinking about what they want to say.

Discussion: What I want my family and close friends to know about chronic illness and disability. Write each person's comments on sheets of newsprint. If the group is too large for comfortable, open discussion, break into smaller groups, then report back. Before the end of the session, encourage each participant to commit to share at least one thing about his or her struggle with a family member or friend. Bless those commitments in prayer and offer thanksgiving for each person, for each person's family and friends, and for the honesty within the group. Include a blessing for the dinner meal.

Session 3—Come to the Light: John 12:46

Preparation. Cover the worship table with a black cloth. In the center, place a tall, lighted candle on a gold pedestal holder. This cross symbolizes Christ. Surround the Christ candle with empty candleholders, evenly spaced. Prepare a basket of white taper candles (one per person). Cut apart sections of the prayers on Handout 1 and place them on the seats of people who will read the parts of this prayer.

Read Psalm 38:9-11, 21-22; 43:3. Then lead the group prayer activity: "I will begin and end a prayer. If you have a slip of paper on your chair, you are to read your portion of the prayer when you are ready. Do not worry about the order in which these are read. If your prayer tells the name of an author, you also do not need to read that part. Read when you are ready. I will be closing the prayer."

Sing verses one and two of "Lo, a gleam from yonder heaven," *HWB* 591.

Invite participants to come forward to take a candle from the basket as a tangible symbol that Christ is the light of the world. People may light their candles at the worship table and place the candle in one of the holders. They may pray there or at their seats. Play soft instrumental music and lower the lights in order to enjoy the candlelight.

Close with a prayer of blessing. You may want to choose a prayer from one of the books mentioned on Handout 1.

Session 4—What I Want My Congregation to Know

Provide an opportunity for participants to discuss what they want the congregation to know about chronic illness and disability. Make a list on newsprint sheets. Is the group willing to share with the retreat leaders present? At the end identify the three most important suggestions for improvement in congregational sensitivity and awareness. End the session with a prayer of thanksgiving for each person's honesty.

During the personal quiet time: Write a letter to your family or to God; write a prayer, take your hymnal outside in the woods and sing; or write about how you have met Jesus this weekend.

CLOSING WORSHIP

 Visual elements. Cover the worship table with a white cloth and a smaller gold cloth. Light the Christ candle used in session 3. For communion add grape juice in a pottery pitcher, small paper cups, and bread on a plate. Add petals of flowers from the arrangement used on Friday evening, and two vials of olive oil.

Play meditative music as people gather. When all have gathered shut off the music and say: "The candle has been lit, the juice poured, the bread baked, the oil of anointing prepared. Come. for everything is ready now."

Sing, "Come, let us all unite to sing," *HWB* 12. Read Isaiah 43:1-3a, 4a, 5a. Then sing "Children of the heavenly Father," *HWB* 616.

Give a short homily growing out of the weekend sharing. You may want to wait to plan this until Saturday evening so that it reflects the work of the Holy Spirit during this retreat. Mark 1:9-11 may be a helpful passage for your reflection.

Share in an anointing service for those who want to participate. People may mention specific needs for which they desire anointing. Place oil on each person's forehead in the shape of a cross while saying, "_____, you are God's beloved son/daughter."

Open a time for anyone who wants to share how God has ministered to them or spoken to them throughout the weekend. Then invite all to come to the table for communion.

Closing prayer. "Beloved sons and daughters: May the Christ who invited you to this table meet you each day as we go from this place. Go in love. Amen."

Sing, "Come, come ye saints," *HWB* 425, and lead in the following benediction:

May God bless and keep you.

May the very face of Jesus shine on you and be gracious to
    you.

May the presence of Christ embrace you

and give you peace, hope, love, and joy.

Handout 1

"Come to the Light" Group Prayer

Leader: Jesus, we know you have called us to "Come." Here we are!
You know that we struggle with our illnesses and disabilities.
They are our darkness. We ask you to hear the prayers of our hearts:

Jesus, Divine Physician and Healer, we turn to you.
Comforter of the troubled, alleviate our worry and sorrow.
> —p. 215, *The Hem of His Garment* by Laurence J. Gesy. Our Sunday Visitor Publishing, 1996

Can't you do anything for your wounded ones? We are the ones who
walk in loneliness. We are the ones full of fear. We are the ones whose
lives are in upheaval. We are the ones who kneel before you.
> —p. 84-85, *Psalms of Lament* by Ann Weems. Westminster John Knox Press, 1995

Sometimes, Jesus, my mind is not able to concentrate on you. My heart
is not able to remain centered, and it seems as if you are absent and
have left me alone.
> —From Henri Nouwen p. 21, *All Will Be Well: A Gathering of Healing Prayers* by Lyn
> Klug, ed. Augsburg Fortress, 1998

I dream of a day when I no longer feel distress in my body. I cry out to
you to hear me to stretch your arms of compassion to me and to
embrace me with your comfort.
> —p. 131, *Praying Our Goodbyes* by Joyce Rupp. Ivy Press, 1988

Jesus, you know how overwhelming life can sometimes be. You know
the darkness of my soul.

There is a deep canyon of desolation in me. Be my strength so that I will
not give up. Be my vision so that I can see how to live in this suffering.
> —p. 157, *Praying Our Goodbyes* by Joyce Rupp. Ivy Press, 1988

Jesus, where shall we find you?

Leader: You have heard the prayers of our hearts, O Lord. We give you
thanks for the privilege of sharing them with you. Amen.
Here now these words of assurance: Christ, the light has illuminated
the darkness of the world and the darkness in our lives. "What has
come into being in him was life, and the life was the light of all people.
The light shines in the darkness, and the darkness did not overcome it.
Jesus is the true light, which enlightens everyone. In him there is no
darkness at all. If we walk in his light as he himself is in the light, we
have fellowship with one another. Jesus calls you out of the darkness
into his marvelous light."
> —from John 1:3b-5, 9; 1 John 1:5b, 7a

A Well-Watered Garden:
A Daylong Retreat for Women

Contributed by Jane Halteman

PURPOSE

This day of refreshment and relaxation offers participants a change of pace from their day-to-day work. Spending time with God in the garden becomes a metaphor for the rest God gives and the transformation God works in open hearts. Plan this retreat for the spring of the year.

MATERIALS NEEDED

- Music: Recording of "In the bulb there is a flower," *Songs to Live By II: Passing on Hymns of Faith*. Faith & Life Press. (Call 1-800-743-2484 to order.)
- Food: Arrangements for a simple but hearty lunch
- Indoor garden: Potted plants, bedding plants, flowering plants, a fountain, single stem roses (one per person), and garden stakes
- Book: *May I Have This Dance?* by Joyce Rupp (Ave Maria Press, 1992)
- Art supplies: Paper for journaling; crayons, colored pencils, and other drawing supplies, construction paper, poster board, and glue for guided art prayer
- Worship center: Low table, glass bowl, candle, butterflies (one per person), votive candles (one per person)

SCHEDULE

9:00 a.m.	Arrival
9:15	Gathering activity
10:00	Break
10:15	Session 1 – Abiding in the Garden
10:45	Journaling
11:30	Prayer of reflection
12:00	Lunch
12:45	Session 2 – Discerning God's Voice
1:30	Group sharing
2:00	Break
2:15	Closing worship
2:45	End of retreat

GATHERING ACTIVITY

Visual environment. Create an indoor garden with potted green and flowering plants, bedding plants, a fountain, single stem roses in a glass vase, wind chimes, garden stakes. Arrange chairs in a circle.

Welcome participants as you play nature sounds and "In the bulb there is a flower" on a CD recording.

Introduce the day's schedule and theme. Read these Scriptures to introduce the theme of a well-watered garden: Isaiah 58:11, Jeremiah 31:12 and Isaiah 44:3. Some may not be familiar with spiritual retreats. Suggest that the retreat will offer opportunities to pray, journal, and share stories. When sharing with each other we will find that we are not alone in our seeking. Explain that we will resist the temptation to solve problems as we listen, seeking to be open to God's presence and to one another.

Get acquainted by asking participants to tell their names, the churches, and the towns in which they work and worship. If this is geared toward professional women, they may also want to share one thing about their work they would like other participants to know.

RETREAT ACTIVITIES
Session 1—Abiding in the Garden

Room arrangement. Set up chairs around tables in a room next to the indoor garden. Allow plenty of table space for writing and creating with art supplies.

Lead a guided meditation using the chapter, "Watered Gardens," in the book *May I Have This Dance?* by Joyce Rupp. Set the stage by asking participants to consider a difficult part of their work or home life. God wants to transform those difficult places, wants to offer each of us the water of God's loving presence in the garden where God can begin the transformation process within our souls and circumstances.

Journaling is a time to tell God what you are thinking, a time to listen for God's response. Some may wish to respond with art rather than writing. Say, "What are the well-watered places in your life where transformation is taking place? Where do you see signs of dryness? You may use some of the journaling time to rest or take a walk."

Prayer of reflection. Gather in the indoor garden. Introduce participants to soaking prayer and Christian contemplative prayer if they are not already familiar with these. Then invite them to find a comfortable place to pray in solitude.

Soaking prayer, often used in praying for healing, is a form of intercession that is ongoing. We hold the person for whom we are praying in God's presence over an extended period of time. Soaking prayer is not so much a matter of words as of intent and longing. We long for the person to be held in the center of God's love and creative power.

Christian contemplative prayer is the opening of our whole being to God. It is prayer beyond words. Contemplative prayer is a prayer of silence, an experience of God's presence.

Lunch

Visual environment. Use beautiful tablecloths and bedding plants centerpieces. This attention to beauty communicates hospitality and God's refreshment in the lives of these women.

Session 2—Discerning God's Voice

Return to the tables. Provide sheets of colored construction paper and poster board. Give this explanation:

- Think about some of the things that make up your life and tear shapes that represent the various aspects of who you are. You are, no doubt, a many-faceted woman. Sometimes you may feel as though your life is a juggling act when you balance relationships at home, at work, and in volunteer settings. As you choose a piece of poster board and three or four sheets of construction paper, think of this exercise as a prayer form, not an art experience.

- Listen for God's voice inside of you as you tear. Begin by tearing the shape of your life at work. Are you the point person for other employees? Are you drained by constant interaction or rejuvenated by interesting conversations? Do you have too much or too little free time? Are you generally harried or usually working at an even pace with little or no interruption? Perhaps you wish for more patience, or work with people you wish had more patience with you.

- Tear the shape of your life at home. Perhaps you are also a busy neighbor, or wife, or mother. Do you feel too tired to cook at times? Do you have children who look forward to spending quality time with you at the end of the day? Maybe you want to be a good neighbor to the convalescent down the street or welcome the latchkey kids around the corner.

- Think about your relationship with yourself. Are you at ease with who you are or do you have unfulfilled expectations? Think of your interior life in relation to God. What shape would best describe that relationship? Think of yourself in your physical garden or your interior garden.

- When you have created three or four shapes that describe facets of who you are, arrange them in a collage on the poster board and move to the circle in the indoor garden area.

—This guided art prayer is adapted from an idea in the book, *When the Heart Waits: Spiritual Direction for Life's Sacred Questions* by Sue Monk Kidd (HarperCollins, 1992)

Without drawing attention to yourself, gather discarded scraps into a glass bowl for use during the closing worship.

Group sharing. Invite participants to share with each other about their collage and the prayer experience. Then take a short break.

CLOSING WORSHIP

Visual environment. Arrange the chairs in the indoor garden into a semi-circle facing a table prepared as a worship center. Add a candle, some type of beautifully crafted decorative butterflies, the glass bowl of discarded scraps, and votive candles.

Play "In the bulb there is a flower" as people assemble for the closing worship. Light the single candle.

Review the day. Remind participants that God is interested in the desires expressed in their collages, but that God also wants to transform the scraps they left behind. Lift up the glass bowl and ask God to open our hearts to new areas of transformation and growth. Thank God for the promise of new growth in well-watered gardens.

Offer a blessing appropriate to the day: "May you sense God's transforming touch as you return to your home and place of employment." Give each one a votive candle lit from the worship center candle. Send each participant home with a rose from the indoor garden, a butterfly from the worship center, and a candle.

Option: For a slightly longer retreat, add a movement activity before the closing worship. Play meditative instrumental music and ask participants to spend time in prayer, visualizing that God is calling them to move into a well-watered garden. There, God is calling them to new and vibrant life. Invite those who feel comfortable to express themselves with movements while the music is played.

Prayers for Healing: A Weekend Retreat for Women

Contributed by Claire Ewert Fisher

PURPOSE

This retreat invites women to encounter God's healing power and discover anew how God's love is active in our lives. Participants will be invited to pray in a variety of ways, share with each other, and participate in an anointing service.

MATERIALS NEEDED

- Music: CD player, recorded instrumental music such as *Let All Who Thirst* by Lucia Unrau and Peter Terry (available from Faith & Life Resources, 1-800-743-2484); *Hymnal: A Worship Book* or other hymnals.
- Worship elements: Basins of warm water for hand washing service and hand towels; small vials of olive oil for anointing service; bread and juice for communion service
- Other: Sheets of newsprint for introduction activity, paper, pencils, pottery jug
- Additional preparation: Assign small groups of 6-8 participants and prepare small group lists; arrange for a worship leader to choose hymns in keeping with the theme. Read *Prayer, Stress, and Our Inner Wounds* by Flora Slosson Wuellner (Abingdon Press, 1985) and *Simple*

Ways to Pray for Healing by Matthew Linn, Sheila Fabricant Linn, Dennis Linn (Paulist Press, 1998). Some of the prayer activities have been adapted from these books.

SCHEDULE

Friday

6:30 p.m.	Registration
8:00	Gather
	Coffee and snack

Saturday

8:00 a.m.	Breakfast
9:00	Session 1 – God's Activity in Our Lives
11:15	Break
12:00	Lunch
1:00	Quiet time
2:00	Nature walk or recreation
5:30	Supper
7:00	Session 2 – God in Our Relationships

Sunday

8:30 a.m.	Breakfast
10:00	Session 3 – Healing Today and Tomorrow
11:00	Closing worship
12:00	Lunch
1:00	Clean up and farewells

Schedule may be adjusted to include a time for fun according to some chosen theme. Laughing together as well as sharing together about our lives builds a community of trust and healing.

GATHERING ACTIVITY

Welcome women to this retreat. Take care of any hospitality matters such as an introduction to the facilities.

Introductions. Assign the small groups and give each group a sheet of newsprint. Each small group meets to introduce themselves to each other. Their first task is to find three things they all have in common. They may need to ask lots of questions of each other until they come up with three. Their second task is to give their group a name and tell why. Names may or may not relate to what they have in common. Their third task is to decide who is willing to be the group facilitator for sharing times and who will introduce the group name. Write the three things and the group name on the sheet of newsprint.

Groups stand and a designee from the group gives their group name and the three things they all had in common. Post the group paper on the wall.

Introduce the retreat theme by telling a story or describing prayers of healing. Explain that the weekend will involve Bible stories, praying in a variety of ways, a hand washing service, anointing for healing, and a communion service. Assure people that they may participate in each experience to the extent that they feel comfortable. They may wish to take part in even though it is unfamiliar. They may decide that some part of the experience is not for them.

Also talk about some underlying understandings about confidentiality. This weekend we will be looking at four stories that demonstrate God's activity in our lives. The first three are Bible stories. The fourth story will be your own. You will be invited to share parts of your own story in your small group to the extent that you feel comfortable. When we hear another's story we must treat it like a prized possession. It is not ours to share with anyone else. It is not a topic for conversation or debate. Sharing means we express who we are, how we feel, and how we experience life. Discussing means we talk about something.

Pray on behalf of the retreat, inviting God's healing presence.

RETREAT ACTIVITIES
Session 1—God's Activity in Our Lives

Begin with a time of singing. Sing hymns that focus on God's love and faithfulness.

Tell the whole story of Naomi in your own words: a) Point out that in one decade Naomi's life changed from being a hopeful young mother to a life of loss and economic insecurity. Give enough cultural background for hearers to understand Ruth and Naomi's economic dependence on men; b) When telling about Ruth's decision to accompany Naomi, read the words in Ruth 1:16-18; c) Emphasize that Naomi left "full" and returned empty; d) Point out that going to the threshing floor was a risk that Ruth took for the sake of Naomi's well being.

The telling of the story may incorporate identification with our own experiences or these can be pointed out afterward.

- •Those who have suffered loss can probably identify with Naomi. The feeling of emptiness is a huge part of the grieving process. She feels lonely; she feels as if nothing matters anymore. She fears that these deaths might be divine judgment on her life. God seems so far away.

- •The text talks about Boaz as a redeemer, but clearly it is Ruth who takes the risks, behaves in a questionable manner, and lives in a selfless manner to save her mother-in-law. (It was, after all, considered scandalous to lie on the threshing floor at night with a man who was not your husband.) From this vantage point it is easy to see how God was active in Naomi and Ruth's lives. Yet, to live a life of faithfulness is not necessarily easy.

- •At times we are keenly aware of God's call and purpose for our lives. At times we can see the hand of God only in retrospect. Even then, we may not be sure. Life lived with God is an adventure. We don't always know where we are going and rarely, if ever, do we know the end from the beginning.

Invite participants to a time of individual prayer and reflection. Play soft music on the CD player for a bit to demonstrate the signal you will use to let people know when it is time to rejoin the larger group. Distribute sheets of paper and give the following explanations:

- •In prayer, ask God to bring to mind some of the events of your life. There will no doubt be some memories that are pleasant, times when you were keenly aware of

God's presence and leading in your life. There will probably also be some times when you felt very alone, as if God had abandoned you. Other memories will probably include times of pain, with the awareness that God was supporting you, carrying you.

- Once you have spent some time with God praying your history, take the sheet of paper and divide it into sections for the decades of your life to form a timeline. Now mark the memories that have come to mind. Mark an X above those places when you felt close to God. Mark and X below those times when you felt far away from God and empty.

- Spread out to find a comfortable and quiet place to pray. Allow any tension or anxiety to leave your body as you pray and become aware of God's love. Listen for a music signal that it is time to return to the group.

Play music to call people to form into their small groups. Share parts of your prayer in your small group if you wish to do so. This could include talking about where you have placed Xs and why. Remind participants that this is a time for mutual support and a time to deepen relationship with God. This is a time to listen in a nonjudgmental way. It is also a time to listen rather than discuss. The information shared is confidential.

Sing "Lord, listen to your children," HWB 353, as people return from the small group sharing to rejoin the entire group. Lead in a communal prayer. Invite participants to select one of the memories that they have just shared in the group. In your mind's eye bring it back to memory. Now imagine God's light and God's love surrounding that memory. Rest gently in this surrounding light. Together with the Psalmist, we say: "For with you is the fountain of life; in your light we see light" (Psalm 36:9).

Session 2—God in Our Relationships

Begin with a time of worship. Sing hymns of God's faithfulness. Read Romans 8:38-39.

Tell the story of Martha. Draw from Luke 10 and John 11.

- Note Martha's practical bent and her ability to get things done.
- Highlight Jesus' affectionate tone when he says, "Martha, Martha." He did not scold her for having a conflict with Mary but he did name her distraction and worry.
- Tell of Lazarus's death, Jesus' tears, and Martha's response at the tomb.
- There are no limits to God's healing work. Even death does not inhibit God's activity.

Relate the Martha story to our lives today. The leader may want to share personal experiences of facing woundedness and finding healing.

- The loss of someone or something dear to us causes a serious wound. Death comes in many forms: illness, divorce, loss of job, or unexpected challenge to one's status or ideas.
- Most of us have been wounded, some by deliberate acts, others by the circumstances of life.
- In the healing of memories, we sometimes find ourselves identifying with Martha as she pleads with Jesus not to open that tomb. The stench will be terrible. It may seem better not to disturb the past.

Talk about healing and forgiveness. Even if we deeply desire to forgive the offending person, the hurt may remain. The *feeling* of forgiveness and release will most likely not happen until the pain of the memory has been healed. When deep inner healing has begun, the old feelings of persistent anger and resentment melt away. The healing process requires patience and hope, courage and stamina. But this is Jesus' invitation to us. He surrounds us with his love. No pain is so long-standing that the love of God cannot reach it. Every shock, every anger, every grief is encompassed by God's love and transformed by God's love. Read Romans 8:38-39 again.

Meet in small groups to share. Where do you identify most with Martha's story? What longings does this story raise for you? Rejoin the entire group at the designated music signal.

Lead participants in a guided prayer. Any guided prayer for healing must be done with great love. It must also be done with sensitivity to the fact that some may not be ready for this. Reassure the group that God's love will surround each of us and guide us toward healing. Give freedom not to participate in this guided prayer if it does not feel right. Leave plenty of time for each part of this guided prayer.

1. Close your eyes and breathe in the love of God that surrounds you. Visualize yourself in a garden or meadow. Notice Jesus coming down a path toward you. Greet each other in whatever way seems appropriate to you. Listen to what Jesus says to you.

2. With your right hand make a fist. Let that fist become as hard and immovable as the stone that covered Lazarus's tomb. Who or what is behind that stone? Who has wounded us, or what resentment lies behind that stone?

3. Before asking Jesus to help you move the stone, share with him how you feel. It may be anger or fear or betrayal. Whatever you feel, tell Jesus about it. Then listen to what Jesus most wants to say to you.

4. When you feel ready, push back the stone with Jesus. Ask Jesus how he wants to bring life out of what has been pain and death and grief to you.

5. When you feel ready, say good-bye to Jesus and leave the meadow. When you feel ready, open your eyes.

6. You may wish to write a letter or journal after this meeting. You may wish to spend time with someone here, sharing your experience. Or you may wish to draw or write a poem. Respond in whatever way the Spirit is leading you.

Invite participants to a hand washing ceremony to signify a desire for deep healing from past hurts and a desire to forgive. Prepare one or more basins of warm water ahead of time. Provide fluffy hand towels. People may come alone or with someone else. Be available to wash the hands of those who come alone. While people come to the basin, play an appropriate piece on the piano or play a recording of "O healing river" from the CD, *Let All Who Thirst*.

Close with a prayer thanking God for the courage to continue the process of healing. Thank God for surrounding us in love.

Session 3—Healing Today and Tomorrow

Begin with a time of worship. Sing hymns of gathering. Read an appropriate psalm of praise, such as Psalm 116.

Tell the story of the woman at the well from John 4. Hold a clay pot or jug as a visual element to introduce the story. Here are some points where the story may touch our lives.

- •This remarkable story illustrates how we are able to come to healing. One day, in the middle of our busyness, we encounter Jesus. We do not really have the time or the desire to talk to him. We are too busy carrying around our water jar filled with our problems. But Jesus calls out to us and if we are brave enough or desperate enough, we respond. Bit by bit the old bothersome wounds are poured out as the living water bubbles up.
- •Jesus looked at this woman whom society described as "an enemy." He looked at her with love. He communicated acceptance and truth. She experienced healing.
- •The good news is that the power of God's healing love encompasses not only the past but also the future. God's love can transform the past into a source of new strength for the future. God is present in our futures to love and to heal. As we soon leave to go home and into a world that may remind us of past hurts and fears, we know that God's love accompanies us.

Read all or parts of Psalm 139 as an affirmation of God's love, and gather for a final time in the small groups. Pray for each other, then rejoin the large group for the closing worship.

CLOSING WORSHIP

At the end of the session lead an anointing service. Invite people to come forward. Place oil on each forehead in the sign of the cross. Speak the words, "In the name of Jesus Christ, receive this sign of healing." Another alternative is to put the oil on the back of each woman's hand. If the group is large, you may need to ask several others to help. Sing hymns about God's healing love as people come forward.

End with a communion service.

Shaping the Christian Male:
A Weekend Retreat for Men

Contributed by Ted Koontz

PURPOSE

This retreat is designed as a mutual exploration to clarify our calling as Christian men. Participants will reflect on their identities as men in a world of shifting roles and cultural changes. We will base our meditation and sharing on the parable of the prodigal son and be led toward finding our true home in God. Thus, we will be empowered to bless others.

The group leader will need to do significant preparation in order to present concepts from the book, *The Return of the Prodigal Son: A Story of Homecoming*, by Henri J. M. Nouwen, and to a lesser extent, *The Male Predicament: On Being a Man Today*, by James E. Dittes.

MATERIALS NEEDED

- Resources: *The Return of the Prodigal Son: A Story of Homecoming* by Henri J. M. Nouwen (Image Books, reissue edition, 1994); *The Male Predicament: On Being a Man Today* by James E. Dittes (Harper Collins, 1985). Reproduction of Rembrandt's, "The Return of the Prodigal Son." (Available from Internet sites such as barewalls.com or artposterstore.com. Since this art is on various websites, you may want to use it electronically by projecting it onto a viewing screen instead.)

- Room arrangement: Prepare signs for small group meeting areas. This may be the various corners or spaces within the larger group meeting room or they may be separate locations close by. You may want to prearrange the groups so that all find a small group with whom to connect. This is especially true if men are coming from various congregations.
- Music: *Hymnal: A Worship Book* or other hymnals
- Copies: Schedule, Handouts 1-4

SCHEDULE
Friday night

	7:00 p.m.	Arrive, settle into room
	8:00	Gathering
	8:30	Small group sharing

Saturday

	8:30 a.m.	Breakfast
	10:00	Session 1 – The Younger Son
	10:45	Reflect, write, share
	12:00	Lunch
	1:00	Session 2 – The Older Son
	1:45	Reflect, write, share
	3:00	Free time
	5:30	Dinner
	Evening	Free time

Sunday

	8:30 a.m.	Breakfast
	9:30	Session 3 – The Father
	10:15	Reflect, write, share
	11:30	Closing Worship
	12:00	Lunch, leave for home

GATHERING ACTIVITY

Extend welcome and talk briefly about the purpose of this retreat. Indicate the importance of exploring our calling as Christian men. How we live our lives is especially important when we remember that we don't live forever. In order to illustrate the power of men in shaping the next generation, share a personal story of mentoring by a father, father-in-law, or other men. What blessings do we hope to pass on? Will our lives be a true, albeit very small, window to God?

Pray on behalf of the retreat and participants. Ask God for freedom to offer ourselves, our experiences, and our understandings to each other. Ask God for grace to walk together on this journey in which none of us is an expert.

Songs to be sung throughout the weekend include: "Far, far away from my loving father," *HWB* 139; "For God so loved us," *HWB* 167; "Here, O Lord, your servants gather," *HWB* 7; and "Heart and mind, possessions, Lord," *HWB* 392.

Locate this generation of men within the massive societal shifts in such areas as roles of women, mobility, stress, and affluence. Ask for a show of hands on these or similar questions, then note that in the midst of these changes we live with less security and stability than sometimes in the past. Thus we need to take the time to look inward, upward, and toward some close friends, rather than only outward to the world of action.

> Are you more or less connected to a larger network of relatives than your grandparents were?
>
> Are you more or less dependent on your immediate family?
>
> How many of you suspect that you work more hours and spend more time away from home than your parents' generation did?
>
> How many of you have a higher level of education than your parents had?
>
> How many of you have a close acquaintance or family member who has gone through a divorce?
>
> How many of you have moved more often than your parents have?
>
> How many of you had mothers who worked full-time for pay outside the home?
>
> How many of you have spouses who work full-time outside the home?

Explain the structure of the sessions. Tonight we will set the stage and get acquainted. The rest of the weekend sessions will be based on the parable of the prodigal son and reflections from Henri Nouwen's book on this parable. After each session we will share our own journeys with each other in a smaller group. We will remain in the same small groups throughout the weekend. There will also be time for personal reflection, prayer, and writing throughout the weekend.

Read Luke 15:11-32 against a backdrop of Rembrandt's painting, "The Return of the Prodigal." Show this by projecting it electronically, by making a color slide of the art print to show on an overhead projector, or by posting the art print where all can see.

Pray a prayer of night blessing, focusing on becoming men who bless those around us. After this closing prayer, gather in small groups. Invite people to meet God by meeting with others, and by praying and journaling tonight and in the morning.

Gather in groups of five to eight. Distribute the questions for the group to answer with each other (Handout 1). Encourage honesty and depth of sharing. Ask groups to make a commitment to confidentiality with what is said in the groups and to honor each other's choices about the level of sharing. Dismiss for the night from these groups.

RETREAT ACTIVITIES
Session 1—The Younger Son

Sing songs, then read Luke 15:11-32, this time introducing it as the parable of two sons and their father.

Introduce Henri Nouwen's treatment of this parable in his book, *The Return of the Prodigal Son*. Explain the way in which he discovered Rembrandt's painting (see the introduction of the book).

We are each in various ways, the younger son, the older son, and the father. One way to describe a Christian man's journey is to talk about it as the journey from being the son toward becoming the father, the one who blesses. Though we will be talking about fathers and sons, this is not limited to biological relationships, nor to relations only with males.

Compare Rembrandt and the younger son. Rembrandt had all the characteristics of the younger son and then came a period of much suffering. Nouwen's book is a good resource for information about Rembrandt's life. You may want to show Rembrandt's earlier painting with the younger son in a brothel.

There are many fine qualities in men who are like the younger son. They are ready for adventure, eager to experience the world, aware of themselves, alive, not shut down. However, note these negative aspects as well. These summaries are taken from Part 1 of Nouwen's book.

- A Radical Rejection notes that the joy of return is deeply related to the pain of rejection. "The 'distant country' is the world in which everything considered holy at home is disregarded" (page 36).
- Deaf to the Voice of Love can be rebellion against family and a physical leaving, but is not limited to these. "Leaving home," says Nouwen, "is living as though I do not yet have a home and must look far and wide to find one" (page 37).
- Share quotes from Nouwen's insights on pages 37-39 about coming home with God and ways we identify with the choices of the younger son.
- The goal is to come home with God. Continue by sharing insights about the prodigal's repentance and return. Repentance is related to believing in unconditional, total forgiveness.

Share stories from within your own community or experience that show leaving and returning. Coming home is one of the hardest and most courageous acts we can undertake. Can we identify with the younger son through our longing for the embrace of the Father? Do we know his weariness, needing to be held, loved, and healed? Can we identify with Nouwen's description of leaving, without physically leaving, to find approval, love, and esteem somewhere other than God?

Distribute Handout 2. Give thirty minutes to reflect and write, then signal to gather in the small groups to share.

Session 2—The Older Son

Identify characteristics of the older son. Use Part 2 of Nouwen's book in much the same way as you did in session one. What are the good things about the older son? How does he feel toward his brother? What is his self-esteem based on?

Talk about friendship and loneliness in the context of the older brother. It is very hard for people who get their self-worth from being better than others to have satisfying friendships that overcome loneliness. Friendship is based on acceptance, on mutuality, on being authentically who we are. We can't do that if we remain in the stance of the elder son.

Confront the issue of power and control. Power since the fall of humans (Genesis 3) has often become a dominating type of power. This "lording over" power is the kind of power we exercise when we order our children around. This power has rested on covering up vulnerability, hiding the truth of the "powerful" one's own vulnerability and woundedness. *The Male Predicament: On Being a Man Today* by James E. Dittes offers these valuable insights about the subtle ways we maintain power and control. Expand on these concepts. Examples from the presenter's own life will be helpful in illustrating these points.

- We create the illusion that we are whole and powerful by making sure there are others who are less powerful than we are.
- We focus on another's weakness and don't look at our own.
- We maintain a position of having the resources and strength, while assuming that she has the needs and the weakness.
- We condescend by being sacrificial and moving down to her level.
- We always have an answer, the last word.
- We blame the victims for creating problems when they raise a grievance.

Talk about the picture of God we create. Elder sons give their children a picture of a God who is judgmental. This picture shows a God whose love is conditional based on performance; who may lash out at them if they fail; who does not see and understand the significance of a report card, or a game of catch after school.

Describe aspects of what it takes for an elder son to return to God's loving embrace. It is hard for us to come to the loving embrace of the father. We may ask: Who needs this mushy love stuff? What? Me? In need of forgiveness? Here are some aspects of what it takes for an older brother to return.

- Tears of recognizing that we have been going on the wrong road
- Seeing the dead-end of our way of life
- Letting go of the need to control and dominate everything
- Cultivating a spirit of gratitude instead of resentment

Close with prayer of thanksgiving for the gift of life and the Father's love.

Distribute Handout 3. Give thirty minutes time to write, then signal to gather in the small groups to share.

Session 3—The Father

Open with singing and a prayer of thanksgiving for the gift of life.

Read Luke 15:11-32. Invite four men to read it using roles of narrator, younger son, older son, and father. If you have been showing Rembrandt's painting on an overhead or as an electronic projection, do so again. Otherwise, refer to the print you have posted.

One way to describe a Christian man's journey is to talk about it as the journey toward becoming the father, the one who blesses. Who is this father? How do we know more about him? How do we know God's character?

Read the words of Jesus in John 14:1-11a. This text clearly tells us where to look when we want to understand God.

Describe a new kind of power, not just the renunciation of the dominating type of power. Opening ourselves to become the father will lead us into a much deeper acquaintance with the pain of the world than we have known before. We will know far more of the hidden suffering around us and empathize far more deeply with the suffering we already know about. We will find ourselves knowing a bit of the cross, of suffering, of what it means to die with Christ.

The father passes on the blessing through the generations. This call to pass on the blessing is one way of describing the general calling of God's people. Though not an exclusive call or prerogative of fathers and men, the father metaphor is especially relevant for us. This blessing we pass on is marked by:

- Friendship, equality, and sharing
- Empowerment of others rather than maintaining control
- Recognition of mutual gifts versus an assumption that others need our strength because they are weak
- Focus on God rather than on us humans.

Suggest some blessing practices. These are not meant to be definitive but to spark ideas: Cards, notes, calls, evening rituals with children, special celebration of a son or daughter's twelfth birthday, singing as a family, writing birthday blessings, writing a journal of experiences to share with children, taking your father or someone else out to eat just to talk, celebrating your mother's birthday.

Distribute Handout 4. Give thirty minutes time to write, then signal to gather in the small groups to share. After another thirty minutes, signal to gather in the larger group for the closing worship.

CLOSING WORSHIP

Sing several songs that you have sung throughout the weekend.

Read Exodus 3:1-6a. Passing on the blessing is our call.

Taking my place in the chain of blessing started with Abraham and Sarah is my calling, your calling, the calling of God's chosen people. Pray on behalf of the group as they leave and dedicate themselves to this calling in their daily lives.

Gathering Activity—Questions

Introduce yourselves: name, employment, family, location (origin, current)

List five words describing the character of each of these
    a. your father

    b. yourself

    c. sons (if you have any)

    d. God

What do women and children close to you like about your character? What do they tell you or signal to you that they wish would be different about you?

What do you like about who you are? What would you like to be different about who you are?

The Younger Son—Questions

We vary in the ways in which we are like and different from the younger son in rejecting the Father. Likewise our returns can take many forms. Write in response to these questions. You will be invited to share in the small groups to the degree that you are ready to share.

How are you the younger son
    in leaving home?

    in longing to come back home, but fearing to do so?

    in coming home?

What turning and conversion is or was necessary for the younger son in you?

Have you tried to return and not experienced the welcome experienced by the son in the story?

How do you differentiate the Father from church, family, and others?

Do you know yourself as the beloved son? Do you know the Father's embrace? Do you seek it? Can you accept it? Does it invite you or repel you?

The Older Son—Questions

We vary in the ways in which we are like and different from the older son. Write in response to these questions. You will be invited to share in the small groups to the degree that you are ready to share.

Do you identify with the older son? How?

Do you have friends?

Do you cry? Laugh? When?

What makes you most deeply satisfied, happy, or joyful?

What do you want to do or say before you die?

Do you know tears of repentance?

What do you need to do to accept the embrace of the father?

The Father—Questions and Suggestions

Write a blessing, a thank you, or an affirmation to someone.

Who are your "fathers," those who have blessed you? What can you learn from them?

What are ways you practice passing on the blessing?

What other ideas do you have for how to bless?

How are you nurturing your journey toward fatherhood? How will you?

Seeker-Friendly Church Campout: Including Our Friends and Neighbors

Contributed by David Kniss

PURPOSE

This weekend fellowship retreat is designed for inviting friends and neighbors who do not attend church. The secret to a successful retreat is to have all spiritual aspects remain informal and natural. Campfire singing, games, hiking, and genuine hospitality provides an atmosphere of friendship, trust, and welcome. Prayer at mealtimes and a Sunday morning service provide specific spiritual content, but are done in a way that is considerate of those unfamiliar with the Bible and Christian terminology.

MATERIALS NEEDED

- Equipment: Athletic equipment for ball games, table games
- Food: Traditional campfire foods and lots of hearty, healthy, homemade soups, breads, cookies, and other food for meals
- Music: Guitars, other musical instruments
- Setting: The setting can be any relaxing location in keeping with the resources of the congregation. State parks often

provide camping spaces in blocks. Retreat centers may offer meals if you choose to be free of food preparation duties.

•Campfires: Find out if the retreat location provides wood
•Copies: Schedule and "Leave with a Blessing"

SCHEDULE

Friday

Evening	Arrive after supper
9:00	Campfire

Saturday

8:30	Breakfast
Morning	Hiking, fishing, biking, free time
12:00	Lunch
Afternoon	Free time, organized ball game and children's games
5:30	Supper
Evening	Campfire, table games

Sunday

8:30	Breakfast
10:30	Worship service
12:00	Lunch
	Return home after lunch

Schedule may be adjusted according to the recreational facilities available and the schedules of a particular retreat center.

GATHERING ACTIVITY

The preparation for this time away from normal routines actually happens a long time ahead of the retreat in the internal preparation of the congregation. Many congregations already have an annual fellowship retreat. The goal of this retreat is for each household to invite one set of friends who do not attend church. It will be their individual responsibility to stay in touch with their guests and not leave them to fend for themselves. They will be introducing them and helping them make connections within the group. However, it is the corporate responsibility for each church member to think inclusively, to plan and act in ways that take into consideration how a person who has never been to church would feel.

Possible Bulletin Announcement

ANNUAL CHURCH RETREAT

This year we encourage you to bring a friend or family who does not go to church. We would like for each of you to invite someone as your guest. You will be responsible to pay their costs as well as responsible to see that they are included and comfortable in this setting. This is a tremendous opportunity to reach out to others in our community.

Hospitality and welcome. Make sure your retreat location is well marked and that several people are available to welcome and give the hospitality directions (such as cabin location, main gathering area, or where to set up camp). Hand out the weekend schedule plan as people arrive, even if you have distributed these ahead of time. Have coffee, tea, and other drinks available.

Campfire. Pastor or planning committee may want to give an official welcome and encourage people to introduce themselves as they meet others throughout the weekend activities. Guitarists take the lead on singing campfire songs. These will be both Christian songs and secular songs. The important thing to remember is how it feels to be new to a group and not know the "insider" language, songs, or practices. Many will likely not know church camp songs. Let the group suggest songs, and if someone suggests "Yankee Doodle" then all will join in. Roasting marshmallows or apples may follow, along with more songs if the group is interested.

RETREAT ACTIVITIES

Mealtime prayers. This is an important but unobtrusive way to demonstrate the Christian practice of prayer. Along with mealtime prayers, sing the same mealtime blessing at each meal so that those who are new to your group have the opportunity to learn and participate. A mealtime prayer is listed below, but any similar blessing would fill the same need.

> Thank you, God,
> for the abundance of this earth,
> for the beauty of our land,
> and for our companions on this journey
> Touch our spirits with your love and compassion,
> that we might be generous
> with all you have provided. Amen.

Present plenty of large group and small group options during the free time. Allow those who have made a Christian commitment to be salt and light in the normal interactions of a fellowship retreat. Those who do not have a personal relationship with Christ will still have fun. They will be drawn by genuineness, informal stories of God's care, and the inner freedom of those who know themselves to be God's beloved sons and daughters.

The campfire on Saturday evening will follow much the same plan as on the first night. Invite people to stay around the campfire to talk after the singing stops.

CLOSING WORSHIP

The Sunday morning worship time marks the close of this fellowship retreat. For some it may be a first introduction to a Christian church service. Scripture reading, a short meditation or drama, and lots of singing offer a comfortable introduction to a worship service. Choose Scriptures that may be recognized by people who are thoroughly secular. The story of the Exodus and Psalm 23 are both reasonably well known. Or read a gospel story of Jesus' healing ministry or the story of Jesus' resurrection. Jesus' story of the Good Samaritan in Luke 10 is yet another possibility.

Provide hymnals or song sheets so that those who are unfamiliar with the songs will be able to participate.

Pastoral prayer. Allow time for sharing joys and concerns. Pray for specific needs in the congregation and community.

Thank God for friendships old and new. Ask God to bless each person in the coming weeks.

Benediction. Close with Numbers 6:24-26 and distribute a copy of this blessing to everyone as they leave the worship service on their way to the final meal together.

Expectations. Not everyone will find someone who says yes to an invitation. Encourage congregational members to attend the retreat weekend even if they can not bring guests. The important thing is to extend the invitation, wholeheartedly live the welcome, yet be aware that someone may decide to say no, even at the last minute.

> Leave with a blessing:
> The Lord bless you and keep you;
> The Lord make his face to shine
> upon you, and be gracious to you;
> the Lord lift up his countenance
> upon you, and give you peace.
> —Numbers 6:24-26

ADDITIONAL IDEAS

Flea Market. The contributor suggests an annual flea market to defray the costs of a church retreat. This lowers the cost per person considerably and helps people be more willing to pay for friends who attend.

The flea market gives additional opportunities for neighbors to relate to church members on an informal basis. Add a prayer tent to your flea market where people can go to request prayer for special needs. Offer coffee and juice at the prayer tent.

Consider the Lilies:
A Retreat for People with
Developmental Disabilities

Contributed by Dawn Ruth Nelson

PURPOSE

This overnight retreat provides an opportunity to experience God's love while being in nature. Participants with developmental disabilities will be invited to trust that God cares for them and their needs just as God cares for the birds and the flowers.

MATERIALS NEEDED

- Copies: Song "Consider the lilies"
- Games: Parachute, card games, simple board games
- Food: Arrange for meals at the retreat center, snack foods that suit the medical needs of participants
- Medications: Make sure people bring their regular medications
- Craft materials: Card stock in various sizes and colors, markers, stickers
- Music: Guitar or piano; CD player; recording of "His eye is on the sparrow" (also available as a free download from Amazon.com if you do not find a CD to purchase)
- Video: *Miracle in Lane Two* (available for purchase at Amazon.com if you cannot rent it locally)

•Worship center: Low table, rich blue cloth, picture of Jesus, small cloth or silk flowers, small stones, small colored feathers

Note: Attention to Hospitality. You will need to schedule a few volunteers who are trained in CPR, first aid, and medication administration. This need not be intimidating. It just means finding a few people who regularly work with people with developmental disabilities. Request that a family member or friend accompany each person. You will need to establish a buddy system for your time on the retreat. Pair people who are disabled with someone who is not disabled.

SCHEDULE
Day One

10:15 a.m.	Leave from designated spot for retreat center
11:30	Arrive at retreat location, assign rooms, take walk with buddy, free time
12:30	Lunch
1:30	Gathering
2:00	Craft activity
2:30	Parachute games or other games
3:00	Group picture (Give picture to each participant afterward.)
3:15	Snack
3:30	Video (Give medications for those who need them.)
5:15	Bird-watching session
6:15	Supper
7:15	Talent show
8:00	Board games and card games
10:00	Lights out

Day Two

8:00 a.m.	Breakfast
9:00	Worship – Consider the Lilies
9:30	Closing worship
10:00	Pack up
10:30	Leave retreat

GATHERING ACTIVITY

Welcome all the participants. Sing "Consider the lilies."

Open your Bible to Matthew and paraphrase Jesus' words from Matthew 6:25-34. For example:

> A group of people gathered round to hear what Jesus had to say. He told them, "Do not be anxious and worried. Look at those birds. They don't have to worry. God takes care of them. And God will take care of you."
>
> Then he said, "Look at the lily. It's a beautiful flower. The flower doesn't have to worry either because God takes care of it."
>
> God takes care of the flowers and the grass. God takes care of the birds. What do you think? Don't be anxious. Do not worry. God loves you more than he loves the birds, so God will take care of you.

Introduce yourselves. Tell your name to the group. Then the group repeats the name, saying "Matt, we welcome you."

RETREAT ACTIVITIES

Craft Activity

Use card stock paper of various colors and sizes. Choose the one you want. Write down a phrase you remember from the Bible story such as, Do Not Be Anxious. Then draw birds and flowers around the words and decorate with stickers. You may want to have people go to their rooms with their buddies for this project. This provides a little time away from the stimulation of the group.

Video

Miracle in Lane 2 is a Disney production based on the real life story of soapbox derby champion Justin Yoder. Twelve-year-old Justin accepts the limitation of his spina bifida but still wants to win a trophy. This is a 1½-hour video. This is a good time to give medications to people individually.

Bird Watching Session

Adjust schedule to the time of year and location. Birds usually feed at about sundown. Explain that birds look for food at this time of day. Describe any birds you think might be commonly seen. Show pictures from a Field Guide or encyclopedia, if possible. Emphasize remaining very quiet. Go outside to watch for birds.

Talent Show

Ask people to show and tell. Some may want to show their craft project, others may want to sing a song or do a skit. Others may play an instrument.

Worship—Consider the Lilies

Visual element. Place a rich blue cloth on a low table. Set up a cross or picture of Jesus. Scatter multicolored feathers and small silk or cloth flowers onto the table.

Begin with the song, "Consider the lilies." Sing other familiar songs. Play a recording of "His eye is on the sparrow."

Talk about common worries. Then hand out little stones to represent what worries us. Then go around the room and let everyone tell a worry. Talk again about Jesus saying, "Do not worry."

Invite people to come up and exchange the stone for a flower and a feather to take home.

Sing another song or repeat "Consider the lilies" again.

CLOSING WORSHIP

End the worship time with thanksgiving. Ask each person to add one thing they are thankful for about the retreat. Make up tune to go with the phrase, "Thank you, Lord, for giving us _____." Sing it as many times as you need to give everyone the opportunity to add his or her contribution.

Consider the Lilies

Matthew 6:25-34
Adapted by Jean Goeboro

Music by Jean Goeboro

REFRAIN

Con - sid - er the lil - ies of___ the field; they nei - ther toil nor spin.___ Yet I tell you that e - ven Sol - o - mon was not___ ar - rayed like these. these.___

1. What shall we eat, Lord? What shall we drink?___
2. Birds of the air___ don't toil or reap,___
3. If God so clothes___ grass of the field,___
4. Do not be anx - ious ⁊ for to - mor - row.

What shall we put on to - day?
yet our good Fa - ther feeds them.
which is a - live and then burned,
Let each day's trou - ble suf - fice.

Is not life more than food,___ the
Are you not of more worth___ ⁊
will He not much___ more___ give
Seek___ first His___ king - dom, and

bod - y more than clothes?___
in the eyes of God?___
clothes___ to His chil - dren?
all things will be yours.___

to Refrain

Experiencing God: For Sunday School Classes or Small Groups

Contributed by June Mears Driedger

PURPOSE

This retreat plan is especially appropriate for a group that knows each other and has a commitment to each other, such as a Sunday school class or other small group that meets on a regular basis. Through Scripture reading, meditation, personal prayer, and contemplation, we will experience God more deeply and reflect on those experiences with each other.

Either a retreat facility or a large cabin will be suitable for this weekend retreat.

MATERIALS NEEDED

- Visual elements: Open Bible, candles, loaf of bread, grape juice and chalice
- Music: Copies of *Hymnal: A Worship Book*, CD player and recorded music
- Copies: Schedule and Handouts 1-3

SCHEDULE
Friday night

7:00 p.m.	Arrive, settle into rooms
8:30	Gathering

Saturday

8:30 a.m.	Breakfast
9:15	Session one – Experiencing God
10:00	Silence and solitude
10:45	Session two – Under the Eye of God
11:30	Walking meditation
12:30	Lunch
1:00	Silence and solitude
2:30	Session Three – God's Touch in My Life
3:15	Free time
6:00	Dinner
Evening	Free time

Sunday

8:00	Breakfast
9:00	Silence and solitude
10:15	Closing worship – Experiencing God Through Communion
11:30	Leave for home

GATHERING ACTIVITY

Create the environment for worship. Set chairs in a semi-circle, arrange candles, an open Bible, and any other visuals. Play quiet music on a CD player.

Once all are gathered, welcome the group and begin with a prayer of blessing for the weekend. Share hopes and expectations for the weekend.

Explain any details of the retreat center, such as geographical concerns, where the dining room is located, and any boundaries that should be respected. Distribute schedule outline. Review the schedule, answer questions, change schedule if needed. Lead the group in a discussion of community understandings such as, "everything shared is confidential" and "honor each other's silence and privacy."

Present the goals of the weekend
- To meditate on and pray the Scriptures
- To reflect on our experiences with God in the ordinary and extraordinary happenings of our lives
- To encourage one another by sharing those experiences

Dismiss the group with the instructions to complete the sentence: "When I think of experiences of God, I think of _____." Invite participants to write as many experiences as they want. Close with prayer and extinguish the candles. Go to rooms in silence.

RETREAT ACTIVITIES
Session 1—Experiencing God

When all have gathered after breakfast, light the candles and allow for a time to sit quietly. Open with prayer.

Lord, Creator of the ends of the earth,
You have sustained our lives to see a new day.
Guide our time together with you and with each other.
Amen.

Sing "Creating God, your fingers trace" and "They that wait upon the Lord," *HWB* 168 and 584. This is a time for sharing our thoughts and insights from the question of last evening. Sometimes people feel they must participate because it is expected of them. Assure the group that silence together is fine, and specifically give permission to remain quiet.

During this day, which we have set aside for experiencing God, we may benefit by learning more about Lectio Divina. We will be using this way of praying in our next group session and the time that follows. Distribute copies of "Praying the Scriptures" and outline the four points.

Silence and solitude. Dismiss the group to spend time hiking, walking, or writing in journals. Blow out the candles and leave quietly. The Lectio Divina sheet may be left in the meeting room.

Session 2—Under the Eye of God: Isaiah 40:28-31

As the group gathers, relight the candle and play quiet music. Distribute copies of Handouts 1 and 2. Read Isaiah 40:28-31 out loud from two different translations. Read slowly, deliberately, and expressively. Briefly discuss Handout 3. Then invite group members to leave in silence. We will return for lunch, but our time of reflection will extend through lunch and beyond.

Lunch

Move the candles from the worship center to the lunch tables, indicating God's presence in our quiet reflective mood of gathering at the table. Thank God for the simple, practical strength of healthy food and clean drinking water. Respect each other's reflection and silence at lunch. Invite participants to continue meditation, prayer, and contemplation on the Isaiah text.

Session 3—God's Touch in My Life

Gather in silence. Continue the patterns of silence, prayer, and singing begun in the previous session. Invite those who wish to share their experiences from the walking meditation to do so. Respect the quiet of those who choose not to share.

Introduce and distribute copies of Handout 4, "God's Touch in My Life." Invite the group to spend time today and tomorrow morning to reflect on God's presence in their lives using the questions on this sheet as a guide.

CLOSING WORSHIP—Experiencing God Through Communion

Worship center. Add the elements of communion (a single loaf of bread and a chalice of juice).

When people have gathered in silence, relight the candles.

Sing "What is this place" and "God is here among us," *HWB* 1 and 16.

Share thoughts and experiences, either in relation to Handout 3 or from the weekend as a whole. Use these questions to guide the sharing.

- Offer a word or phrase to describe the weekend experiences with God.
- What did you discover about yourself?
- What did you experience of God either this weekend or in the past?
- What invitation do you sense as a result of your experiences with God?
- What will you take with you as you leave?

Share communion. After praying, gather in a circle around the worship center. Break pieces from the loaf of bread and dip them into the single chalice.

> O God,
> Your steadfast love has been ours for generations.
> Through Christ, you brought us out of the abyss of death
> and into the light of eternal love.
> With joy and thanksgiving, we proclaim our salvation,
> remembering Christ's death and resurrection,
> until he comes again.
> As we break bread and share the cup together,
> may Christ be present with us,
> and may the Spirit bind us together
> as Christ's body in this world. Amen.
> —*Hymnal: A Worship Book*, 786

Close with a prayer of thanksgiving for Christ's presence and the Spirit's guidance in our midst.

Isaiah 40:28-31

Have you not known? Have you not heard?

The Lord is the everlasting God,
      the Creator of the ends of the earth.

He does not faint or grow weary;
      his understanding is unsearchable.

He gives power to the faint,
      and strengthens the powerless.

Even youths will faint and be weary,
      and the young will fall exhausted;

but those who wait for the Lord shall renew their strength,
      they shall mount up with wings like eagles,

they shall run and not be weary,
      they shall walk and not faint.

          Isaiah 40:28-31

Hast though not known? hast thou not heard, that the everlasting God, the Lord, the Creator of the ends of the earth, fainteth not, neither is weary? there is no searching of his understanding.

He giveth power to the faint; and to them that have no might he increaseth strength.

Even the youths shall faint and be weary, and the young men shall utterly fall:

But they that wait upon the Lord shall renew their strength; they shall mount up with wings as eagles; they shall run, and not be weary; and they shall walk, and not faint.

          Isaiah 40:28-31, KJV

Walking Meditation

We have read the text slowly out loud, the first step of Lectio Divina. You may want to repeat that step before moving on to the other steps. Here are some other suggestions as you meditate, pray, and contemplate the Isaiah text.

1. Take a word or phrase from the Isaiah text and begin repeating it with your lips, although not audibly.

2. Begin to walk and breathe in cadence with words or phrases from the Isaiah text. Take the time you need to establish an easy, steady rhythm of word, breath, and walking pace.

3. Continue the rhythm of word, breath, and walking pace but turn your attention inward and observe what is happening in your mind. Become aware of inner noise.

4. Notice persistent thoughts and allow anything that seems particularly insistent to surface for full attention. Let this moment's central concern surface and present it to God. Reflect on it and explore it.

5. Offer everything you have pondered to Jesus. You may wish to lift up your hands and/or arms as an expression of offering your concerns and reflections.

6. Be open to whatever God might offer to you in the silence.

7. Return to lunch and then the meeting room at the appointed times.

God's Touch in My Life

Review this list and select one of the following incidents:
  I was seriously ill
  I held an infant in my arms
  I helped someone express their deepest hopes or fears
  I chose a new vocation or job
  I embarked on a new friendship
  I cried in sorrow or joy
  I wondered if this is all there is to life

Write your reflections on that incident:

My feelings at that time were _____

The questions it raised about my life were _____

The persons who "walked alongside" me then were
_____

Is there a person in the Bible who felt and questioned as you did?

Does that story reveal anything about your story or challenge you in any way?

How do I feel touched by the moment in retrospect? Is there an insight or healing from that incident for me today?

The invitation I sense on reflecting on this incident today, is to do or be _____

Topical and Thematic Retreats

Retreat settings encourage people to delve into a topic and find God's direction in their lives. Such retreats can be planned around almost any topic that impacts Christians.

Topical retreats follow a simple recipe. Start with a retreat setting to get people away from their busy world of activities. Add information about a stimulating topic. This may be a book study or a speaker. Mix with plenty of opportunities for discussion and sensitivity to God's Spirit. The result: life-shaping decisions.

"God Shapes Our Lives" focuses on a biblical image rather than a stimulating idea. It is less a topic to be discussed than an event to be experienced with all five senses. As such, it may be used as a pattern for similar contemplative experiential retreats. Those designing their own retreats might want to use: Candle making (Jesus as light of the world), pottery (God as master potter), or a quilting retreat (God's design for our lives).

Use these retreats in their present form, but also think of them as templates or master plans for a variety of topics. You may want to come back to them again and again, making your own variations.

RETREATS IN THIS SECTION INCLUDE:
- God Shapes Our Lives: Contemplative Bread Making
- Overcoming Evil with Good: A Peace Retreat
- Dollar$, Faith, and Centsibility: A Young Adult Stewardship Retreat
- Freedom Fences: A Marriage Retreat
- Finding the Heart's True Home: A Prayer Retreat

WHEN PLANNING A THEMATIC OR TOPICAL RETREAT

Aspects of Planning	*Special Suggestions*
PURPOSE	Experiencing and doing in order to draw near to God Learning about some important current topic Hearing God's call to faithful living
SCHEDULE	Usually involves a balance of information and discussion Include needed times of worship
GATHERING ACTIVITY	Introduce the topic only briefly during gathering Topical retreats work best when people know each other beforehand
RETREAT ACTIVITIES	Plan for significant blocks of time dedicated to presentation of material and discussions Information about a topic can come from an expert (outside speaker) or from a book study Leave some space for rest and reflection in topical retreats Thematic contemplative retreats should include longer blocks of solitude than topical retreats
CLOSING WORSHIP	Some aspects of the closing worship can arise from the group Create litanies or prayers that speak of new commitments and new directions for the future

God Shapes Our Lives: Contemplative Bread Making

Contributed by Miriam Frey

PURPOSE

Bread is a rich image for God's providence. During this retreat, participants will bake bread and reflect on God's call and provision. Through silence and the experience of making, shaping, smelling, and tasting the bread, our hearts will be opened to see ways God is caring for us and shaping us.

This retreat is limited by the amount of oven space available. Count how many loaves can be baked at one time and limit participation to that number. The retreat space should have several ovens, space for making bread, and space to spread out for times of reflection.

MATERIALS NEEDED

- Music: Copies of *Hymnal: A Worship Book*, CD player and recorded music to signal time to return to the group.
- Bread-making supplies: Lukewarm water, yeast, whole grain flour, butter, and salt. Add other ingredients according to the recipe you use. Bread pans, mixing bowls, utensils, and measuring cups.
- Visuals: Various kinds of breads in a basket, a single white pillar candle against the background of a cloth of rich earth tones.

- Furniture and arrangement: Long tables or counter space for mixing, kneading, and shaping bread, warm space for bread to rise, and a room next to the kitchen area for worship. Chairs should be arranged in a semi-circle facing the worship table.
- Copies: Schedule, recipe, Handouts 1-3. Bread recipe should be for two loaves.
- Other: Paper, writing and drawing supplies. Breadboard, knife for slicing bread, butter and knives for spreading. Squares of muslin large enough to wrap loaves of warm bread for the journey home.

SCHEDULE

8:30 a.m.	Arrive and prepare for the day
9:00	Gathering – Opening worship
9:30	Session 1– Give Us Today Our Daily Bread"
10:15	Reflection (punch down bread after 30 minutes)
11:15	Session 2 – God Shapes Our Lives
11:55	Reflection time
12:15	Lunchtime – Sack lunches (preheat oven; 12:30 place bread in oven)
1:15	Take bread out of the oven
1:20	Session 4 – I am the Bread of Life
1:40	Reflection time
2:30	Closing – Be Present at our Table, Lord
3:00	Close of retreat

You may need to adjust schedule to fit the bread recipe you are using.

GATHERING ACTIVITY

Prepare a worship center on a small table in a room next to the kitchen. Invite people to gather. Ask participants to introduce themselves briefly to one another.

Review the activities for the day. Distribute schedule. Explain the rhythm of experiencing and reflecting, then sharing.

After each of the sessions we will receive suggestions for use in the reflection time. We will write, draw, rest, or walk during this reflection time. We will play music on the CD player when it is time to rejoin the group.

Light a candle and lead a prayer on behalf of the group and their experience with contemplative bread making. Share the purpose of the retreat:

- To reflect on God's provision and care.
- To reflect on God's shaping, nurturing role in our lives as we experience the process of bread making.
- To understand more deeply that Jesus is the bread of life.

Read the following slowly, with pauses between each reading: Luke 11:1-4, Luke 13:20. Sing together "God of our life," *HWB* 486.

Invite participants to a time of silent reflection while reading the texts of two hymns that use the imagery of bread. "Break thou the bread of life," *HWB* 360, and "I hunger and I thirst," *HWB* 474 (verses 1 and 2), are possible choices. Close with this prayer of entreaty based on "Break thou the bread of life."

> Break now the bread of life,
> O Lord, to us
> We seek you Lord,
> our spirits long for you. Amen.

RETREAT ACTIVITIES
Session 1—Give Us Today Our Daily Bread

Stretch before continuing. Making bread will use our muscles and strength. It will involve our senses of smell, taste, and touch.

Gather in the kitchen where all of the ingredients are laid out and easily identified. Talk about smells, tastes, and textures of each ingredient before mixing the bread. Introduce the ingredients of bread: lukewarm water, yeast, whole grain flour, butter, salt, and any other ingredients you will use. Discuss the purpose of each ingredient in bread. Provide recipes and work in pairs to mix the bread.

Note: It will save time to have a pot of lukewarm water ready for use. The leader should be making loaves of bread to demonstrate as well as for use in the closing worship.

Knead the bread. Encourage participants to reflect quietly on how God's hands hold us and knead us. Set the bread in a warm place for rising. Leave quietly for a time of reflection using questions on Handout 1. Pairs will decide which one returns to quietly punch down the dough halfway through this reflection time.

Session 2—God Shapes Our Lives

Take the first ten minutes to share thoughts about the questions. The experiences with God should be handled as the sacred gift they are. Only those who wish to share should do so. Assure the group that there is no undue pressure to talk or to fill the silence.

Move to the kitchen to punch down the dough a second time and shape it into loaves. Guide those who have not done this before. When the bread is in the pans and the kitchen cleaned up, distribute Handout 2. Participants leave for a time of silence and reflection.

Session 3—I Am the Bread of Life

Place two warm loaves of bread on a cutting board at the worship center. Leave the other loaves to cool in the kitchen. Invite participants to talk about their experience of making bread. How can bread be life giving? How does God provide our daily bread? Tell a story or invite participants to share experiences of God's provision in daily life.

Read John 6:30-40 in two sections. Read verses 30-34, and then verses 35-40. After each section is read, follow with a few minutes of silence; invite participants to share what speaks to them in Jesus' words about bread. You may want to read John 6:22-29 first to give the setting of the text.

Distribute Handout 4 for the reflection time.

CLOSING WORSHIP

Light the candle. Sing, "I am the Bread of life," *HWB* 472, or "I hunger and I thirst," HWB 474. Prayerfully read Matthew 4:3-4 and Luke 22:14-20. Sing "Become to us the living bread," *HWB* 475. Slice the loaves of bread baked by the retreat leader. Serve with butter.

Go to the kitchen to pick up each participant's fresh loaf of bread. Wrap them in squares of muslin. Gather in a circle for the closing blessing. Read the first verse of "Become to us the living bread" as the closing prayer. All raise loaves heavenward and repeat the word, "Alleluia."

Reflection Questions—Give Us Today Our Daily Bread

You will need to punch down and turn your dough 30 minutes into your reflection time.

Read Exodus 16:4-8, 35.

- God provided manna for the Israelites. How have you seen God's provision in your daily life?

- What does it mean to you to rely on God for daily sustenance?

- What new meaning do you bring to the prayer, "give us this day our daily bread"?

- How does bread connect all peoples and cultures around the world?

Remember the feel of the bread in your hands as you kneaded it. Think about it as a metaphor for your relationship with God.

- If you are the dough and God were kneading you, how would you imagine God feeling?

- What areas of your life reflect God's kneading process?

As you complete your meditation, please return to the meeting room at the appointed time.

Reflection Questions—God Shapes Our Lives

He (Jesus) told them another parable: "The kingdom of heaven is like yeast that a woman took and mixed in with three measures of flour until all of it was leavened." Matthew 13:33

•In what ways is the kingdom of heaven like yeast?

•It takes time to mix and knead the bread. It takes time to let it rise as it is doing right now. Reflect on this aspect as it relates to your life with God.

Think about the experience of shaping the dough into loaves as a metaphor for your own life with God.

•How is God shaping you?

•What role are you playing in this process?

•What part is God's part?

As you complete your meditation, please return to the meeting room at the appointed time.

Reflection Questions—I Am the Bread of Life

So they said to him, "What sign are you going to give us then, so that we may see it and believe you? What work are you performing? Our ancestors ate the manna in the wilderness; as it is written, 'He gave them bread from heaven to eat.'"

Then Jesus said to them, "Very truly, I tell you, it was not Moses who gave you the bread from heaven, but it is my Father who gives you the true bread from heaven. For the bread of God is that which comes down from heaven and gives life to the world."

They said to him, "Sir, give us this bread always." John 6:30-34

Jesus said to them, "I am the bread of life. Whoever comes to me will never be hungry, and whoever believes in me will never be thirsty. But I said to you that you have seen me and yet do not believe. Everything that the Father gives me will come to me, and anyone who comes to me I will never drive away; for I have come down from heaven, not to do my own will, but the will of him who sent me. And this is the will of him who sent me, that I should lose nothing of all that he has given me, but raise it up on the last day. This is indeed the will of my Father, that all who see the Son and believe in him may have eternal life; and I will raise them up on the last day." John 6:35-40

How have today's activities of mixing, kneading, shaping, and baking the bread added to your understanding of Jesus as the bread of life?

In what ways is Jesus the bread of life to you?

What words of Jesus from John 6 have special meaning for you?

Overcoming Evil with Good: A Peace Retreat

Submitted by Andre Gingerich Stoner

PURPOSE

This weekend peace retreat teaches a creative response to violence and enemies. Based on Jesus' teaching in Matthew 5:38-48, it conveys the message of God's love and active non-violence through storytelling, Bible study, and times of response. This retreat provides structured sessions, yet allows space for you to plan your own workshop options and recreational activities according to the needs of the group and local retreat facilities. Though originally designed as a junior or senior high retreat, it can easily be adapted for adults.

MATERIALS NEEDED

- Music: *Hymnal: A Worship Book* or other hymnals. Arrange for a music group to lead singing.
- Resources. Books: *The Powers that Be* by Walter Wink or *Engaging the Powers* by Walter Wink (Fortress Press, 1992), or *Threatened with Resurrection* by Jim S. Amstutz (Herald Press, 2002); Peace story sources: *Peace Be with You* by Cornelia Lehn, *Coals of Fire* by Elizabeth Bauman, *What Would You Do?* by John Howard Yoder; Videos: optional, see list in session three
- Other: Large piece of blank poster board for gathering activity, several large peace pledge posters (see text

below), copies of Handouts 1-3, colored water based markers, index cards, pencils, and colored cardstock cut into 3 inch puzzle shaped pieces
- Visual and worship elements: low table, black cloth, white cloth, wooden cross, basket
- Arrange for games, snacks, and recreation options. Include youth in the planning.

SCHEDULE

Friday

6:30 p.m.	Arrival, registration, settle in
7:00	Gathering Activities
8:00	Session 1 – Telling Peace Stories
9:00	Snack, games, and conversation

Saturday

8:30 a.m.	Breakfast
9:30	Quiet time for personal devotions
10:30	Session 2 – Jesus Teachings
11:30	Free time
12:00	Lunch
1:00	Session 3 – Peace Workshops
3:00	Recreation (activities depend on season and camp facilities)
5:00	Supper
7:00	Session 4 – Jesus' Life and Death
Late Night	Snack, games, and conversation

Sunday

9:30	Brunch
11:00	Closing Worship – Resurrection Power

GATHERING ACTIVITY

Welcome the youth or adults. Introduce the schedule. If people are unfamiliar with the facilities, explain key meeting places. This is the time of transition from their busy schedules to a calmer retreat setting. Youth will likely feel the tension of peer acceptance and wonder if this will be a safe environment.

Arrange for a music group or music leader in advance. Or ask the camp or retreat center to arrange for music leadership. Sing for 30 minutes or longer to create a sense of community and welcome. This also provides a better transition for those who arrive late.

Introduce yourselves with thumbprint cards. If the group is large, divide into smaller groups for the introduction activity. Provide index cards and brightly colored water-based markers. Each person places their thumbprint and creates a distinctive drawing as their signature for the weekend. Ask each one to put their names on the card along with the thumb signature. Ask them to place these on a large poster as they introduce themselves. Example: "Hi, I'm Missy Lucas. My thumb signature is a smiley face with sunglasses on."

Include other icebreakers as desired. The kinds of gathering activities depend on the size of the group and the level of comfort and acquaintance with each other.

RETREAT ACTIVITIES
Session 1—Telling Peace Stories

Briefly introduce the theme of overcoming evil with good. Christians are people who orient their lives around Jesus. He is our leader, our example, and the one who saves us. In what ways are Christians supposed to be like Jesus? Be a carpenter? Wear sandals? Remain single? Travel around a lot? Speak Aramaic? Have long hair? No! The way Christians are called to be like Jesus is to love like he did. Like Jesus, we are invited to open ourselves to God's love and let that love flow through us into the world. God's love is a powerful force that can change people and it can change the world. It is a love that overcomes sin, injustice, and evil. This weekend we want to learn about that love and how we can be part of it.

Tell several peace stories. Stories are powerful vehicles for communicating a message. Let these stories stand on their own without much introduction or commentary. A fitting hymn or song between each story gives a chance for the story to soak in and gives space between the stories. For example, you may want to sing "Amazing grace" after telling "Love of Enemies in South Africa." Draw from the following list of ideas.

- Tell a story from your own experience of someone returning good for evil. Or draw from the stories told in your extended family. For example, my family has a story about my Grandpa Beachy's response to someone stealing his watermelons.
- Tell the story of John 8:2-11. This dramatic story of Jesus' third way is very effective when memorized and told with a few simple gestures or motions, such as pausing, kneeling down and writing on the ground with your finger.
- "Love of Enemies in South Africa" (included at the end of this retreat)
- "St. Francis and the Sultan" (included at the end of this retreat)
- "Dirk Willems" (included at the end of this retreat)
- Tell other stories from *Peace Be with You* by Cornelia Lehn, *Coals of Fire* by Elizabeth Bauman, or *What Would You Do?* by John Howard Yoder

Other possible songs to sing include "This little light of mine," "You are salt for the earth," and "Will you let me be your servant," *HWB* 401, 226, and 307.

Invite the group to join you in reading the Peace Pledge you have posted. Note that the first line of the pledge is the theme of the weekend.

Invite participants to read Matthew 5:38-48 during the personal devotional time tomorrow morning. Give handouts of the peace pledge with room to journal thoughts about the Matthew passage or a response to the stories.

Before dismissing for snack time, ask for three volunteers to stay and rehearse a short skit for the next session. (See Handout 1.) Close with a prayer of blessing for the participants and the retreat time together.

Session 2—Jesus Teachings

Make copies of the peace pledge (Handout 3) and post them at drinking fountains, restrooms, and around retreat facility

Gather the group with a time of singing. Arrange for the music group to lead singing.

Read Matthew 5:38-48 aloud. Base this Bible study session on the following comments and activities.

Biblical Background. This teaching draws from the writings of Walter Wink. He works extensively with this text in chapter 5 of *The Powers That Be* and in greater depth in chapter 9 of *Engaging the Powers*. Read one of the sources and assimilate the concepts in preparation for this session. Wink's interpretation is also summarized in chapter 11 of *Threatened with Resurrection* by Jim S. Amstutz.

Over the centuries, Christians have used these verses to teach acquiescence to evil. Wink recovers Jesus' original meaning. In each of the examples Jesus tells his audience, "Look, there is a creative way to respond. Don't be subservient and don't fight. Instead, highlight the oppression. Take actions that force your oppressor to see your humanity. Take actions that show up the evil."

Notice the examples Jesus gives. A dominant person who is used to backhanding a servant on the cheek is suddenly confronted with the other cheek. It's physically impossible to backhand the left cheek with the right hand so he is left looking rather foolish. (Remember, this is a culture where left hands are used only for wiping.) To use a fist would indicate that the person is an equal. The master or dominant person is caught short, facing a person who has by this one small action asserted equality.

Similarly, in a culture where viewing another's nakedness was humiliating, giving the undergarment puts the cloak taker in an awkward position. The person giving the undergarment is at the very bottom economically. Only the poorest would get sued in a court of law for a cloak as collateral for a loan. Something is wrong with the system that leaves people landless with only a cloak to offer. Yet this all has the air of legality and fairness. So when the poor person strips naked and gives the undergarment, too, it is a powerful statement that shows up the oppression.

And, finally, anyone who walked the second mile carrying the pack of an occupying Roman soldier would leave that soldier flustered and confused. He is suddenly no longer in control, despite all his apparent power. In fact, according to the law, he could be reprimanded or punished if he makes someone carry his pack more than a mile. The pack carrying Jewish peasant has just asserted his own ability to take charge of the situation in a way that is neither violent nor subservient.

Begin the Teaching. Phrases from this Scripture have become everyday expressions and part of popular culture.

Ask the group: "What does it mean when you hear someone say, 'go the second mile'?" (Generally it means to be extra nice.) "What does it mean when someone says, 'turn the other cheek'?" (Generally it means to let someone walk all over you.)

Say, "This Scripture has been used to train Christians to be cowards. Christians are taught to tolerate and accept evil. I don't think this is what Jesus wanted to teach. Let's take another look."

Study the Bible Text. Read verse 38. Point out that this injunction is already limiting violence. Instead of unlimited retribution, the Mosaic law said you can only match wrong for wrong.

Verse 39: Highlight the words, "Do not resist evil." How could Jesus have meant that? Jesus constantly confronted injustice and resisted evil. He cast out demons, deliberately broke Sabbath laws, rebuked scribes and Pharisees, and cleansed the temple. *Anti-sta-ni* is the Greek term translated "resist" in this verse. It is a technical military term referring to armed resistance or violent struggle. A better translation might be, "Do not resist violently. Don't mirror your opponent (eye for an eye)." The Scholars Bible translates this verse: Do not react violently to someone who is evil. Or another way of saying it would be, "I will not use a weapon to settle a dispute." Jesus says, "But do this . . . and then gives examples.

Use the following demonstration, skit, and explanation to illustrate Jesus' three examples.

Turn the other cheek. Ask for a volunteer from the audience to help you demonstrate this. The volunteer will stand before you. You are the one who will do the striking in slow motion, explaining as follows:

The text says, "If someone strikes you on the ..." what? (The answer is "the right cheek.") You have to know this is a right-handed culture. The left hand is used only for wiping! Now if I punch the other person with my right hand, I'll hit him/her on the left cheek. So how am I going to strike the volunteer on the right cheek with my right hand? (The answer is "backhand." *Demonstrate striking backhand in slow motion.*) This is not about a fistfight. This is about someone in power dominating someone else. Who usually backhands whom? (Someone with power backhands someone with less: master-slave, in some cases adult-child or man-wife.) This is about how a powerful person would treat someone less powerful.

So let's pretend I'm the master and the volunteer is the slave. If I backhand him, what kind of response am I hoping to get? I want the slave to bend their head, shuffle their feet, say "yessir," and grovel. If I am the master I want the slaves to accept the humiliation and stay in their subservient place. But let's suppose that instead of groveling this person turns the other cheek. (*Ask the volunteer to turn the other cheek and show how it would impossible to backhand him or her on the left cheek.*) It's important to remember that this is a right-handed culture. Left hands are used only for wiping. Also, to hit with an open hand or fist would communicate equality.

What other choices does the slave have? He could hit me back, but that's suicidal, because I've got all the power. What does Jesus say you should do? (Look the master in the eye, turn your other cheek.) In doing so, the slave is saying, "I am a human being. You can not rob me of my dignity. It didn't work the first time. Try again if you wish. But it won't work this time either." It's like telling a bad joke twice.

Go the second mile skit. Practice this skit (Handout 1) with three volunteers after the Friday evening session. Leader should be the narrator.

Give your cloak as well. Jesus' second example will probably be a bit harder for your participants to understand. If you plan to explain, you may want to draw on the following explanation from page 80 of *Threatened with Resurrection* by Jim Amstutz.

> By Jewish law if you are so in debt that you can't pay, or if you borrowed something of value from someone, your cloak, used as a coat for protection and warmth but also for your blanket at night, was given as collateral. Because of this double usage it had to be given back by sundown (Exodus 22:26). Your tunic on the other hand was the garment worn next to your skin, your shirt. "Give them the shirt off your back" probably comes from this verse. So what is Jesus saying? It appears to be, if rich creditors push to the point where they are suing you for your clothes, go all the way. The economic system was so bad and people so poor that Jesus says expose it— literally! Clown a bit. Offer him your tunic as well and parade around bareback. The shame when someone is naked was not on the one without clothes, but on those who see him without clothes.
>
> —Herald Press © 2002. Used with permission.

Conclusion of the Teaching. Sum up Jesus' teaching in Matthew 5. Two standard responses to threats or violence are fight or flight (hit back or run or grovel). Jesus shows us a third way, which is neither fight nor flight. Seek the help of the group to write a list. What does this third way look like? Your list might include:

- refuse to give up your dignity
- seize moral initiative
- use your imagination
- meet force with humor, curse with blessing
- expose injustice of situation

• be willing to suffer rather than retaliate
• seek oppressor's transformation and well-being
• use weapons of truth and love

We might sum it up by saying, "There's nothing wrong with fighting but don't use sticks and fists. Fight with your head and your heart (the truth and love). It's neither fight, nor flight, but Jesus' Third Way—active nonviolence." Refer to lines two and three of the Peace Pledge you have posted.

Point out that in this teaching Jesus is not so much presenting rules as offering examples. There is nothing deadlier than applying teachings legalistically. Telling a child who is being bullied to literally "turn the other cheek" is just asking him to let himself be a victim. It damages his self-respect and encourages cowardice. Only out of a position of self-worth and inner strength can he find a response more creative than slugging it out.

Jesus gave examples, three examples. But God's people have shown us many more creative responses. We need to learn this third way and tell each other many more stories. Here is just one. "Bishop Desmond Tutu was walking by a construction site on a temporary sidewalk the width of one person. A white man appeared at the other end, recognized Tutu, and said, 'I don't give way to gorillas.' At which Tutu stepped aside, made a deep sweeping gesture, and said, 'Ah, yes, but I do.'" Thus, he used humor rather than weapons.

We must also remember not to use this approach vindictively, as another way to defeat our opponent. Jesus' teaching continues with the words, "Love your enemy." Jesus' third way seeks the well being of the oppressor. Martin Luther King Jr. said, "Our capacity to love is stronger than your capacity to hate."

Have the skit volunteers help with the reading of Matthew 5. Stand a distance apart from each other at the front of the room. See Handout 2.

Sing a closing song, such as "You are salt for the earth," *HWB* 226.

Session 3—Peace Workshops

Choose from the following options.

• Invite a number of people to lead workshops on a range of topics such as video games, praying for your enemies, stories of conscientious objectors from WWI to the present, or conflict resolution skills.

• Fill out the peacemaker registration form available at http://www.mcc.org/ask-a-vet/peacemaker.html. Allow 30 minutes to fill it out, and discuss responses in small groups.

• Adult participants may be interested in such topics as Jesus' third way in family relations or business relations, restorative justice, or death penalty. This will vary with the audience and current issues they are facing.

• Show videos that relate well to this topic.

Non-Violence in a Violent World is a 40-minute video with study guide appropriate for junior and senior high youth.

It's Not Just a Job: The Realities of Military Life is a 22-minute video that looks at the dehumanizing effect boot camp has on recruits. Ex-military people tell what life in the military is really like and encourage youth not to join the military. Excellent for junior high and high school age youth.

A Voice on the Hill explores how advocacy for just government policies grows from service. Designed for viewers from grade 11 through adults.

War: Anybody's Son Will Do is a Canadian Broadcast Corporation production by Gwynne Dwyer on how young people are trained to be able and willing to kill. You may only wish to watch the first 35 minutes because it becomes somewhat repetitive.

Change of Command presents the stories of military veterans whose inner voice clashed with their military duties. Divided into five sections, each section may be viewed and discussed separately. Study guide included.

Also available in Spanish under the title *Cambio de mando.*

• Show a segment from *A Force More Powerful* about Nashville sit-ins. This shows how young black students tried to put Jesus' teaching into action to challenge the evil of segregation. It shows the importance of training and discipline in the way of active nonviolence. This segment is about 25 minutes long. To order *A Force More Powerful* on home video, contact Mennonite Central Committee.

*Note: All videos mentioned above are available on free loan from Mennonite Central Committee. In the United States, call toll free 1-888-563-4676. In Canada, call 1-888-622-6337 or e-mail sam@mcc.org. Visit their on-line resource list at http://domino18.prominic.com/A5584F/Resource_Catalog.nsf for other options.

Session 4—Jesus' Life and Death

Worship center. On a low table place a black cloth and a wooden cross, large enough for all to see.

Experiencing God's love. Share your own story of God's love and grace. This session works best if the leader is willing to share his or her own story. We can love like Christ did when we open ourselves to Christ's love for us. Tell how that became real for you. This may be the story about the events that led to your decision to make a commitment to follow Jesus and be baptized. It may be a story of love demonstrated in the Christian community. When did you realize that God knew you, loved you, and had profoundly touched your life? That is the story to tell.

Explain that being a Christian is not just a matter of deciding to live a certain way, but opening ourselves to God's love and letting that guide our lives. Sometimes that is dramatic. Usually it is gradual. Either way, Jesus calls us to open our lives to God's love so that we become more and more like him.

Invite participants to open themselves to God's unlimited love. "God knows you, and loves you and calls you by name. I don't care how messed up your life is, God is walking toward you, ready to embrace you, forgive you, claim you as a beloved son or daughter."

Pray: "Thank you for your love. I pray that I would grow in the knowledge of your love each day. Thank you that you know each of us and you meet each of us in a special way. I pray that each person here would open themselves to receive your love, which you are waiting to pour into their lives. Amen."

Joining Jesus' way of love. Read 1 Corinthians 1:18 and share the following story to illustrate the message of the cross. Note the contrast between cruise and cross as two different ways of encountering the enemy. The cross is a symbol of God's love. Jesus went to the cross because he confronted evil and sin. Not because he was a wimp. Not because he was a robot just playing a part. He stood up for the weak, the poor. He challenged the wrongs of his day. But he didn't use human weapons. He used the weapon of love. He chose a third way. The cross is a symbol of that love. The cross is God's nonviolent response to evil. The cross is a symbol of Jesus' willingness to pour himself out in love.

From 1987 to 1991, Andre Gingerich Stoner lived in the Hunsrueck region of what was then West Germany as a volunteer with Mennonite Central Committee. There were dozens of U.S. military bases in the area. He lived together with other Christians about a mile from a large base where 96 U.S. cruise missiles with nuclear weapons were deployed. Each Sunday afternoon, he would gather with other Christians outside the base to pray for peace. He would often look across the fence at the bunkers and contemplate the destructive potential of those weapons. On that one base alone, there was more than four-times the destructive firepower of all the weapons used in World War II. Many people worked hard to get rid of those weapons. There were prayer services, petitions, huge demonstrations, even blockades.

A local farmer who owned a field next to the base wanted to set up many crosses on the field—a symbolic graveyard to highlight the power of death buried in the bunkers. After talking with Christian friends, she decided to set up 96 large crosses as a contrast to the 96 cruise missiles. When guests came to visit him, Andre would often take them on a tour of the area and we would stop at the field of crosses. With the barbed wire and the bunkers in the background they would read 1 Corinthians 1:18. "For the message of the cross is foolishness to those who are perishing, but to us who are being saved it is the power of God."

As they stood there they often reflected on the way of the cruise and the way of the cross. Cruise missiles are incredibly sophisticated computer-guided weapons, which can fly below radar for thousands of miles, hugging the contours of the ground, and strike with tremendous firepower within feet of their targets. This is the world's wisdom. This is the world's way of dealing with enemies—to threaten them and in the last resort be willing to destroy them. God's way is the way of the cross, meeting enemies with love, compassion, and service, and in the last resort being willing to give your life for them. Many think this is foolishness, but for Christians the way of the cross is the power of God. Sometimes Andre would stand with others in front of the base with a sign that said, "The cross is stronger than the cruise." Jesus invites us to believe that and to live that out.

Ten years later Andre went back to Germany. In the meantime, many prayers had been spoken and many Christians and others of good will had struggled diligently for peace. The wall between East and West Germany had been torn down. The cruise missiles in the Hunsrueck had all been removed and destroyed. Small businesses use the buildings and bunkers on the base for storage. Once a year, tens of thousands of youths swarm across the base for a giant rock festival. The crosses are still standing. The cross is stronger than the cruise.

Jesus' way of love doesn't always look most effective in short run. But it is the power of God. Jesus is calling you and me to join him, to take up our cross, to be this kind of loving, healing presence in the world. The way of the cross is a movement of love so deep and profound that it changes the world.

Allow time for silent reflection, then pray or sing, "Strong, righteous man of Galilee," *HWB* 540. The text of this hymn by Harry W. Farrington can also be found at http://www.cyber-hymnal.org/htm/s/t/stronrmg.htm.

CLOSING WORSHIP—RESURRECTION POWER

Worship table: Keep the cross on the table. Drape a white cloth around the bottom. Add a basket of puzzle pieces, index cards, and pencils.

Arrange for the music team to lead in singing. After the singing, distribute the puzzle pieces, index cards, and pencils. Explain that these will be used later.

Read and talk about John 20:19-23. Jesus comes back to the city that killed him, friends who deserted him. What does he do? We might expect him to say, "Confound you scoundrels! You are all cursed." We might expect that he finally let them have it? Instead, he stretches out his hands and says, "Peace be with you." The love of God is relentless, persistent. Jesus comes back again and again with a word of forgiveness, with an open door to begin a new life.

Jesus sends us into the world. He said, "As the Father sent me, so I send you." No matter how messed up we are, no matter how weak we are, no matter how much we've disappointed ourselves or God, Jesus calls us and sends us. He entrusts his mission to us! He sends us into the world to love like he loved, to be like he was in the world, to say to the world, "Peace be with you." Confronting wrong, evil, injustice, and sin with relentless and persistent love.

We are not on our own, or alone. Jesus sends us. Jesus gives us his Holy Spirit, who is always there to strengthen us, to guide us, and to work through us.

Closing blessing. Recite the Scripture to verse 22 while walking through the group saying to them, "Peace be with you" and "As the Father sends me, so I send you." And then breathe on them and say, "Receive the Holy Spirit." Continue walking through the group saying these things to them. As you do so, the song leader from his/her chair begins leading the song, "Spirit of the living God," *HWB* 349.

While singing, ask retreatants to write on their puzzle piece one way they want to live out the peace pledge, or one part of the peace pledge to which they want to commit themselves. As they are ready, come forward and glue their puzzle piece around a peace pledge poster mounted on large poster board. Have a colorful water-based marker available to add their distinctive thumb signature. Use the index cards for anyone who wants also make a copy of their commitment to take along home.

ADDITIONAL RESOURCES

Find more peace resources and information at www.mph.org and www.peace.mennolink.org.

Peace Pledge posters, t-shirts, and individual peace sheets available at http://peace.mennolink.org/resources/toorder/index.html#prayacttshirt. Look under peace pledge in the product list.

STORIES
Love of Enemies in South Africa

Imagine this scene from a recent hearing of the Truth and Reconciliation Commission in South Africa: A frail black woman stands slowly to her feet. She is something over 70 years of age. Facing her from across the room are several white security police officers, one of whom, Mr. Van der Broek, has just been tried and found implicated in the brutal murders of both the woman's son and her husband some years before. She was made to witness her husband's death and heard his last words: "Father, forgive them."

And now the woman stands in the courtroom and listens to the confessions offered by Mr. Van der Broek. A member of South Africa's Truth and Reconciliation Commission turns to her and asks, "So, what do you want? How should justice be done to this man who has so brutally destroyed your family?"

"I want three things," begins the old woman, calmly, but confidently. "I want first to be taken to the place where my husband's body was burned so that I can gather up the dust and give his remains a decent burial."

She pauses, then continues. "My husband and son were my only family. I want, secondly, therefore, for Mr. Van der Broek to become my son. I would like for him to come twice a month to the ghetto and spend a day with me so that I can pour out on him whatever love I still have remaining with me."

"And, finally," she says, "I want a third thing. I would like Mr. Van der Broek to know that I offer him my forgiveness because Jesus Christ died to forgive. This was also the wish of my husband. And so, I would kindly ask someone to come to my side and lead me across the courtroom so that I can take Mr. Van der Broek in my arms, embrace him, and let him know that he is truly forgiven."

As the court assistants come to lead the elderly woman across the room, Mr. Van der Broek, overwhelmed by what he has just heard, faints. And as he does, those in the courtroom: friends, family, neighbors—all victims of decades of oppression and injustice—begin to sing, softly, but assuredly, "amazing grace, how sweet the sound, that saved a wretch like me."

—This story was first told by Stanley Green, CEO of Mennonite Mission Network, and published in the Spring 2000 issue of *Missions Now*

St. Francis and the Sultan

Francis of Assisi was deeply troubled. A large army of Christians had sailed to Egypt in order to fight the "unbelievers'"–the Muslims. Many people died; children starved; there was no end to the murdering.

Francis went to the commander of the Christian troops, Cardinal Pelagius. "For Christ's sake, stop the murdering," he said. But Pelagius responded, "We must fight unbelievers. They are Christ's enemies." Without a further word he dismissed Francis.

"If Pelagius will not listen, I must speak with the Sultan," said Francis. Without fear he entered the enemy encampment.

"What do you want?" asked the Sultan. "Did you come to murder me?"

"No," said Francis, "I came to ask you to please stop the war. The Christians will not listen to me, therefore I have come to you."

The Sultan was surprised. He had never met this kind of Christian before. Francis stood before him without weapons or threats and without fear.

"Jesus is my Lord and master," said Francis. "He loved the world, and that is why he suffered for it. He taught us that we should also love our enemies and not fight them."

"I've never met Christians who live like that," said the Sultan. "They all lie and murder. But because you have shown me otherwise, I want to send many riches with you when you go. Take as much gold as you can carry."

Francis cried out in alarm, "I don't need any gold. But please, make peace with your enemy."

"This is the first time that I have met a Christian who doesn't want money," the Sultan exclaimed. He could not forget this strange man for a long time.

The Sultan tried to negotiate a peace, but the Christian commander Pelagius would not accept his terms. After a mighty battle the Christian army was defeated. The Sultan took Pelagius and 12,000 men captive.

The Sultan called for Pelagius to appear before him. "Listen closely," the Sultan said. "I swore not to leave a single Christian alive. I wanted to kill you all. But some time ago a Christian named Francis of Assisi visited me. He is the only person whose deeds showed that there might be some truth in your faith. I want him to keep me in good memory. For his sake, and for his sake alone, I will set you and your men free."

—This version of St. Francis and the Sultan is adapted from *Peace Be With You* by Cornelia Lehn (Faith & Life Press, 1981)

Dirk Willems

Dirk Willems was an early Anabaptist living in the sixteenth century. He had been baptized into the Catholic Church as an infant. But later he chose to be rebaptized upon confession of faith. In those days, rebaptism and attending Anabaptist meetings were against the laws of the land and punishable by death.

Dirk undoubtedly did not go around announcing his baptism. The meetings he attended and held at his house were secret meetings. Nevertheless, someone must have noticed that Dirk had decided to follow Jesus in all of life. A thief-catcher was sent to apprehend him, so Dirk ran with all his might, hotly pursued by the thief-catcher. Dirk knew that torture and surely death awaited him if did not escape. He came to a waterway with just a thin coat of ice, for winter had not yet fully taken hold.

Dirk ran quickly across the precarious ice. He had nearly reached the other side when he realized that his captor had followed and broken through the ice. He turned to see him, in the icy water, reaching up for help. At this decisive moment he had one last chance to escape capture. Instead, Dirk quickly returned and aided the thief-catcher in getting out of the icy water, thus saving his life.

As you can imagine, the thief-catcher wanted to let him go. However, the burgomaster very sternly reminded the thief-catcher to consider his oath, so he seized Dirk and turned him over to the authorities. After imprisonment and torture, Dirk was sentenced to death on May 16, 1569. He was burned at the stake outside Asperen in Holland. His story has been told countless times as an example of loving one's enemy.

—Adapted from *Martyrs Mirror* by Thieleman J. van Braght

Go the Second Mile Skit

This skit uses improvisation following prompts given by the narrator.

Characters: Jewish Peasant, Roman Soldier, Centurion, and Narrator

Props: A large canvas bag for a soldier's pack, two chairs or other objects to represent mile markers. Set the mile markers at opposite sides of the room in front of the audience.

Narrator: Palestine in the time of Jesus was occupied territory. Roman legions commanded by centurions were always passing through.

Enter Roman Soldier on one side and Centurion on the other side standing a distance from the mile marker chairs.

Narrator: (*Walk toward and indicate mile marker on the soldier's side.*) There were mile markers (*point to chair*) on the roads and a soldier could legally impress a civilian to let him borrow his donkey or make him carry his pack, which weighed up to 60 pounds. As you can imagine, the people of Palestine were not very happy about the Roman occupation. (*Enter Peasant on the same side as the soldier.*) Peasants of Palestine were the losers in this arrangement. If they were out and about, they got forced to carry soldiers' packs. They hated the arrogance of the occupying troops. Oh, there is a peasant working out in his field. Let's see what happens.

Peasant works the field, ignoring the soldier as long as possible. Soldier comes toward the first mile marker and calls the peasant. The peasant is not happy about this, but not entirely hostile either. Improvise the

scene. What will each say? Will you talk to each other as you go from one marker to the next? What might you talk about? A mile is a rather long time to walk together.

Narrator: (*before they reach the mile marker*) Oh yes, I should tell you. The law said the soldier could require him to carry it one mile, but only one mile, so as not to anger or incite the local population. If a centurion caught a soldier disobeying this law— who knows what he might do. Military law was arbitrary. Maybe he'd lose a month's pay, or maybe he will just be reprimanded. But wait, they're reaching the mile marker now.

Peasant: Okay, I'll just keep carrying this pack another mile.

Peasant continues to walk on past the mile marker still carrying the pack. Roman soldier is uncomfortable? What is this guy up to? He checks to see whether the Centurion has noticed. Improvise the scene. Will the soldier get in trouble? Will you wrestle over the pack? What might each say? What might the Centurion do or say.

Narrator: (*at the appropriate time*) Cut. Let's discuss what happened here. (*Characters and audience join the discussion about the impact of the peasant's action*).

Matthew 5:38-48

Reader 1: "You have heard that it was said, 'An eye for an eye and a tooth for a tooth.' But I say to you, Do not resist an evil-doer. But if anyone strikes you on the right cheek, turn the other also;

Reader 2: and if anyone wants to sue you and take your coat, give your cloak as well;

Reader 3: and if anyone forces you to go one mile, go also the second mile.

All: Give to everyone who begs from you, and do not refuse anyone who wants to borrow from you
.

Leader: "You have heard that it was said, 'You shall love your neighbor and hate your enemy.'

Reader 1: But I say to you, Love your enemies and pray for those who persecute you, so that you may be children of your Father in heaven; for he makes his sun rise on the evil and on the good, and sends rain on the righteous and on the unrighteous.

Reader 2: For if you love those who love you, what reward do you have? Do not even the tax collectors do the same?

Reader 3: And if you greet only your brothers and sisters, what more are you doing than others? Do not even the Gentiles do the same?

All: Be perfect, therefore, as your heavenly Father is perfect."

Peace Pledge

With Jesus' help I will overcome evil with good.
I will not kill
I will not use a weapon to settle a dispute.
I will use the power of nonviolence
I will help build a peaceful world.
I will follow Jesus.

_____

_____

_____

_____

_____

_____

_____

_____

_____

_____

_____

_____

_____

Dollar$, Faith, and Centsibility:
A Young Adult Stewardship Retreat

Contributed by Mark Diller Harder, Claydon Grassick,
Jeff Steckley, and Mike Strathdee

PURPOSE

This weekend retreat is designed to help young adults examine their relationship with money and to increase our awareness of the unspoken ways money functions in our lives. Through activities, Bible study, and sharing with each other we will increase awareness of the unspoken ways money is a part of our lives. We will explore what our faith has to say about how we live.

This weekend retreat for young adults could be adapted for the study of another topic pertinent to young adults. Your plan should include these marks of effective young adult retreats:

- •Young adults themselves should help plan and lead the retreat and sessions.
- •Sessions need to be creative, interactive, and practical. Include plenty of time for discussion.
- •Young adults want flexibility and a relaxed pace. This schedule is a guide. Include adequate free time. Note the large block of free time on Saturday afternoon.
- •Keep the retreat affordable. Cook your own food as a group. Use basic lodging.

- •Start each session with a time of singing. Different groups vary in their musical tastes so no specific songs are suggested here.
- •Bring lots of games, snack food, late night activities.

MATERIALS NEEDED

- •Resource: Several activities come from *Teaching a Christian View of Money: Celebrating God's Generosity* by Mark Vincent (Herald Press, 1997). Recommended as background source for anyone doing this retreat. Session 1, "What's in Your Wallet?," and the money autobiography section were adapted from The Giving Project, a stewardship education initiative also developed by Mark Vincent.
- •Copies: Schedule, Handouts 1-3
- •Other: Wenarri coins made from electrical box punch outs, pebbles spray painted gold or printed on stiff paper and cut out; Flurry of Facts assigned (see below); Mock budgets prepared (see below); Large sheet of newsprint for Putting into Practice public forum.

SCHEDULE

Friday

6:30 p.m.	Arrival, registration, settle in
7:00	Welcome, Gathering Activities
8:00	Session 1 – What's in Your Wallet?
Late Night	Games and conversation

Saturday

8:30 a.m.	Breakfast
9:30	Session 2 – What's in the Bible?
10:15	Break
10:30	Session 3 – Money Autobiography
12:00	Lunch
1:00	Free time
5:00	Supper

7:00	Session 4 – Putting Your Money Where Your Mouth Is
Late Night	Games and conversation

Sunday

9:30 a.m.	Brunch
11:00	Session 5 – Worship Hike: Finding Treasure
1:00	Clean up and departure

GATHERING ACTIVITY

Spend plenty of time singing to establish a sense of community and informality. Introduce yourselves. Invite participants to write their full names on a flipchart for all to see. Explain what your name means and why you were given that name. Take plenty of time because this activity sets the tone for the trust and openness of the rest of the retreat.

RETREAT ACTIVITIES
Session 1—What's in Your Wallet?

Introduce the theme of money and faith using several short exercises.

Flurry of Facts. In reader's theater format, several voices read world facts on poverty and wealth. Designate someone on the planning committee to do the research on this ahead of time. It is not included here because facts change. Enter the words "wealth and poverty" in an Internet search engine for access to data. For example, Oregon State University has an excellent site at http://oregonstate.edu/instruction/anth484/wpout.html.

Read the Parable of the Computer Programmer (based on Luke 12:18ff.):

A university grad named Dave landed a new programming job that paid really well. He decided

"I'm going to max out on my retirement plan, open a high interest savings account, and get a cushy new apartment." And he said to himself, "Now I can relax! I have enough money to live for a couple of years. I can party, have fun and enjoy life!"

But God said to him, "You idiot! Tonight you could die in an accident, and all these things that you collected, who will have them then?"

That's the way it is with people who store up stuff for themselves but aren't rich towards God.

Agree/Disagree. Individuals stand or crouch in agreement or disagreement when the following statements are read.

- Christians have an obligation to give 10 percent of their income to charity.
- Saving lots of money for the future should be a low priority for Christians.
- An important way in which God blesses us is with wealth.
- God chose the poor to be rich in faith.
- There's nothing wrong with buying nice things for yourself as long as you give a reasonable amount to good causes.
- Charging any interest on loans is morally wrong.
- What I do with my money is my business, because I earned it.
- You can't be a Christian and own a Ferrari (Inspired by Tony Campolo.)

What's in your wallet? Ask each participant to take out their wallets and look through them. What do you find? Select one item that is important to you. Why? Share the story of that item with the whole group? What does this sharing say about what we value?

Close with prayer. Invite participants to hold their wallets. Focus on thanksgiving, choices, and challenges.

Before breaking for informal activities, introduce three ongoing weekend activities.

- Wenarri System. Each person is given a random amount of Wenarri coins. Do not offer an explanation except that they will be needed during the weekend. (However, the planners are aware that a special Saturday supper dessert costs five Wenarri. Some people will have more than five Wenarri and others less. What dynamics happen over that supper? Do people hoard or share?)

- Mock Budgets. Each person is given one of four mock budget work sheets, based on the real budgets of a single student, single working young adult, newly married couple, and couple with children. These will need to be prepared ahead of time by a member of the planning committee. How would you manipulate the fixed costs and disposable income? How would you spend the money? What goes to charity? These will need to be prepared beforehand based on realistic prices in the country at the time. Fixed costs include housing, food, and transportation. It may also include repayment of student loans and medical insurance coverage.
- Putting into Practice: Introduce a large sheet of paper on most of one wall. Throughout the weekend participants can write down practical ideas on dealing with money struggles.

Session 2—What's in the Bible?

Begin this morning session with singing. Then review the biblical teachings about Jubilee (Deuteronomy 15:1-18; Leviticus 25:8-55).

Distribute the list of New Testament passages on money, Handout 1. Ask for four volunteers to stand at different corners of the room and rotate reading these verses aloud. What is the overall tone towards wealth and money?

Break into groups of four. Read Mark 10:17-31. What questions would you have if you were a character in the story?

Session 3—Money Autobiography

Welcome people back. Sing to begin the session.

Begin a money autobiography exercise by having three young adults who have prepared beforehand share their money autobiography. Distribute Handout 2. Spend time alone answering money autobiography questions. Then gather in groups of three or four to share.

Close with a song of blessing for the noon meal.

Supper—Five Wenarri Dessert

At supper time people will have opportunity to spend their wenarri for a special dessert or maybe a choice of desserts. Later you will discuss what happened among the table groups in which people had unequal wealth in wenarri.

Session 4—Putting Your Money Where Your Mouth Is

Fish bowl debate. Place four chairs in the middle of the room in pairs facing each other. An ethical money situation is read and only those in the four chairs can debate it. Anyone in the large outside circle can bump one of the four and enter the debate. Distribute Handout 3 so that everyone has a copy of the situation.

Spend time in small groups of three and four in regard to the ongoing exercises introduced on Friday night. What did you notice when it came to spending your wenarri? What did you learn about yourself? Has the mock budget exercise been helpful? What questions does it raise for you? What have you learned from others' comments on the Putting into Practice sheet?

Evaluate the weekend. Use both verbal response and written evaluation forms. What have we learned? What will you take home with you? What will you put into practice?

CLOSING WORSHIP

Close the weekend with a worship service that takes the form of an outdoor hike. Stop at various points to sing, pray, and share stories. Halfway through, read the Parable of the Talents (Matthew 25:14-30). What does the story sound like from the perspective of the four characters? Hike some more. End at a quiet place with a time of communion.

Return to the retreat center for clean up and good-byes.

What's in the Bible?

No one can serve two masters; for a slave will either hate the one and love the other, or be devoted to the one and despise the other. You cannot serve God and wealth. Matthew 6:24

And the crowds asked him (John the Baptist), "What then should we do?" In reply he said to them, "Whoever has two coats must share with anyone who has none; and whoever has food must do likewise." Even tax collectors came to be baptized, and they asked him, "Teacher, what should we do?" He said to them, "Collect no more than the amount prescribed for you." Soldiers also asked him, "And we, what should we do?" He said to them, "Do not extort money from anyone by threats or false accusation, and be satisfied with your wages." Luke 3:10-14

Now a bishop must be above reproach, married only once, temperate, sensible, respectable, hospitable, an apt teacher, not a drunkard, not violent but gentle, not quarrelsome, and not a lover of money. 1 Timothy 3:2-3

But those who want to be rich fall into temptation and are trapped by many senseless and harmful desires that plunge people into ruin and destruction. For the love of money is a root of all kinds of evil, and in their eagerness to be rich some have wandered away from the faith and pierced themselves with many pains. 1 Timothy 6:9-10

You must understand this, that in the last days distressing times will come. For people will be lovers of themselves, lovers of money, boasters, arrogant, abusive, disobedient to their parents, ungrateful, unholy. 2 Timothy 3:1-2

Keep your lives free from the love of money, and be content with what you have; for he has said, "I will never leave you or forsake you." So we can say with confidence, "The Lord is my helper; I will not be afraid. What can anyone do to me?" Hebrews 13:5-6

As he (Jesus) was setting out on a journey, a man ran up and knelt before him, and asked him, "Good Teacher, what must I do to inherit eternal life?" Jesus said to him, "Why do you call me good? No one is good but God alone. You know the commandments: 'You shall not murder; You shall not commit adultery; You shall not steal; You shall not bear false witness; You shall not defraud; Honor you father and mother.'" He said to him, "Teacher, I have kept all these since my youth." Jesus, looking at him, loved him and said, "You lack one thing; go, sell what you own, and give the money to the poor, and you will have treasure in heaven; then come, follow me." When he heard this, he was shocked and went away grieving, for he had many possessions. Mark 10:17-22

Handout 2

Money Autobiography

Who were/are your money management role models (parents, friends, etc.)?

How was money talked about in your family? What did you not talk about?

Do you approach your relationship with money from an abundance or scarcity mentality?

What are your strengths and challenges in your current money management practices?

Fish Bowl Debates

1. Four of you share a household together. You all have different incomes and financial situations. You each pay an equal amount for rent, and have a loose "pot" system for groceries. Receipts are sometimes forgotten. One person tends to be the most reliable at putting money in the pot and making sure the rent is paid on time.

One evening when you all happen to be sitting around the living room together, someone suggests that maybe each person should just buy their food on their own and keep separate cupboards and fridge shelves. The four of you continue that conversation.

2. You just graduated from university with a sizable student loan. You have a decent part-time job that pays the bills, but only makes a dent in the student loan. This is a major weight on your mind. You also volunteer at a downtown community agency. You have an offer for another part-time job, but to take it would mean quitting the volunteer placement. You've also wondered about simply taking two years now to volunteer with a service organization that would put your loans on hold. What should you do?

You discuss this with three of your friends.

3. You are on the music committee at your church. The piano is very poor quality and you have just had the offer that someone in the church will donate a Yamaha Grand Piano. The only stipulation is that the donor wants to put a recognition plaque in a prominent place on the side of the piano. What should your committee do?

4. You have recently started attending a church where you have felt very comfortable. You have started to get involved and get to know people. You even have your own mailbox. One Sunday, you receive a letter from the treasurer of the church. It's a budget letter, talking about how much money will be needed for the new church year and giving an expectation that to meet the budget, each participant should donate "X" amount of money, which is the budget divided by the number of participants. There is even a pledge card to fill out and return to the treasurer. How do you respond to this letter?

5. You have decided to donate $1,000 to your local Cancer Care Center. That money could provide cancer care for one person now, likely saving that life. You can also give the money to a new promising experimental study. The brochure proclaims, "$1,000 now will save 100 lives in 10 years." Which will you choose?

6. You live in a large household of young adults, or in a dorm setting. Pete owns one of the only cars around and someone is always borrowing his car. Lots of carpooling happens with the car. Few people offer to pay for gas, let alone for repairs and upkeep. One evening, three different people drop by Pete's room at the same time, all wanting to borrow his car that night. If you are Pete, what to do you do? If you are one of the three people without a car how will you respond?

7. You are a board member for a non-profit organization that provides counseling and support to various individuals on the margins of society. Because of a shortage of funds, the organization is beginning to turn away clients. The board has begun discussing the possibility of applying for a $50,000 grant to meet the demand from a foundation that generates its dollars from gambling and casinos (the Trillium Foundation is an example in Ontario). What do you say at the board meeting?

8. You have just returned from an extended period of time in a service assignment outside of North America. The family you lived with barely had enough to survive and you ate only rice and beans, yet you were treated with amazing hospitality. Your first week back you attend a family reunion at a fancy hall. There's tons of food and probably half of it will go to waste. One family member comments to you, "Isn't it great to have some decent food again!" What kind of conversations will you have?

Freedom Fences: A Marriage Retreat

Contributed by Gerald and Marlene Kaufman

PURPOSE

This weekend retreat will help couples discover how marriages can be strengthened through the appropriate setting of boundaries. Among this community of believers, participants will discern boundary wisdom for their marriage. Sessions and discussions are based on the book, *Freedom Fences*.

MATERIALS NEEDED

- Resources: *Freedom Fences: How to Set Limits That Free You to Enjoy Your Marriage and Family* by Gerald W. Kaufman ed. (Herald Press, 1999). Leader will need to read the book and prepare presentations.
- Other: *Hymnal: A Worship Book*, Bibles, flip chart or newsprint sheets, tree seedlings (one per family)

SCHEDULE

Friday

7:00 p.m.	Gathering activity
7:30	Session 1 – Freedom Fences
9:00	Refreshments and informal gathering

Saturday

8:00	Breakfast
9:00	Session 2 – Topic selected by leader
10:15	Break
10:30	Session 3 – Topic selected by leader

12:00	Lunch
1:00	Free time
5:30	Dinner
7:00	Session 4 – Topic selected by leader
8:30	Activities or games

Sunday

8:00	Breakfast
9:30	Worship Service – Amazing Grace
10:00	Session 5 – Marriage as Covenant
11:00	Closing – Departing as Partners in Freedom Marriage

Note: After leading many marriage and family retreats, the contributors encourage planners to remain open and flexible. Each group has different needs. God does not have a cookie cutter pattern in place. A retreat plan should not be so tightly scripted that there is not room for the fresh wind of the Spirit in your midst.

GATHERING ACTIVITY

Welcome the participants and make introductions as necessary. The form for this varies with the group. If the group is from a single congregation, introductions may not be necessary.

Sing songs of gathering and praise. Songs especially fitting for use throughout the weekend are "Amazing grace," *HWB* 143; "Gentle Shepherd, come and lead us," *HWB* 352; "Will you let me be your servant," *HWB* 307; "God loves all his many people,"*HWB* 397; and "Guide my feet," *HWB* 546.

Explain that each of the sessions involves a presentation by the leader, followed by the opportunity to discuss the material. If the group is very large, form small groups of six to eight people that will meet for discussion.

Reassure participants that no one will be put on the spot or put into embarrassing situations. We want to learn from each other but at this retreat people are not under pressure to perform, nor will they be asked to reveal things that will embarrass them. A lot of people are quite anxious about marriage retreats.

They have heard stories of other retreats. They may be afraid of having to tell intimate details of their lives in front of a group or of having to write extensively, even if they do not know quite what they are supposed to say.

RETREAT ACTIVITIES
Session 1—Freedom Fences

Read Scripture passages that relate to the tensions of freedom and responsibility: 1 Peter 2:16, 1 Corinthians 10:23-24, Genesis 2:16, and Galatians 5:13. Present background and concepts from chapters one and two of the book, *Freedom Fences*.

Distribute Handout 1 and break into smaller groups to discuss questions. Rejoin the large group and share some of your group insights.

Sessions 2—4

Continue to use this or a another suitable format to cover the chapters of your choice. Choose three of the following chapters. Chapter 3, the chapter on permanence, will be the basis of the last session.

Chapter 4: Freedom and Conflict in Marriage

Chapter 5: New Roles in Marriage

Chapter 6: Lifestyle Choices

Chapter 7: Balancing Work and Family

Chapter 8: Spiritual Fences for Freedom

Chapters 9-11 deal with the impact of parenting on marriage

Follow this format or make variations depending on the size and needs of the group.

1. Begin with singing and the Scripture readings given at the beginning of the chapter.
2. Leader presents background information on the specific topic.
3. Small groups process the impact of the topic on marriage. Choose from these two options or use a combination:
   a) Use the questions for discussion at the end of each

chapter; b) Or, ask groups to come up with a list of Freedom Fences for the specific topic covered by the leader. The authors give a list of Freedom Fences at the end of each chapter. You may want to list one or two from the book and let the groups create more.

4. Bring ideas to the larger group to share.

5. Some activities work well as individual activities. Spouses may choose to discuss their answers with each other. Create handouts so that all participants have a copy of the discussion questions.

During session four ask each couple to create their own version of Ecclesiastes 3. For example: "For everything there is a season and a time for every matter under heaven: A time for conflict and a time to resolve conflict." Ask them to bring their lists to the closing worship tomorrow.

Worship Service—Amazing Grace: God's amazing love and grace upholds us as we seek to be faithful in our marriages and family commitments. Sing hymns appropriate to the weekend. See the suggestions made under Gathering Activity.

Prepare a ten-minute homily based on the ways that you sense the Spirit moving in the group. It is best to wait to prepare this until Saturday evening. The homily should arise out of the spirit of the group. Listen to concerns of the group and the movement of God's Spirit, then plan the homily.

Session 5—Marriage as Covenant

Present chapter 3, "Permanence in Marriage." List the ten Freedom Fences on pages 66 and 67. Distribute Handout 2 and break into small groups to discuss. Groups may pick which of the questions they wish to discuss.

CLOSING WORSHIP—DEPARTING AS PARTNERS IN FREEDOM MARRIAGE

Lead a group Ecclesiastes 3 Litany. Begin by reading Ecclesiastes 3:1, then invite participants to share lines from their own versions if they wish. Close by rereading verse one.

In the foreword of *Freedom Fences*, Shirley Showalter suggests that family fences are somewhat like hedgerow fences, or privet hedges. They live and grow and represent the "safe, permeable, organic nature" of healthy family life. Read Psalm 1:1-3.

Benediction. "Go forth as partners in freedom marriage. May you be like trees planted by canals of flowing water, living, growing, and yielding pleasant fruit. Amen." Give each couple a tree seedling as a reminder of God's blessing and promise.

Session 1—Freedom Fences

Group Discussion Questions

1. When you hear the word "freedom," what does it mean to you?

2. When you hear the word "restraint," what does it mean to you?

3. How do you compare with your parents on a freedom restraint continuum, where one indicates "total freedom" and five means "complete restraint"?

4. Give examples of current situations where you have benefited from some of the new freedoms. Also describe where it has been helpful to have some fences.

5. God gave humans freedom of choice and God also gave the Law. The early church also struggled with the tension between freedom and boundaries. In response, write ten new commandments that would create fences needed for today's society.

Individual activities you may want to discuss with your spouse: Make a list of the freedoms you enjoy. Then make a list of the restraints that are imposed on you by yourself or by others. What do these lists tell you about yourself? Which list is longer? What, if any, changes are needed?

—From *Freedom Fences* by Gerald W. Kaufman, L. Marlene Kaufman, Anne Kaufman Weaver, and Nina Kaufman Harnish (Herald Press, 1999), pp. 35, 49-50

Session 5 – Marriage as Covenant

Group Discussion Questions

1. Why is it so important to keep marital promises?

2. Who is affected when marital promises are broken? In what ways?

3. How can family and friends be helpful when they have serious concerns about someone's marriage? How would their involvement limit the freedom of the couple?

4. We can have meaningful relationships with many people. In what ways can those relationships be a threat to marriage?

5. Marriage is the association of separate individuals with separate needs. How much can spouses be expected to give up for the sake of the relationship?

—From *Freedom Fences* by Gerald W. Kaufman, L. Marlene Kaufman, Anne Kaufman Weaver, and Nina Kaufman Harnish (Herald Press, 1999), pp. 67-68

Finding the Heart's True Home: A Prayer Retreat

Contributed by June Mears Driedger

PURPOSE

This weekend retreat is designed for a small group. Time away from the distractions of home and work will allow members of the group to spend time in prayer and silence, as well as in community and conversation. It might be held at a retreat facility or at a large cabin with participants sharing in meal preparation and clean up. We will explore various forms of prayer outlined in Richard Foster's book, *Prayer: Finding the Heart's True Home*,

This retreat will require advance preparation for the leader who will present the material from Richard Foster's book. It serves as a model for retreats using study materials on any topic related to spiritual growth.

MATERIALS NEEDED

- Music: Hymnals and/or Taizé song books, portable CD player and recorded music; Taizé music and recordings are available on the Internet. Visit the Taizé website at http://www.taize.fr/en/index.htm, then click on *Learning the songs* and *Sound clips and RealAudio*.
- Visual elements and furnishings: Candles, open Bible, and a cross arranged on a worship table at the front of the room; place chairs in a semi-circle facing the front

•Copies of *Prayer: Finding the Heart's True Home* by Richard
    Foster (HarperCollins, 1992)

SCHEDULE
Friday night

7:00 p.m.	Arrive, settle into rooms
8:30	Gathering together

Saturday

8:30 a.m.	Breakfast
9:00	Session one – Moving Inward with Prayer in Silence and Solitude
9:45	Silence and solitude
11:15	Session two – Moving Together in Reflection
12:30	Lunch
1:30	Session Three – Moving Upward with Prayer
2:15	Silence and solitude
3:45	Session Four – Moving Together in Reflection
4:00	Free time
5:30	Dinner
Evening	Free time

Sunday

8:00	Breakfast
8:45	Session Five – Moving Outward with Prayer
9:15	Silence and solitude
10:15	Closing Worship – Moving Together in Reflection
11:30	Leave for home

GATHERING ACTIVITY
Before people arrive, set chairs in a semi-circle, arrange candles, open Bible, and place any other visuals in a way that
can be seen by everyone. Have quiet music playing. As people
arrive, invite them into the circle. Once everyone is seated,
light the candles and open with a brief prayer.

Welcome everyone and then explain any details about the
retreat center. Distribute schedule outline. Review the schedule,
answer questions, change schedule if needed. Lead the group in

a discussion of community understandings, such as "everything shared is confidential" and "honor each other's silence and privacy."

Share hopes and expectations for the weekend. Move into the focus of the weekend—exploring different methods of prayer. Discuss the different kinds of prayers and how they will be approached during the weekend. Dismiss the group with the instructions to write words or phrases that describe their understandings and experiences of prayer. Close with prayer, extinguish candle(s), and go to rooms in silence.

RETREAT ACTIVITIES

Session 1—*Moving Inward with Prayer in Silence and Solitude*

Open with prayer. Light candles. Sing two hymns or songs together. Summarize Foster's chapter on "Moving Inward: Seeking the Transformation We Need" and the chapter on "Prayer of Examen." Allow time for discussion. Dismiss the group to experiment with this form of prayer. Remind participants this is not a test of our spirituality but rather it's a time to explore what ways of praying meet our spiritual needs.

Session 2— *Moving Together in Reflection*

As the group gathers, sit quietly with music playing. When all have gathered in silence, invite people to share their prayer experiences. Assure participants that times of silence within the group are okay. Conclude the session with prayer and extinguish the candles.

Session 3—*Moving Upward with Prayer*

Continue the pattern of leading an opening prayer and singing songs. Summarize Foster's chapter on "Moving Upward: Seeking the Intimacy We Need" and the chapter on "The Prayer of Adoration." Allow time for discussion. Dismiss the group to experiment with this form of prayer.

Session 4—Moving Together in Reflection

Follow same instructions as session two.

Session 5—Moving Outward with Prayer

Continue the pattern of leading an opening prayer and singing songs. Have the candles lit before people gather. Summarize Foster's chapter on "Moving Outward: Seeking the Ministry We Need" and the chapter on "Intercessory Prayer." Allow time for discussion. Dismiss the group to experiment with this form of prayer.

CLOSING WORSHIP

Follow same instructions as session two. After 30 or 40 minutes move into sharing perspectives on the entire weekend. Lead a group prayer time followed by hymns and songs chosen by group members. Conclude with "You shall go out with joy," *HWB* 427. Bless each participant as you say good-bye.

Spirituality Retreats

Retreats in this section focus on direct experience of God's presence. More contemplative in approach, these designs emphasize silence, prayer, and worship. They include teaching on spiritual disciplines such as solitude, a variety of forms of prayer, Scripture meditation, and journaling. A number of the retreats in this section connect with the Christian year. In those cases, either the title or subtitle identifies the season. They vary in length, and though most are designed for groups, each could easily be adapted for a personal retreat.

"In the high-stress world in which many people live, the best retreat may be the one that provides space to meet God and opportunity to refresh thirsty souls with living water," says Marlene Kropf, who contributed "Thirsting for God." That, indeed is the gift and intent of these retreats.

RETREATS IN THIS SECTION INCLUDE:
- Waiting for God: A One-Day Advent Retreat
- Zechariah, Elizabeth, Mary, and Joseph: An Advent Retreat
- Thirsting for God: A Lenten Prayer Retreat
- Jesus Walked This Lonesome Valley: A Good Friday Retreat
- The Risen Christ: Prayers and Scriptures for Easter Monday
- Called by Name: A Half-Day Retreat for Eastertide
- Labyrinth Ritual for Ascension Day: A Mini-Retreat for Times of Transition
- Exploring Creativity: A Retreat for Ordinary Time
- Lead Me to the Rock: A Daylong Personal or Group Retreat
- A Day of Rest: Meeting Jesus in a Gospel Story
- Encountering the "I Am": A Spiritual Formation Retreat

WHEN PLANNING A SPIRITUAL RETREAT

Aspects of Planning	*Special Suggestions*
PURPOSE	Providing space to meet God Learning life-giving spiritual disciplines Experiencing God's presence by reflecting on a particular time in the church year
SCHEDULE	Balance brief thoughts shared by the leader with times of reflection and times of sharing See the plan as a rhythm that creates wholeness Plan for the meal time to reflect the purpose of the retreat
GATHERING ACTIVITY	Show God's welcome by paying careful attention to that which communicates beauty, wholeness, and holiness (a time set apart with God)
RETREAT ACTIVITIES	Significant blocks of time devoted to solitude Pay attention to each detail, much is communicated by symbol, mood, visual elements, and tone of voice Choose hymns and music that capture the soul of the retreat, as well as the theme Use Scripture, well chosen words, prayers, and poetry, perhaps the words of the spiritual guides from the past
CLOSING WORSHIP	Participants share the fruit of their reflection End with Christian rituals such as communion or anointing or symbolic action

Waiting for God: A One-Day Advent Retreat

Contributed by *Jennifer Davis Sensenig*

PURPOSE

This retreat is designed for a group of five to twenty adults. It should take place at the beginning of the Advent season. Through silence and contemplative prayer, this six-hour retreat prepares participants to wait on God's revelation.

MATERIALS NEEDED

- Music: CD player and recorded music; *Hymnal: A Worship Book* or other hymnals
- Visual elements: Greenery, several small decorative birds, candles, open Bible, Advent wreath, blooming amaryllis or Christmas cactus.
- Furniture and room arrangement: Semi-circle of comfortable chairs; worship center on table at one end of semi-circle; arrange table with visual elements except for the blooming plant
- Other: White votive candle for each participant arranged on a tray; plain paper and pencils; colored pencils and attractive paper

SCHEDULE

9:00	Gathering
9:20	Session 1 – Awake to God
9:45	Quiet solitude
10:30	Session 2 – Hidden Birds
11:00	Quiet solitude
12:00	Silent lunch
12:45	Session 3 – The World Waits
1:15	Quiet solitude
2:30	Closing worship
3:00	Close of retreat

GATHERING ACTIVITY

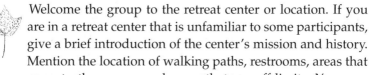

Welcome the group to the retreat center or location. If you are in a retreat center that is unfamiliar to some participants, give a brief introduction of the center's mission and history.

Mention the location of walking paths, restrooms, areas that are open to the group, and areas that are off-limits. You may want to mention artwork in the building or on the grounds related to your retreat theme. Indicate the location of hot beverages, if available, and any rules, such as "no food in the chapel." Ask whether there are questions about the place.

If they haven't done so already, ask participants to introduce themselves. Briefly outline the goals of the day and distribute the schedule. If you have a signal for return to the group time such as a bell, indicate that. If not, ask participants to be responsible to return from the times of quiet as indicated on the schedule.

Talk about the discipline of silence. Explain that the group will keep silence during the retreat. You may tell something about your own experience of being silent, such as, "It usually takes me some time to settle into the silence. At first it feels awkward to say nothing. The quiet can be a welcoming, refreshing release from my habit of chatting all the time. At times, though, the silence feels rather hollow and lonely. I encourage you to stick with the discipline of silence during our retreat, because

God can use silence to get our attention, and God is really the one who prepared this retreat time for us." Allow time for questions about procedures or the retreat center.

RETREAT ACTIVITIES
Session 1—Awake to God

Light the number of candles according to which week of Advent this retreat is being held. Sing "O come, O come, Immanuel," *HWB* 172.

Read Psalm 130:5-7 slowly.

Explain the meaning of Advent. Advent comes from the Latin word *adventus,* which means coming. Jesus is coming in the celebration of his birth at Christmas. Christ is coming into our lives personally and powerfully as we yield ourselves. And Christ is coming again to judge and to save this world which God loves.

According to the Gospels, Jesus made a habit of retreating in solitude for prayer and for time with God. Sometimes he brought some of his closest friends with him, and sometimes he was entirely alone. Read Mark 1:35.

Awake to God. Use this spiritual exercise to prepare to wait in silence. Relax each part of the body. Begin with palms down during the first part of the prayer. Turn palms up during the receiving part of the prayer. Close eyes and rest hands in lap with palms down. "Just as we have begun to relax our body, we also need to begin relaxing our mind, letting go of some of the things that may preoccupy us. Each of us has left some things behind to come to this retreat. With your palms down let go of the things you have left behind. Perhaps there are people or children you've left at home today. Perhaps you need to let go of some concerns or stresses. We can release these to God. (Pause.) Perhaps there are responsibilities or obligations that you need to set aside in order to wait for God. We'll spend a few minutes in silence. When you have let go of whatever might prevent you from focusing on God today, then turn your palms up to receive what God has for you. We will wait together." (Retreat leader then waits and watches for upturned hands.)

End the time with this quote from Henri Nouwen: "To pray means to open your hands before God. It means slowly relaxing the tension which squeezes your hands together and accepting your existence with an increasing readiness, not as a possession to defend, but as a gift to receive." (*With Open Hands*, Ave Maria Press, 1972, p. 154.)

Prayer of thanksgiving. "God, we thank you for preparing this time and place for us. We thank you for preparing us, forming us in your hands. Amen."

Make a transition to the time of solitude by singing verse one of "O come, O come, Immanuel."

Session 2—Hidden Birds

Light candles. Sing verse 3 of "O come, O come, Immanuel." Recite Psalm 130:5-7.

In the book, *Century of the Wind: Memory of Fire Volume III*, Eduardo Galeano tells the true story of a Uruguayan political prisoner and his five-year-old daughter. God surprises us by entering with us into times of deprivation and despair. Read this adapted account of that story.

> Schoolteacher Didasko Perez had been imprisoned for certain ideological ideas. The prisoners were not allowed to whistle, smile, sing, or greet each other. They were also not allowed to make or receive drawings of pregnant women, couples, butterflies, stars, or birds.
>
> Five-year-old Maya entered this restrictive world to visit her father. On one visit she mistakenly brought a drawing of birds, which the guards promptly destroyed. On the next visit, she brought a drawing of trees. Her father asked about the colored circles scattered in the tree-tops. There were also circles half-hidden in the branches. At first he thought they were fruit. Then the little girl whispered to her father that she had drawn the eyes of the birds, birds she was smuggling in to her father.

God is sometimes like the daughter who smuggles in a message, an image of hope. Read Isaiah 61:1-3, 10-11, twice, listening for the word or phrase that is addressed to you. Read the passage a third time asking, "How is my life touched by this word?" During a fourth reading ask, "Is there an invitation here? Pray silently for the person beside you in the circle. Ask God to help that person respond to the invitation."

Enter the time of solitude to reflect on Isaiah 61 or to look for "hidden birds" in your life as you walk outside.

Silent Lunch—Play recorded music if you desire, but do not feel that you must fill the quiet with sounds.

Session 3—The World Waits

Light candles. Sing verse 6 of "O come, O come, Immanuel." Instead of singing you may want to play a recorded version while lighting the candles. Or, play it on a flute.

Speak the first verse of "Come, Thou Long-Expected Jesus," *HWB* 178 as a prayer. Or pray another Advent prayer.

Mention the prophets, Mary, Elizabeth, Zechariah, Simeon, and Anna as Bible characters that waited. We wait because the world is not whole. The world awaits the coming of Christ in every place.

Make line drawings. Participants need paper and pencil. Fold paper into eight squares by making three folds. With each word spoken by the leader, the group responds with a line drawing in one of the boxes to represent that word. Words to use: gift, waiting, silence, holy, peace, hope, time, joy. Turn the paper over for more words, such as comfort, power, fear, and captive. Add your own words as you wish.

Enter the time of solitude. Perhaps one of the words is the hidden prayer of Christ within you. Stay with that word, repeating it silently to yourself as you walk or rest. Or continue an image from one of your line drawings. Provide colored pencils and attractive paper for participants who wish to expand their line drawing. Encourage participants to look outdoors and follow the lines of nature that may help them pray and wait. Notice whether any of your lines appear in nature.

CLOSING WORSHIP

Add the blooming plant and the votive candles to the worship center.

Break the silence. Lead a time of group participation by asking, "What gifts did you receive today?" Read Psalm 126. This is a psalm for people returning home.

Sing verses 1, 3, 5, and 6 of "O come, O come, Immanuel." Distribute candles to use at home during Advent.

Zechariah, Elizabeth, Mary, and Joseph: An Advent Retreat

Contributed by Wendy J. Miller

PURPOSE

The season of Advent invites us into prayerful waiting and anticipation of God's coming among us in Jesus. Participants are invited to open their hearts and minds to God's presence and call upon their lives.

MATERIALS NEEDED

- Music: CD player and recorded music (used during silent lunch and as a signal); hymnals
- Copies: Schedule and Handouts 1-4
- Worship center: Incense burning in fire-proof dish (Zechariah); tablecloth spread on table and plate of finger food (Elizabeth); dark blue candle and cross (Mary); pair of sandals and a hammer placed on the floor alongside a blanket (Joseph)
- Food: Arrange for a noon meal; cups, napkins, plates, tea, coffee, hot chocolate, sugar, milk, and finger foods for afternoon gathering.

SCHEDULE

8:30 a.m.	Arriving and settling in
9:00	Gathering
9:30	Session 1 – Zechariah, Elizabeth, Mary, and Joseph
10:15	Prayerful Solitude – Entering the Narrative
11:30	Silent lunch
12:30	Session 2 – Listening for God's Invitation
1:00	Prayerful Solitude – Being with God
	Walk or rest
3:30	Closing worship
4:30	Departure

Note: This daylong retreat can be adapted to four separate two-hour mini-retreats, which could be held at a church. Adaptation plans are included.

GATHERING ACTIVITY

Welcome people as they arrive, and invite them to be seated. Explain that the day will include time spent together and in solitude, times for quiet reflection on Scripture, journaling, and prayer. Distribute the schedule.

Take a few minutes to explore the participants' past experience of silence. This will help those who have been "silenced" or who have received "the silent treatment" to feel supported. It is also helpful to speak to the noise we discover within us when we move into silence. Explain that the guidance being offered in the times of prayerful solitude can help us move beyond much of the inner noise. Invite participants to be patient with any frustration they feel in the silence, and to be open to God's presence and invitation during this day. Demonstrate the music signal you will give when it is time to gather after times of solitude.

Offer the opportunity for people to have conversation or spiritual guidance with you or other spiritual directors if they so desire.

Have people introduce themselves, inviting each one to give

their name, to mention one particular thing that they left behind in order to be present at this retreat, and to express what they desire from this retreat experience. After listening to people voice what they have left and what they desire this day, bring these items to God in prayer. Pray for the participants. Invite the Spirit of God.

RETREAT ACTIVITIES
Session 1—Zechariah, Elizabeth, Mary, and Joseph

The Gospel narratives invite us into the lives and experiences of four people who were waiting: Zechariah, an aged priest; Elizabeth, his wife, well on in age and still childless; Mary, a young woman who is engaged to be married; and Joseph, a carpenter and Mary's fiancée. Each of these people knew and loved God and waited in expectancy for the coming of the Messiah. However, when God invited them to participate in Jesus' coming, each one—Zechariah, Elizabeth, Mary, and Joseph—discovered that to welcome and embrace the Christ child would change their lives in ways they had not expected.

Distribute and explain the four handouts. Today you are invited to choose one of these characters, and to enter into his or her story. Each is the story of God's visitation and the character's response. The Scripture references are given at the beginning of each handout.

- You might choose to be present in the temple with Zechariah, who no longer believes that God can answer his prayers. He receives an angelic visitor and is led into nine months of silence and waiting on God. To believe, and to say yes to God would mean breaking with hundreds of years of family and religious tradition. For John would not become a priest, but would be a prophet speaking for God in the desert.
- Or you may feel led to be in the house of Elizabeth to experience the loneliness of being childless, and the pain of being shamed by her neighbors because she is without child. Notice how being hospitable to God's gift to her

includes making space within herself for pregnancy in old age, for Zechariah and his silence, for Mary and her need for refuge, and for her neighbors as they come to celebrate the naming of this baby.

• You may choose to be in Nazareth with Mary, who discovers that saying, "Yes, I am the Lord's servant," places her hopes for marriage and even her life at risk. As she leaves her village and walks that long journey to the house of Elizabeth, you may choose to reflect on who the people are in your own life who offer space and give you soul care when your own "yes" to God brings you into new and untried territory.

• Or, you may decide to enter into Joseph's struggle as he seeks to figure out how to make the right decision. Just when he thinks he is doing the good and right thing, God meets him in a dream. Embracing Mary and the unborn child will thrust him out of his house, his carpenter's shop, and into the life of a refugee, guided by dreams rather than carpenter's plans.

During the afternoon session you will be invited to move more deeply into the narrative experience of your own life as you respond to the reflection questions given on the handout.

During this first period of prayerful solitude, read the Scriptures listed along with the descriptive reading given for the person of your choice. Read the Scriptures twice, slowly, and then enter into the narrative. Does it draw your heart and mind in a particular direction? Pay attention to who else is present in the story. Listen. Simply be present.

Leave for the time of prayerful solitude.

Session 2—Listening for God's Invitation

This afternoon you are invited to move more deeply into the gospel narrative you have chosen. Take some time to read the Scripture narrative once more and the reflection material on the handout of your choice. Then spend the rest of the time responding to the reflection questions offered on the handout.

You may choose to write in your journal as a way of responding or to take a walk and be aware of God's presence as you ponder each question. You may feel a need to rest or to sit quietly. Arrange to ring a bell or play soft music fifteen minutes before the end of the time period. This allows people to bring this reflection and prayer time to a close without abruptness.

CLOSING WORSHIP

Prepare drinks and finger foods so they are ready as people return. Include the food symbolizing Elizabeth and her hospitality. As the group eats together, invite them to reflect aloud on their experience during the retreat. Give people permission to remain silent. Give opportunity for those who wish to speak. Use these questions to guide this time of sharing experiences.

Which person's narrative did you enter into today?

How has God met you in that place?

What spoke to you in a personal way today?

At the close of this time, invite people to think about the places, people, and concerns to which they are returning. Encourage them to consider God's invitation to them as they return to their own "house," and as they continue their pilgrimage within the Advent season.

Conclude with a familiar Advent hymn such as "Come, thou long-expected Jesus," *HWB* 178, or "Comfort, comfort, O my people," *HWB* 176. Close with a prayer of benediction.

Closing worship should end by 4:15 so that participants can gather their things and be ready to leave by 4:30.

ADAPTATION FOR FOUR SEPARATE MINI-RETREATS

Introduce the first retreat by welcoming people for the Gathering Activity, and then using the first paragraph of the Retreat Activities. Continue by giving participants the first handout: Zechariah. Read part of the Zechariah Scripture narrative, and then the short descriptive piece on the handout.

Invite people to read the Scriptures listed on the handout,

twice, slowly, and then to enter into the narrative. Invite them to notice what parts of the text they feel drawn to, and to pay attention to who else is present in the story, to listen, to be present. (45 minutes)

Play some music (without words) on a CD or cassette player to signal to participants that it is time to draw this time of prayer and reflection to a close.

Read the descriptive material one more time, and invite participants to be in prayerful solitude and to respond to the reflection questions given on the handout. (45 minutes)

Again, play some music to signal that it is time to draw this time of reflection to a close.

Closing Worship: See description above, focusing the sharing on Zechariah's story and experience, and how God is speaking to participants personally.

Do one character each week. Use a similar format for each of the characters. The worship table each week would reflect the character for that session. Move the Joseph items to the table draped with a blanket rather than placing them on the floor. During the Elizabeth session, the food on the worship center becomes the food for the refreshments.

Waiting in Silence with Zechariah
Luke 1:1-25, 57-79

Zechariah was born into a family of priests
    whose family tree was rooted in soil 1,200 years old,
and whose taproot was Aaron, brother of Moses.

Tradition had nurtured, pruned,
    and shaped his lot in life since birth;
and his work as priest was scheduled by lot.

When his lot came, Zechariah stood alone
    at the altar of incense in the holy place
to pray for the people.
But in his heart he carried another prayer—
    a longing he had voiced over and again.
Somehow the pain of waiting had become dulled by doubt,
    and even though he said the words,
his heart hid from the God who did not seem to listen . . . and so

Zechariah was not ready for God's answer—
    or the birth announcement Gabriel carried from God.

God leads his servant into silence—a desert
    pregnant with the struggle of revisioning:
learning to see as God sees;
    and birthing: for Zechariah enters the silence
as a priest who stands alone to speak to God for the people;
    but he emerges as a prophet
who sits among the people of his community to speak for God.

Reflection
What is your lot in life?

As you sit alone and listen, what are the longings of your heart?

If God answered the prayer of your heart, what would you need to
encounter and surrender within yourself?

Waiting with emptiness with Elizabeth
Luke 1:5-7, 24, 25, 39-66

For long, long years Elizabeth had been obedient but remained
barren.

Now she was elderly, but shamed by her neighbors because she
was without a child.

The lonely hours and days carve deep spaces in her soul. Not
allowing anger and bitterness to trap her heart, Elizabeth
learns to sit in the pain of that space, and thus the table of
compassion and hospitality is spread within her.

When God answers her prayers, her solitude blossoms into a
safe space—for Zechariah and his silence, for the new life
within Elizabeth, for Mary, a young woman needing refuge,
for her neighbors, and forming of community as they celebrate together the naming of John.

Reflection
What emptiness do you bring into this quiet space? Feel wel-
comed, safe, heard.

Who are the Elizabeths who are helping you to recognize the
name, the sign of God within you?

Waiting in Servanthood with Mary
Luke 1:26-40

A young woman who lived in a village was engaged to a carpenter.
   He was not wealthy or well known, but he was a good man.
She was preparing for the wedding
   and was engaged in hopes for home, family, security . . .
until an angel knocked at her door.

"Peace be with you!"
   (What is God's peace like, she wondered. Why is my heart pounding so?)
"The Lord is with you and has greatly blessed you.
   Don't be afraid! You will conceive and bear a son,
and you shall call his name Jesus." (Jesus? In me? How?)

"The Holy Spirit will come upon you,
   and the power of the Most High will overshadow you."
And Mary said: "Yes, I am the Lord's servant."

Her engagement to the carpenter and her hopes
   were all at risk as she journeyed
into the hills of Judah,
   to calm the pounding of her spirit in the house of Elizabeth.

When we say, "Yes, Lord; I am your servant,"
   our lives will never be the same again.
For Jesus will be born in us, his Spirit will overshadow us,
   and we will give birth to God's kingdom in the stable of this world.

Reflection
As you look back on your life, reflect on the Gabriel moments.

What word did God speak to you?

Who are the people who have created safe space for you to speak and to explore the word, the birthing?

Where is saying, "Yes, Lord," taking you?

Waiting for Guidance with Joseph
Matthew 1:18-25; 2:13-15, 19-23

He was a carpenter, and able to read plans
    for building of ploughs, houses, carts.
And he was engaged to be married, and making
    plans for the wedding, their house, and their life together.
But now Mary was pregnant . . . A SCANDAL!!
    in the eyes of the town folk and the Law.
Joseph's reason kept him on the side of the town and the Law;
    his goodness guarded her life (it wasn't his child she was carrying).

Joseph was a good man, obedient to the law
    until his obedience was shattered by a dream!
Now he wasn't used to reading dreams—visions of the night
    which evaporate like mist in the clear light of day.
Carpenter's plans are concrete, square,
    touchable, predictable.
But the dream troubled his goodness, his safety, his respectability:
    THE SCANDAL WAS EMMANUEL: GOD WITH US!

Joseph repented of his obedience to the Law,
    took Mary within his embrace, and with her, the Christ-child, JESUS.
He thought he had embraced the unborn,
    but now his life was held and directed by the tiny child.
THE MIGHTY GOD, THE PRINCE OF PEACE.

Now he became a refugee, his life guided by dreams.
    He thought he would build safe houses,
but now he was protector of Mary and the child,
    a safe presence guided by dreams given by God.

Reflection
How are you allowing Jesus to embrace and direct your life?

What risk is God calling you to embrace?

How is your understanding of God changing as you respond to the dreams God has placed within you?

Thirsting for God:
A Lenten Prayer Retreat

Contributed by Marlene Kropf

PURPOSE

Especially appropriate during the Lenten season, this daylong retreat is designed to increase awareness of our desire for God and deepen our longing for communion with God. Through silence, prayer, simple rituals, and meditation on Scripture, we will be led through parched deserts to rivers of living water. There our thirst will be quenched and our souls revived.

MATERIALS NEEDED

- Food: A variety of muffins or breads, a basket of fruit, coffee, tea, and juice for morning refreshments. A simple tasty menu for lunch.
- Room and furnishings: low circular table for the center of the room, comfortable chairs arranged in a circle
- Worship centers for the table: Session 1—light gray cloth, dark or dull colored pot or vase, bare black branches, small white votive candle; Session 2—small crystal bowl, salt, small spoon; Session 3—silky blue cloth, clear bowl, water, white votive candle, fresh sprigs of green ivy; Session 4—pale blue cloth, silky blue cloth, blue bowl or pitcher, several white votive candles, sprigs of ivy, tray with small clear plastic cups filled with cold water

- Copies: Schedule, handouts
- Music: *Hymnal: A Worship Book*, recorded sounds and music (see plan for suggestions)
- Other: Water poem (see suggestion), paper and pens

SCHEDULE

8:30 a.m.	Gathering
9:00	Session 1 – Walking Meditation: Psalm 63:2
10:15	Session 2 – Thirsting for God: Psalm 42:1-2
11:30	Silent lunch (in a separate location from retreat gathering space)
12:30	Session 3 – Water Blessing: Mark 1:9-11
2:15	Session 4 – Rivers of Living Water: John 7:37-39
3:30	Closing worship and reflection
4:00	Close of retreat

*Note: If you choose, this retreat can be extended overnight. You could begin in the evening with Session 1 and conclude the day with an evening prayer service; Sessions 2 and 3 could take place in the morning, and Session 4 and closing worship in the afternoon.

GATHERING ACTIVITY

Visual environment. On a center table is spread a light gray cloth (a pattern on the cloth resembling sand or rocks in a dry creek bed would be appropriate). On the cloth sits a dark or dull-colored vase or pot filled with bare black branches. A small white votive candle is lit.

After participants have helped themselves to food and drink, they may be invited to gather in a circle. If they haven't already done so, ask them to introduce themselves briefly to one another. Present the goals of this day:

- to examine our desires and longings and become more deeply aware of our thirst for God
- to meet and commune with God by entering into silence, prayer, simple rituals, and Scripture meditation, thus satisfying our thirst and reviving our souls.

As you begin, remind the group that an encounter with God can happen anywhere, any time. But just as we set aside time to be with our intimate friends, so we have come apart this day to open ourselves in a special way to God's presence. Lead the following exercise as a way of encouraging people to let go of whatever concerns or distractions might hinder their attentiveness to God and to open themselves to God's desire to meet/commune with them today.

Prayer Exercise. "Palms down, palms up" (adapted from Richard Foster, *Celebration of Discipline: The Path to Spiritual Growth*, Harper & Row, 1978, pp. 24-25)

1. Place your palms down on your lap as a way of symbolizing your desire to turn over to God any concerns over distractions you bring with you to the retreat. As you listen to your heart and life and become aware of each concern, pray, "God, I give to you (name the specific concern); I release … into your hands today." Wait in silence.

2. When you sense you have released your concern into God's hands, turn your palms up as a symbol of your desire to receive God's gift or response. Pray, "God, I receive your (name what you sense God is offering to you)."

3. Repeat the above and continue with this prayer until you feel centered and at rest.

Lead a prayer on behalf of the group and their journey into God's presence.

Distribute the schedule for the day's retreat and discuss the alternating rhythm of group sessions, silence, and gathering. If you have a signal for gathering, such as a bell, let them know what it is; if not, ask participants to take responsibility for keeping track of time.

RETREAT ACTIVITIES
Session 1—Walking Meditation: Psalm 63:2

As we move into a day of retreat, it can be helpful to spend the opening session walking outdoors in silence—noticing our surroundings, our bodies and our movements, and our inner world. Encourage people not to hurry, but rather to slow down their thoughts and movements. When they meet others on a path, they can offer a prayer on their behalf. This time serves as an introduction into a deeper quietness, a more profound openness to God.

Read Matthew 5:6: "Blessed are those who hunger and thirst for righteousness, for they will be filled." Leave space for silence. Read the text again.

Distribute Handout 1, "Walking Meditation." Call attention to the suggested meditation on Psalm 63:2. Listen to the hymn, "I hunger and I thirst," *HWB* 474, on *Hymnal Selections*, Vol. 3. Invite people to leave and return in silence.

Session 2—Thirsting for God: Psalm 42:1-2

Visual environment: Remove the lit candle from the table. Beside the pot of bare branches, put a small crystal bowl filled with salt, along with a very small spoon.

As people return, again play the hymn, "I hunger and I thirst."

Lead a time of reflection on desire. What do we know of desire? Of yearning? Or longing? Some examples of ordinary human longing may help us get in touch with the strength and character of desire: the anticipation of children for Christmas or of lovers for their wedding; dreaming about a new house or of the birth of a son or daughter; hopes for a job change or for resolution of a long-standing conflict; a deep longing for inner peace.

It may be surprising to some to think of God's longing for us. God's desire for a relationship with us precedes our desire and, in fact, arouses our longing for God. Mechthild of Magdeburg describes both the soul's desiring and God's desiring. She says the soul speaks to God:

> *God, you are my lover,*
> *my longing,*
> *my flowing stream,*
> *my sun,*
> *and I am your reflection.*

God answers the soul:

It is my nature that makes me love you often,
for I am love itself.
It is my longing that makes me love you intensely,
for I yearn to be loved from the heart.
It is my eternity that makes me love you long,
for I have no end.

> —From *Beguine Spirituality*, Fiona Bowie, ed. Crossroad,
> 1990, pp. 55-56. Used by permission.

All our human desires, wants and longings—when fully uncovered or expressed or recognized—lead ultimately to the Divine Beloved. Sometimes we are afraid to face or feel our very deepest longings, mistrusting their goodness and fearing they may somehow be unholy. Yet if we habitually suppress them, we may never discover the true core of our longing, which will lead us to God. Thus, to grow spiritually and to come closer to God, we need to allow our desires to become more conscious.

Increasing intimacy with God actually heals our distorted and misplaced longings. Gradually our superficial wants and desires are peeled away, and our hearts become more open to God, more free to enter the spacious place where God dwells. On a day of retreat, we can pray to see and know our true feelings, hopes and desires. In such vulnerability, God can touch us and transform us.

Announce that after the next period of silence, people will gather for a silent lunch. Make sure details are adequately explained so participants will know how to get food and how to respond to others without speaking or intruding on their silence.

Distribute Handout 2, "Thirsting for God." Call attention to the suggested meditation on Psalm 42:1-2 and the opportunity to write a psalm. If you have access to *Hymnal Subscription Service*, use the following song as a focus for prayer: "As the deer pants" (964, *Hymnal Subscription Service* 2000:1).

As another time for solitude begins, sing together, "I sought the Lord," *HWB* 506. When the hymn is finished, ask participants to come to the table one by one, spoon a bit of salt into their hand, and invite them to leave in silence, tasting the salt and becoming more keenly aware of their thirst for God.

Lunch

Visual environment: Simple, tasty food for lunch should be set out on a table with beverages and necessary tableware. Copies of the hymn, "Come, ye disconsolate," *HWB* 497, should be placed at each table setting. After people have served themselves, play a recording of the hymn. If you choose, you may also read Psalm 42 in its entirety or other appropriate Scriptures or readings while people are eating (do not feel that you need to fill the space with sounds).

Session 3—Water Blessing: Mark 1:9-11

Visual environment. Remove the pot of bare branches. Swirl a silky blue cloth across the gray cloth to suggest flowing water. Place a clear bowl filled with water on the table. Bring back the white votive candle, and surround it with fresh sprigs of green ivy.

As the group gathers, read a poem about water, such as "Water" by Philip Larkin from *Collected Poems*, edited by Anthony Thwaite (Faber & Faber).

Distribute Handout 3, "Water Blessing." Read Mark 1:9-11. Tell the group you will lead them in a guided prayer experience, using the story of Jesus' baptism as the framework for the prayer (don't mention in advance the ritual of blessing at the end of the prayer; rather, let it happen as a natural outgrowth of the prayer).

Invite everyone to close their eyes. Say to them:

> Imagine that you are standing on the banks of the Jordan River. In your mind's eye, see what the river looks like; notice the sky and surrounding terrain. Feel the temperature, the sun, the wind. Listen to the sounds of people walking by or conversing with one another.
>
> Then imagine you see John the Baptist standing in the river; notice his posture and clothing; listen to his voice. Imagine you see Jesus walk into the river and that you watch John baptize him. As he walks out of the water, you hear the voice from heaven that Jesus hears:

"You are my son, the beloved; with you I am well pleased." What do you see on Jesus' face? What is he feeling?

Coming out of the water, Jesus walks toward you. He motions you to come into the water. You stand facing him, waist deep in water. What do you feel? What do you see in his face?

Jesus says to you, "I want to give you a blessing." With that, he places his wet hands on your head and says to you, "You are my beloved daughter ... my beloved son; with you I am well pleased." How do you respond? Is there anything you want to say to him? Stay in the water with Jesus until you are ready to leave.

After a space of silence, begin playing a tape or CD of water sounds. Invite people to open their eyes. Tell them they may each come forward to receive a water blessing. After they receive the blessing, they may depart in silence and meditate on the words that have been spoken to them by Jesus.

As people come to the center table one by one, dip your finger into the water bowl, mark their forehead with the sign of the cross, and speak to each one, "You are God's beloved daughter ... God's beloved son."

Session 4—Rivers of Living Water: John 7:37-39

Visual environment. Replace the gray cloth with a pale blue cloth. Position a blue bowl or pitcher so it is tilted; place the swirling blue cloth (from the previous session) so it looks as though it is flowing from the pitcher. Set white votive candles and sprigs of ivy along the blue water-cloth. On one side of the table, place a tray of small clear plastic cups filled with very cold water.

As people gather in silence, play the song, "O healing river," *HWB* 372, on *Hymnal Selections*, Vol. 3.

During the last period of silence and prayer, we remembered God's promise that our thirst will be satisfied. Jesus, endless source of Spirit, promises rivers of living water, a never-ending supply of thirst-quenching water.

Read Isaiah 35:1-2, 6-7. Note that the desert, an image of dryness and thirst, is a place of profound encounter with God. What sustains us is the promise of water. As the ancient Israelites discovered, from the most unpromising flinty rock, God pours forth a stream.

Distribute Handout 4, "Rivers of Living Water." Give instructions for the dialogue with Jesus. Play "O healing river" again as people leave in silence.

CLOSING WORSHIP

When people have gathered in silence, read Matthew 5:6, "Blessed are those who hunger and thirst for righteousness, for they will be filled." Leave space for silence. Read the text again.

Invite the group to share with one another the fruits of their day of silence, reflection, and prayer. Encourage them to leave spaces of silence between the sharing as a way of receiving and honoring each one's contribution. Emphasize that no one is required to share a reflection, but remind the group that each one's testimony will be a gift to the others with whom they have shared the day. Questions to guide the sharing:

1. What was the silence like for you? Offer a word or phrase to describe the silence.
2. What did you discover about yourself today? About thirst?
3. What did you experience of God? Share your reflections, your psalm, your dialogue, or a song.
4. Do you have any questions about what happened today? What will you take with you as you leave?

Distribute Handout 5, "Closing Worship." Invite the group to stand. Sing "Oh, have you not heard," *HWB* 606, and then read Isaiah 41:17-20 and Revelation 7:17; 22:17 responsively. Carry the tray of cups around the circle; serve each one a cup of water, and invite all to drink together.

Invite everyone to repeat Matthew 5:6 together, "Blessed are those who hunger and thirst for righteousness, for they will be filled." Close with a prayer of thanksgiving for God's rich gifts; ask God to continue to bless each one.

Walking Meditation

1. Take a walk in which you notice:
    •Your body and its movement
    •Your surroundings
    •Your inner world
If thoughts or feelings about other matters seem to want to intrude on your awareness, push them aside very gently and come back to noticing what is immediately at hand.

2. Near the end of the time period, find a place to sit or rest and spend at least five minutes pondering these words from Psalm 63:1
    O God, you are my God, I seek you,
    my soul thirsts for you; my flesh faints for you,
    as in a dry and weary land where there is no water.

3. Return to the meeting room at the appointed time.

Handout 2

Thirsting for God

As a deer longs for flowing streams.
so my soul longs for you, O God.
My soul thirsts for God,
for the living God.
When shall I come and behold
the face of God?
Psalm 42:1-2

During this time of silent meditation, write your own psalm based on Psalm 42:1-2 on the back of this paper. As preparation for your writing, consider the following:
    1. Become aware of your longing for God. To what might you compare this longing?
    2. What makes you thirsty for God? Where are the dry or barren or empty places in your life? What might be the ways you attempt to satisfy your God-thirst with other food or drink.
    3. What do you desire from God? What is your deepest longing? The deepest cry of your heart?

As you complete your meditation, return to the meeting room at the appointed time.

Handout 3

Water Blessing

In those days Jesus came from Nazareth of Galilee and was baptized by John in the Jordan. And just as he was coming up out of the water, he saw the heavens torn apart and the Spirit descending like a dove on him. And a voice came from heaven, "You are my son, the beloved; with you I am well pleased." Mark 1:9-11

Handout 4

Rivers of Living Water

On the last day of the festival, the great day, while Jesus was standing there, he cried out, "Let anyone who is thirsty come to me, and let the one who believes in me drink. As the Scripture has said, 'Out of the believer's heart shall flow rivers of living water.'" Now he said this about the Spirit, which believers in him were to receive. John 7:37-39a

1. Read the above story several times and then try to imagine yourself as a participant at the festival. Create the scene in your mind, the setting with its colors, smells, sounds, the crowd, and especially the figure of Jesus. What does Jesus look like?

2. Imagine that Jesus calls out to the crowd, "Let anyone who is thirsty come to me, and let the one who believes in me drink." What does his voice sound like? What do you hear in it? What is your response?

3. Imagine that you come to Jesus and ask for a drink. What does Jesus say to you? How do you respond? Let the conversation continue. Write it as a dialogue on the back of this paper.

4. When the conversation feels complete, stop. Reread what you have written. Is there more you want to say to God? Does God want to say more to you?

Complete your meditation and return to the meeting room at the appointed time.

Handout 5

Closing Worship

Leader: When the poor and needy seek water,
  and there is none,
  and their tongue is parched with thirst,

All: I the Lord will answer them,
  I the God of Israel will not forsake them.

Left: I will open rivers on the bare heights,

Right: and fountains in the midst of the valleys;

Left: I will make the wilderness a pool of water,

Right: and the dry land springs of water.

Leader: I will put in the wilderness the cedar,
  the acacia, the myrtle, and the olive;
  I will set in the desert the cypress,
  the plane and the pine together,

All: so that all may see and know,
  all may consider and understand,
  that the hand of the Lord has done this,
  the Holy One of Israel has created it. *Isaiah 41:17-20*

Leader: For the lamb at the center of the throne
  will be their shepherd,
  and he will guide them to springs
  of the water of life.

All: and God will wipe away every tear from their eyes.

Leader: The Spirit and the bride say, "Come."

All: And let everyone who hears say, "Come."

Leader: And let everyone who is thirsty come.

All: Let anyone who wishes take the water of life as a gift.
  Revelation 7:17; 22:17

Jesus Walked This Lonesome Valley:
A Good Friday Retreat

Contributed by Marlene Kropf

PURPOSE

On Good Friday we enter the darkest, loneliest valley of human experience. Standing at the foot of the cross, we cannot escape the horror of seeing a child of God abandoned by the Creator. We cannot escape hearing the cry of grief, "My God, my God, why have you forsaken me?"

Participating in a retreat on Good Friday means entering the dark territory of God's absence. It doesn't mean there will be no shafts of light on such a day. Rather, it means being willing to linger for a time in the suffering and pain of the central story of Christian faith. It requires being willing to face the shadow-side of human experience. Through silence, listening, reflection on Scripture, singing, praying, and sharing with one another, participants will stand with Jesus in his lonely hours of sorrow and wait for the promise of new life.

Essential preparation for leading such a retreat is comfort with suffering—one's own as well as others'. Though the day has been carefully structured to create a safe place for the exploration of suffering, the leader must be attentive to the individual needs of participants and be ready to respond with compassion and understanding.

Though this retreat has been designed for Holy Week, it might also be offered for those who are grieving, those facing death, or those who have lived or are living in the midst of war, violence, or some other suffering.

An ideal location for this retreat is a place where the Stations of the Cross are available. If the Stations are not available, a collection of art prints depicting Jesus' journey to the cross can be arranged on tables around the perimeter of a large room (see Session 2). Set a lit votive candle near each art print, and provide a chair where retreatants can sit to meditate on the visual images.

MATERIALS NEEDED

- Resources: *Walk with Jesus: Stations of the Cross* by Henri Nouwen (Orbis Books, 1990) or "Prayers on the Way of the Cross," in *Prayers of Life* by Michel Quoist (Gill and Macmillan, 1963), pp. 116-135.
- Food: A basket of muffins; coffee, tea, and fruit juice (to be available throughout the retreat); a simple lunch may be served, or participants may bring their own bag lunch
- Worship center: A low circular table for the center of the room; <u>Session 1</u>—Rough-textured brown or gray cloth; plain, dark-colored pot filled with bare branches, a few stones or pebbles, wine or burgundy-colored pillar candle; <u>Session 2</u>—A table-size cross (more rough than elegant); <u>Session 3</u>—Black cloth; <u>Session 4</u>—Red or scarlet scarf, large white pillar candle, basket of smaller white candles, container filled with sand
- Copies: Schedule, copies of the Scripture texts, if you choose
- Music: *Hymnal: A Worship Book* or other hymnbooks, tape recorder or CD player, *Hymnal Selections* Volumes 1, 2, 3 for recordings of hymns
- Other: Paper and pens for writing

SCHEDULE

"Even though I walk through the valley of the shadow of death, I will fear no evil." Psalm 23:4a, NIV

9:00 a.m.	Gathering activity
9:30	Session 1 – Entering the Dark Valley
10:30	Session 2 – Walking This Lonesome Valley
12:00	Lunch
1:00	Session 3 – Dwelling in a Land of Shadow
2:30	Session 4 – Emerging into the Light of Love
3:30	Closing worship
4:00	End of retreat

GATHERING ACTIVITY

As people arrive, offer them muffins and juice or hot drinks. If introductions are needed, make sure participants get acquainted. Many Christians throughout history have kept a fast on Good Friday morning. If observing this fast is more in keeping with your practices, offer only hot drinks. If offering muffins, be sensitive to those who may choose to observe a day of fasting.

When it is time to start, ask everyone to be seated in a circle with a low, circular table in the center.

Visual environment. The central table is covered with a rough-textured brown or gray cloth. A plain, dark-colored pot containing an arrangement of bare branches sits on the table. A few stones or pebbles may also be scattered on the table, evoking images of severity or death. A single wine or burgundy-colored pillar candle is lit.

RETREAT ACTIVITIES

Session 1—Entering the Dark Valley

For the opening words of the retreat, read the account of Jesus praying in Gethsemane while his disciples slept (Matthew 26:36-46 or Mark 14:32-42). Invite the group to sing the song, "Stay with me," *HWB* 242, several times. Offer the following prayer:

Lord Jesus Christ,
in this sacred and solemn week
when we see again the depth and mystery
of your redeeming love,
help us
to follow where you go,
to stop where you stumble,
to listen when you cry,
to hurt as you suffer,
to bow our heads in sorrow when you die,
so that when you are raised to life again
we may share your endless joy. Amen.

> —"Prayer for Holy Week" in *Book of Common Order of the Church of Scotland*, Saint Andrew Press, 1994, p. 437. Used by permission.

Introduce the theme and purpose of the retreat (as described under Purpose). Invite people to prepare to accompany Jesus in his sorrowful journey to the cross and his suffering unto death. Let them know the day may be difficult at times. If they find themselves wanting to turn away from painful reflections, suggest they take a brief break (perhaps a brisk walk outdoors) and then return to their prayer and meditation. If they find themselves overwhelmed, assure them they can come and speak to you at any time.

For the first silent meditation, offer the following suggestions:

1. Take a walk outdoors, contemplating the created world. Look for signs of barrenness or death.

2. Bring back a twig or dried leaf or some other sign of death. Set it on the table.

3. Spend the last 15 minutes of the period of meditation writing about what you have seen or felt. What are the signs of death? How do you respond to death? Where are you barren or broken or dying? What is it like to stay with these images of death for an hour?

4. If you choose, return to the story of Jesus in the Garden of Gethsemane for further meditation.

As people return in silence, play a recording of the song, "Stay with me." Invite each one to speak just one word or phrase that came to them in the silence or describes the quality of their solitude. If they choose, they may comment on the item they placed on the table.

Session 2—Walking This Lonesome Valley

Visual environment. Add a table-size cross to the visual center. A rough cross would be more appropriate than an elegant one. Rearrange items on the table so they do not appear cluttered.

Listen to the song, "Jesus walked this lonesome valley," on a recording, or sing it together. This song is found in many gospel songbooks.

From the Garden of Gethsemane, Jesus is taken to trial. Deserted by his friends, he faces the hostile questions and insults of the high priest and other leaders alone. In the morning he is handed over to Pilate for sentencing. Though the entire story of Jesus' condemnation to death, crucifixion, and dying is not often read in the church (or perhaps even by individuals), on Good Friday Christians around the world read the entire account aloud. During this period of meditation, retreatants are invited to read the entire story from John's Gospel (chapters 18 and 19), which is the traditional choice for Good Friday. Offer a suitable contemporary reading as an additional reflection on the Passion story. Each of the following is a deeply moving story or poem, well worth the extra time of seeking them out.

- "The Face of Love," pp. 43-47, from *The Fire of Your Life: A Solitude Shared* by Maggie Ross (Paulist Press, 1983)
- "The Servant of Christ," pp. 80-82, from *Ragman and Other Cries of Faith* by Walter Wangerin Jr. (Harper & Row, 1984)
- "The Execution," a poem by Theodore Tracy, published in the March-April 1992 issue of *Weavings* magazine

For the second silent meditation, offer the following suggestions:

1. Find a quiet, comfortable place where you can read the Passion story in one sitting. Read the story slowly, paus-

ing to reflect on words, phrases, and images that attract your attention. Write those words or phrases in your journal. Meditate on them, letting God speak to you through them.

2. Spend a block of time walking and meditating on the Stations of the Cross. What draws your attention? What repels you?

3. Near the end of the period of meditation, read one of the contemporary reflections on the crucifixion. Spend some time journaling your responses.

After people return in silence, read the following excerpt from *Showings* by Julian of Norwich. Julian was a 14th-century woman of prayer who lived in England. She was given a vision of Jesus' crucifixion and death, about which she wrote:

"After this Christ showed me part of his Passion, close to his death. I saw his sweet face as it were dry and bloodless, with the pallor of dying, then more dead, pale and languishing, then the pallor turning blue and then more blue, as death took hold upon his flesh. For all the pains which Christ suffered in his body appeared to me in his blessed face ... and especially in the lips. I saw there what had become of ... his freshness, his ruddiness, his vitality and beauty which I had seen. This was a grievous change to watch, this deep dying ... The blessed body was left to dry for a long time, with the wrenching of the nails and the sagging of the head and the weight of the body, with the blowing of the wind around him, which dried up his body and pained him with cold, more my heart can think of, and with all his other pains I saw such pain that all that I can describe or say is inadequate, for it cannot be described. But each soul should do as St. Paul says, and feel in himself what is in Christ Jesus."

—*Julian of Norwich: Showings*, translated from the critical text by Edmund Colledge and James Walsh from The Classics of Western Spirituality, Copyright © 1978 by Paulist Press, Inc., New York. Used with permission of Paulist Press. www.paulistpress.com

Sing together "Jesus, keep me near the cross," *HWB* 617. Do not invite spoken reflections at this time. Rather, let people remain with their own thoughts during the lunch hour. Give whatever instructions are needed for a silent lunch.

Lunch

As people eat silently, play a suitable piece of music, such as Allegri's *Miserere*. This moving setting of Psalm 51, a psalm which is often sung during Holy Week, was a closely guarded composition sung only by the papal choir in Rome until—according to some—Mozart heard it sung, copied it by memory, and shared it with others. Many excellent recordings of this work are readily available.

Session 3—Dwelling in a Land of Shadow

Visual environment. Remove everything from the table except the cross and perhaps a few pebbles or stones. Drape a black cloth around the base of the cross.

Begin with this Good Friday reading from the sixth century:

> O Heaven, be struck with horror;
> earth be plunged in chaos;
> Do not dare, Sun, to behold
> your master on the cross,
> hanging there of his own will.
> Let rock be shattered, for the rock of life
> is now wounded by nails ...
> In fact, let all creation shudder and groan
> at the passion of the Creator.
> Adam alone exults.
> —Joan Halmo and Frank Henderson, *A Triduum Sourcebook I*
>   (Liturgy Training Publications, 1996), p. 109

In his suffering on the cross, Jesus enters the darkest, loneliest valley of human experience. In despair he utters the most terrifying cry any child of God can imagine: "My God, my God, why have you forsaken me?" He hangs in agony, abandoned by all but a group of faithful watchers who look on from a distance. Read Matthew 27:45-50 aloud.

Then read Psalm 22:1-19. After verses 2, 11, and 19, invite group members to respond with the antiphon, "My God, my God, why," *HWB* 248. As an alternative, you might choose to sing a chanted version of the text, "My God, my God, why have you forsaken me?"

For the third silent meditation, offer the following suggestions:

1. Reread Psalm 22:1-19 several times.

2. Then rewrite the psalm as your own lament.

What question(s) are you asking God?

What suffering is demanding your attention?

Who is God to you when you suffer? When the world suffers?

What is your plea or your prayer? Confession? Thanksgiving? Petition?

As people return in silence, read another meditation from *Showings* by Julian of Norwich:

> "And I watched with all my might for the moment when Christ would expire, and I expected to see his body quite dead; but I did not see him so, and just at the moment when by appearances it seemed to me that life could last no longer, and that the revelation of his end must be near, suddenly, as I looked at the same cross, he changed to an appearance of joy. The change in his blessed appearance changed mine, and I was as glad and joyful as I could possibly be. And then cheerfully our Lord suggested to my mind: Where is there now any instant of your pain or of your grief? And I was very joyful; I understood that in our Lord's intention we are now on his cross with him in our pains, and in our sufferings we are dying, and with his help and grace we willingly endure on that same cross until the last moment of life. Suddenly he will change his appearance for us, and we shall be with him in heaven … and then all will be brought into joy. And this is what was meant in this revelation: Where is there now

any instant of your pain or of your grief? And we shall be full of joy. And here I saw truly that if he revealed to us now his countenance of joy, there is no pain on earth or anywhere else which could trouble us, but everything would be joy and bliss for us ... And the reason why he suffers is because in his goodness he wishes to make us heirs with him of his joy. And for this little pain which we suffer here, we shall have an exalted and eternal knowledge in God which we could never have without it.

—*Julian of Norwich: Showings,* translated from the critical text by Edmund Colledge and James Walsh from The Classics of Western Spirituality, Copyright © 1978 by Paulist Press, Inc., New York. Used with permission of Paulist Press. www.paulistpress.com

Play or sing the song, "How shallow former shadows," *HWB* 251.

Session 4—Emerging into the Light of Love

Visual environment. Add a red or scarlet scarf to the base of the cross or drape it across the arms of the cross. Place a large white pillar candle on the table and a basket of smaller white candles nearby. Set a container filled with sand near the cross. Light the large candle.

The amazing reality of Good Friday is that God enters human suffering and does not leave us alone. What's more, God's love triumphs over evil and brings new life. Though we do not yet see the full expression of the resurrection of Jesus Christ, we wait in trust and hope for the completion of God's work. As an affirmation of faith, sing together, "O Love that will not let me go," *HWB* 577.

In the book of Hebrews, Jesus is identified as the great high priest who welcomes our prayers and stands with us in our weakness and suffering. During the final period of meditation, we reflect on God's presence with us in our suffering and offer our love to God in response.

For the fourth silent meditation, offer the following suggestions:

1. Read Hebrews 4:14-16; 5:7-9.
2. Reflect on God's presence with you in the midst of darkness or suffering. What is it like to approach the throne of grace with boldness? How are you experiencing God's love? You may want to write a love letter to God.
3. Reflect on how you are being called to love others as God loves you. Who is God inviting you to love? How is God inviting you to love?

As people return from the final silent meditation, invite them to sing the song with which the day began, "Stay with me," *HWB* 242.

CLOSING WORSHIP

Reflect on the day's journey. Invite the group, as they feel comfortable, to share with one another the fruits of their silence, reflection, and prayer. Begin by offering the question: What was the silence like for you today? Encourage them to offer a word or phrase to describe their experience of solitude and prayer on Good Friday.

Then ask group members to find a partner with whom they can share further reflections on the Scriptures, songs, visual art, and silence. If your group is small, you might choose instead to reflect together as a whole group. Conclude this period of reflection by asking, "What will you take with you as you leave today?"

Gather the group for a concluding time of worship. Throughout the world on Good Friday, the church joins with Jesus' self-giving act of loving the world by offering prayers of intercession on behalf of the sin and brokenness of the world. Open the time of prayer by singing, "Christ, we do all adore thee," *HWB* 105. Then invite retreatants to offer their prayers for the world by lighting a small candle at the large Christ candle, praying silently or aloud, and then placing the small candle in the container filled with sand. If you choose, you can play suitable music in the background during this time of prayer.

As the prayers conclude, sing "Christ, we do all adore thee" again. Offer a blessing for each one as they await the joy of Easter morning.

The Risen Christ: Prayers and Scriptures for Easter Monday

Contributed by Mary Schiedel

PURPOSE

Eastertide is a time of great joy and celebration. On this Easter Monday we will sing, pray, and meditate in a setting of celebration and delight. We will leave this retreat more sensitive to the great power that is ours in the risen Christ.

MATERIALS NEEDED

- The location: This retreat may be held in a large home or at a retreat center. All rooms available to the retreatants should announce the celebrative aspect of the resurrection with color, light, and comfort. It is important that people be able to choose their own comfortable spot for silent retreat.
- Worship area: Arrange comfortable chairs in a semi-circle facing the worship center on which you have placed a cross, a large white Christ candle, and flowering plants that provide large splashes of color. Eastertide is a time of great joy, and the mood created by the worship center should reflect that.
- Food: Hot drinks, cold drinks, hot cross buns or other Easter breads; lunch of hearty soup and bread and/or sandwiches of roasted lamb

- Music: Hymnals, CD player with earphones and recordings of Easter music
- Bring from home: Bibles, journals, pens; some may want to bring drawing pencils and art paper

SCHEDULE

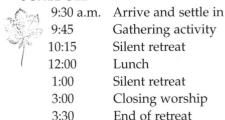

9:30 a.m.	Arrive and settle in
9:45	Gathering activity
10:15	Silent retreat
12:00	Lunch
1:00	Silent retreat
3:00	Closing worship
3:30	End of retreat

GATHERING ACTIVITY

Welcome people to your home or to the retreat center. Introduce retreatants to each other if needed. Offer hot drinks and hot cross buns or other Easter breads. Take care of hospitality issues such as helping people locate the restrooms and feeling comfortable in the meeting place. Show where the coffee and drinks will be found throughout the day. Invite people to gather for the lunch meal if they care to. This is a day of silent retreat with limited structure.

Meet together in the worship area. Invite anyone who wishes to share something significant from the recent Passion Week or Easter Sunday. Then lead in this invocation:

> O Jesus, who called Lazarus from his tomb
> and presented him alive to his friends,
> call me, I pray,
> from the tombs in which I seek to stifle the life I have.
> Remove from me the grave clothes,
> which yet hinder my free movement in your Spirit,
> so that I may truly say, "Alleluia,"
> Through the power of your name. Amen.

RETREAT ACTIVITIES

Celebrate with hymns of Easter and resurrection. Read Psalm 126.

Set a tone for the time of silence and meditation by talking about retreat as a time of knowing Christ so that we may know ourselves, or of knowing ourselves more deeply so that we may be more fully open the Spirit of Christ. We realize who Jesus is in order to know who we are. You may want to read the following quote:

> There is never a time when we can say we are over the peak, we are done. The most precious moments are surely ahead of us. We need to be sensitive to the great power that is in Jesus. He will be with us forever, doing all he can in us. If we could imagine the whole world coming into blossom through one tree, we might have a way to think of each one of us drawing upon the Body of Christ.
>
> —From *Gathering the Fragments: A Gospel Mosaic* by Edward J. Farrell

Ask participants to write down the two Scripture passages for the day in their journals: John 17:1-5 and John 11:17-44. They will be free to take walks, listen to music using the earphones, find comfortable spots to read, pray, reflect, rest, and celebrate the great truth of Christ's resurrection. "This is your space, your time, and God is in this time and place."

The lunch prayer is the Eucharistic prayer for Easter Monday, for in this gathering we too break bread together:

> God, whose blessed Son did manifest himself to his disciples in the breaking of bread; Open, we pray thee, the eyes of our faith, that we may behold thee in all thy works; through the name thy Son Jesus Christ our Lord. Amen.

CLOSING WORSHIP

 Gather again in the chairs around the worship center. Sing more Easter hymns. Invite all who wish to share with their experience or insights with the group.

Close with this prayer of blessing:

> Blessed are you, O God, the author of all sustenance. Fill our hearts with resurrection joy, that in your bountiful providence we may serve you with every good work through Jesus Christ our Lord. Alleluia, Amen.

Called by Name: A Half-Day Retreat for Eastertide

Contributed by Marie H. Stoltzfus

PURPOSE

The season of Easter is the fifty days following Easter Sunday. This retreat should take place sometime in the early weeks of Eastertide. Through prayer and Scripture meditation, we will be invited to listen carefully to what God is saying to us. We desire to hear our loving God calling our name toward faithful living.

MATERIALS NEEDED

- Participants should bring: Bibles, pencil, notebooks or journals
- Worship center: Small table, white cloth with gold ribbon draped across, large white candle, spring plants and flowers
- Other: Small bell or chime to mark time; Play-doh or Sculpey clay and other art supplies
- Music: CD player and meditative music, *Hymnal: A Worship Book* or other hymnals
- Food: Hot drinks; arrange for a simple but nutritious salad lunch. One idea might be to have each participant bring a salad.

SCHEDULE

9:00 a.m.	Gathering activities
9:15	Session 1 – John 20:1-18
10:00	Prayer and solitude
10:30	Sharing
11:00	Session 2 – John 20:19-31
11:30	Prayer and solitude
12:00	Closing worship
12:30	Lunch

GATHERING ACTIVITY

Greet each person as they arrive and introduce participants to each other. Offer hot drinks. Introduce people to the facilities such as restrooms, places where they may spend the time of solitude, and trails or other outdoor spots for silent meditation.

RETREAT ACTIVITIES
Session 1—John 20:1-18

Light the candle at the beginning of each session. Start with centering prayer. Find a relaxed alert posture. Close eyes. Breathe in peace and breathe out tension. Turn your attention to God's presence. Let the mystery of God's presence enfold you. Rest in God's tender love. (Allow ten minutes of silence.)

Introduce the steps of praying the Scriptures if there are people in the group not familiar with this way of praying. (see Appendix A, "Praying the Scriptures")

First reading. Ask one of the retreatants to read John 20:1-18. Listen for a word, phrase, or sentence that touches you. Pause briefly.

Second reading. Have the same reader read the passage a second time. Then beginning with the leader, each person is invited to share the word, phrase, or sentence they received.

Third reading. Choose a different reader. Ask, "What has the Lord said to me in this reading with regard to my life today?

Invite anyone who wishes to share an insight that God has given to do so at this time.

Fourth reading. Choose yet another reader. Read the passage seeking to experience what God is calling us to do now, this day, this week. What are we being called to in our family, our world, in our relationship with God?

Leave and return in silence. Use a small bell or chime to indicate the time to return. Upon return, invite those who wish to share what they sense of God's call and leading. Some may wish to remain silent.

Session 2—John 20:19-31

Use the same process as in session one, followed by a time of silence.

CLOSING WORSHIP

The closing worship may include a brief time of sharing.

Repeat the Lord's Prayer together, then offer this benediction:

> Go out, knowing that you embody the presence of Christ, that you are embraced by God's strong and loving arms, that he knows you and calls you by name as he did Mary and Thomas. Go out believing that you have life in his name. Amen.

End with a nutritious salad meal. Play quiet music that includes hymns of joy and resurrection.

Labyrinth Ritual for Ascension Day: A Mini-Retreat for Times of Transition

Submitted by Nina B. Lanctot

PURPOSE

Ascension is about letting go and listening. Ascension marks a change in the Easter season, moving from a keen awareness of the presence and appearance, the companionship, of the Risen Christ to the absence of the embodied Jesus in anticipation of the coming of the Spirit and Pentecost. It is moving from the known to the unknown, from a familiar way of seeing God in Christ to a new and unknown Spirit. In our lives, we experience many transitions from a known place to an unknown place. In our culture, spring is the time for many of these transitions. Graduations, ending a school year, weddings, and moving are some examples. In our current cultural context we may be moving from a time of relative peace and prosperity to a time of war and insecurity. If we consider the whole year since the last Ascension Day, in our midst will be people who have had many transitions or losses. We all are constantly moving into new times with God.

A labyrinth is a contemplative tool used by Christians for many centuries. Labyrinths are found in many churches in Europe. Walking the labyrinth symbolizes walking with God and walking toward God. The cross is the starting point to construct the classic seven-circuit labyrinth. There is also an eleven-circuit labyrinth design; the most famous is found at Chartes Cathedral near Paris, France.

Note: If you do not have a labyrinth in your area, you can create one. The pattern can be marked out on a canvas that is spread on the floor. See Internet resources below for a picture of both the seven-circuit and eleven-circuit designs. The labyrinth may be used for prayer with a variety of retreat themes. If you choose not to make a labyrinth, you could still have a set walk from one place to the next and back again. You may want to walk to a high area and back. You would need to mark a clear turning around point.

MATERIALS NEEDED

- Helium balloons (one per person); purchase in an environmentally conscious manner. Latex balloons made from rubber trees are biodegradable. If holding the labyrinth walk near the ocean, consider an indoor location. Helium balloons ending in the ocean can harm marine life.
- Food items brought by participants
- Resources: For labyrinth designs, search for "Chartes labyrinth" or "classical labyrinth." To read about one church's experience developing a prayer ministry with labyrinths, see chapter one of *Be Still* by Jane E. Vennard (Alban Institute, 2000).

SCHEDULE

5:30	Arrival
5:15	Gathering Activity
5:30	Walking the Labyrinth
6:00	Fellowship meal and closing worship
7:00	End of retreat

Variation: You may want to have the meal first and end with the labyrinth walk. At the end of the walk, read the John 15 reading and prayer of blessing. This arrangement would more strongly symbolize the movement from the known to the unknown.

GATHERING ACTIVITY

Explain the use of labyrinth as a tool for meditative prayer. Talk about the ways the Ascension theme connects with the personal story of people's lives. For example, for a group of seminary seniors about to graduate you might recall Jesus' presence in the years of study and point to the transitions that are about to take place. We anticipate the new and unknown ways Jesus will be with us during change.

Give a helium balloon to each person. Begin with an opening prayer of blessing for our prayer walk. Share the following instructions.

Now we will be taking a reflective walk in silence. These balloons represent the presence of God in Christ that we have known along the way of our journey up until this day.

RETREAT ACTIVITIES

Read Luke 24:50-53 and Acts 1:6-11.

Walking In

As we walk into the center of the labyrinth, let us remember all the ways God has been with us up to this day on our journey. Be aware of the tug and movement of the balloon. This will remind us of our companion on the journey, Jesus. This may also remind us of other people companions God has sent to accompany us on our way. We may stop or pause in our walking if a particular memory comes to us and we wish to be still and listen along the way. We will take as long as we need to walk into the center.

At the Center

When we come to the center, recall where we are with God on this very day, in this present moment. Allow the balloon to remind us of both your connection with God (through the string) and also God's distance and God's pull on us (as the balloon moves about.) By this time on the walk, the balloon has become familiar to us, just as some ways of experiencing God have become familiar. Give thanks to God for the ways God has been with us.

Letting Go

Our act of faith today will be to let go of the balloon when we are ready. This is not letting go of God or God letting go of us. But it is letting go of the known ways we have been connected to God. We all walk into a future that is unknown. God may want to walk with us in new ways. As you release your balloon, pray a prayer of openness to see God in new ways as our companion in the future. Watch the balloons drift away, and note how it feels to let go of the known.

Walking Out

As we walk out, we will be aware of the absence of our balloon. The path out is our future life. Think of all that is ahead. Continue to pray for an openness to see and feel and imagine the God who is going before us. Listen for the Spirit speaking to us in new ways.

Ending

Before we leave the labyrinth, we give thanks to the God who goes before us.

CLOSING WORSHIP

Share in a simple fellowship meal. Each person could bring soup to be combined into one kettle, and fresh fruit to be combined on a single platter.

After the meal, read John 15:12-13. End with a closing prayer of blessing.

Exploring Creativity: A Retreat for Ordinary Time

Contributed by Judith Guasch

PURPOSE

We are each created in the image of God. This retreat invites participants to explore God's creativity and carry it over into our own lives.

MATERIALS NEEDED

- Food: Hot and cold drinks, cookies
- Music: CD player and recorded meditative music
- Praying with clay: Hand lotion, Indian Red Clay (available in ceramic supply stores and in art stores); form clay into balls and place in small plastic bags (1 per person), cut 4-inch cardboard squares (1 per person)
- Worship center: Candles, wildflowers, blue cloth, large basket and anointing oil for closing worship
- Participants bring: Bibles, journals, pens; two ingredients for a cold lunch to share with the group (loaf of bread, jar of condiments, jam, cheeses, fresh fruits, cold vegetables, salad ingredients—fruits and vegetables should be washed but not prepared into fruit salads or vegetable salads)

•Other: Partnering cards (make pairs of cards with the same flower or bird, these could also be pairs of art print postcards or pairs of cards with matching words like love, faith, hope, peace, kindness); scarves for blindfolds; small bell

SCHEDULE

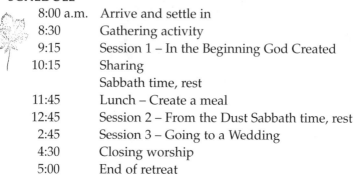

8:00 a.m.	Arrive and settle in
8:30	Gathering activity
9:15	Session 1 – In the Beginning God Created
10:15	Sharing
	Sabbath time, rest
11:45	Lunch – Create a meal
12:45	Session 2 – From the Dust Sabbath time, rest
2:45	Session 3 – Going to a Wedding
4:30	Closing worship
5:00	End of retreat

GATHERING ACTIVITY

Arrange to have two tables, one for lunch items and the other as a hospitality center with hot and cold drinks and summer fruit. Arrange chairs in a circle, with a small table in the middle to hold the worship center. Use your own creativity to arrange the table with candles and wildflowers. Add a cross and a Bible open to Genesis 1.

As people arrive, give them a partnering card and instructions. Retreatants should observe silence, and greet each other without words. They will need to identify their partner with the matching cards.

Gather in the circle around the worship center. Light the candles, as you will at the beginning of each session. Invite people to introduce themselves. Take care of any explanations about the retreat center, such as boundaries of the center. Explain the signal you will use to call people back from the times of silent reflection.

Faith walk. Briefly explain that one partner will be the

leader and lead the blindfolded partner. The object is for the leader to teach or show the blindfolded partner one thing without speaking. Allow ten minutes or so, then switch partners. Afterward discuss what you experienced. What new senses did you use? What creative approaches were you forced to take in this exercise?

RETREAT ACTIVITIES

Session 1—In the Beginning God Created

Read Genesis 1 aloud. Then give these guidelines for the time of silent reflection, which will follow:

- Read Genesis 1 again, counting the words, *created, let, made*
- Read Genesis 1 once more and note what God created. Make a list.
- Reflect on God's response to what was created.
- Reflect on your own response to God's creation. Are there particular places that draw you closer to God? (mountains, lakes, ocean, marshes, prairie)
- Ponder and reflect. Write in your journals if you wish.

Bring together the group with the signal you have arranged. Open this time for about 25 minutes of sharing by those who wish to do so. Read Genesis 2:1-3 and talk about the importance of rest and Sabbath. Leave in silence and return for the noon meal.

Lunch—Create a Meal

Lay out the ingredients brought by participants. Pray a meal blessing. Encourage participants to create a lunch for themselves from the bounty before them. Play meditative music. If the weather permits you may want to have tables outside spread with picnic cloths.

Session 2—From the Dust

Distribute balls of clay in small plastic bags and cardboard squares to each person. Then read Genesis 2:7. Ask people to look at their hands, and examine them for the amazing creations they are. God formed Adam in somewhat the same way that you will be taking clay and creating. Prayerfully listen to God as you hold the clay and work with it.

Invite people to feel the clay, its coolness and its moisture. Invite them to squeeze it and feel how it moves through their fingers. Give these pointers at the beginning.

- •There are no right or wrong creations. This is not about making something good or recognizable but about listening to God.
- •In case you decide to kiln fire it later, you should hollow out thick dense parts or poke vents in the bottom of the clay.
- •You will know when your piece is done. When it is finished, place it on the cardboard and put the plastic bag over it as a tent.
- •When you are finished, wash your hands and thank God for the experience. Clay dries out hands, so feel free to use the lotion.
- •If you finish before the others, please respect their prayer and their silence. You may wish to journal or sit quietly while others finish.

Play soft music during this prayer activity. Afterward, give an opportunity for those who wish to tell about their creation or talk about the experience.

Session 3—Going to a Wedding

Read John 2:1-11 together. Jesus created wine out of water. What would it have been like to be there? During silent reflection reread the passage and imagine the sights, sounds, and smells if you had been there. Where would you be in the scene? What might Jesus say to you? Write the story in your journal from your point of view, or simply take notes on the scene you picture.

Spend the rest of the time until the closing worship in quiet reflection and meditation. You may walk or rest if you wish. During this time, find something from nature that you would like to bring to the group, such as a leaf, a stone, or a wildflower.

(Be aware, however, of any restrictions, and move gently through nature.) Since everyone will be responsible for arriving back on time, set your watches to the same time.

CLOSING WORSHIP

Place a large basket in front of the worship center. Relight candles and play soft music. Sit with your partners in the gathering activity. Allow just a few moments for partners to explain to each other the nature item they found.

Invite participants to a time of sharing and reflection with these questions to guide those who wish to talk about their experiences: "How have you experienced God's creativity today? How might you carry God's creativity into your life as you leave?"

Invite each person to bring the partner's nature item to the basket and give a brief word about why that person chose the item. Anoint the hand of each person with oil. As you place a bit of oil from your fingertip onto the back of the person's hand, pray a blessing of creativity such as, "_____, may God grant you fruitfulness and creativity in your work." Be open to what emerges in the group and allow God's Spirit to move, rather than having a scripted line beforehand for each person. Also, listen for any songs to sing or other words that God would speak to the group.

Suggested benediction:

> Creative God, bless our minds,
> inspire them with your creativity.
> Bless our hands that we might use them
> for your creative purposes. Amen.

Lead Me to the Rock: A Daylong Personal or Group Retreat

Contributed by Joan Yoder Miller

PURPOSE

This retreat is designed to reflect on the biblical images of God as a rock. Through meditation on Scripture and prayerful reflection we will be led to a deeper understanding of God's enduring presence in our lives.

MATERIALS NEEDED

- Music: *Hymnal: A Worship Book* or other hymnals; recording of "Lead me to the Rock." Choose from a variety of artists and styles by exploring the website http://catalog.songsearch.net
- Other: Any time line of historical events; Bibles in various translations; poster with Deer's Cry prayer printed in large letters or an overhead projector and slide with this printed prayer; participants will need to bring Bibles, pens, and paper or journals
- Resources: Optional, *Sing Me Creation* by Desmond O'Grady may be available from a library; *Stone Soup* by Ann Mc Govern (Scholastic, 1987)

- •Worship center visuals: Several draped cloths in earth tones; an assortment of rocks; tall flat candle or a candle fountain with stones; a basket of smaller stones and pebbles for the last session
- •Copies: Schedule and Handouts 1-4

SCHEDULE

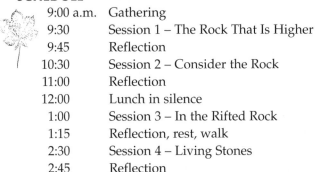

9:00 a.m.	Gathering
9:30	Session 1 – The Rock That Is Higher
9:45	Reflection
10:30	Session 2 – Consider the Rock
11:00	Reflection
12:00	Lunch in silence
1:00	Session 3 – In the Rifted Rock
1:15	Reflection, rest, walk
2:30	Session 4 – Living Stones
2:45	Reflection
3:30	Closing worship
4:00	Close of retreat

This retreat could easily be adapted for a personal retreat. It could also be adapted for spiritual friends in two separate locations who would then share their experiences during their next meeting together.

GATHERING ACTIVITY

Gather participants in a circle. Explain that this is a retreat format that will include times together and alone, times of conversation and silence. The leader will offer suggestions for times of quiet, but the suggestions are an invitation, not an assignment. The aim is to provide a springboard so that participants will be guided in their own prayer and reflection. It is assumed that talking will happen only in gathered times so that a protective space of silence can surround each participant.

Explain that the retreat will focus on biblical images of the rock. Distribute schedule. Get acquainted by sharing your name and a rock you have known (fishing rock or stone in your shoe or landmark rock).

Indicate places to take a walk and boundaries of the retreat center. Some retreatants may need to talk with someone for spiritual guidance. As the retreat leader, be available for a ministry of listening and guidance. Make this known to the group.

Pray an opening group prayer in unison. Post the prayer for all to see.

> I arise today through strength of heaven
> Light of sun
> Radiance of moon
> Splendor of fire
> Speed of lightning
> Depth of sea
> Stability of earth
> Firmness of rock
>
> —"Deer's Cry," an 8th century prayer

RETREAT ACTIVITIES
Session 1—The Rock That Is Higher

Read Psalm 61:1-4. Explain that the direction for the retreat is found in this text, "Lead us, O God, to yourself, the rock that is higher." Play a recording of the song, "Lead me to the Rock."

Distribute Handout 1 and note the guidance for this time of reflection and prayer. Leave and return in silence.

Session 2—Consider the Rock

Read Isaiah 51:1-8. Check to see what other translations of the text are in the group and read the text again from each translation. Notice the nuances of phrases.

Reflect on the enduring quality of rock and on this imagery of rocks as ancestors, as stepping stones for each of us. Say, "I wonder in what ways God is the rock from which we are hewn."

Discuss a time line. Provide a time line of world events with dates to use as markers as people start working on their own personal time lines.

Read verse one of "From time beyond my memory," *HWB* 484.

Read several stanzas from *Sing Me Creation* by Irish poet Desmond O'Grady, if you can find a copy of the book. Especially note the phrase, "found the whole story cut in stone."

Move into a time of prayer and reflection. Distribute Handout 2. Also give markers and long sheets of paper for time lines. Participants will also want to take a Bible with them. Leave and return in silence.

Lunch

At a meal of vegetable soup and hearty breads, provide quiet music or read *Stone Soup* by Ann McGovern.

Session 3—In the Rifted Rock

Listen to or sing a hymn such as "In the rifted Rock I'm resting," *HWB* 526, or "Rock of ages, cleft for me."

Read Exodus 33:12-23. Distribute Handout 3. Note the questions for reflection and the need for a Bible. Leave and return in silence.

Session 4—Living Stones

Read 1 Peter 2:4-10. Talk about how stones differ from the rock imagery we've looked at in the Bible.

At the worship center table, pour several handfuls of pebbles around the rocks, then distribute Handout 4. By now retreatants are familiar with the rhythm of group time and times of solitude.

CLOSING WORSHIP

Invite the group to reflect on their experience of rock and stone during the retreat. Explain that it is not required that they speak. This time is being offered for those who wish to talk. A question might be posed, such as "How does rock or stone connect you with God?" or "What kind of stone has been in your pocket today?" To move things along, the sharing could simply go around the circle; at each person's turn, they take their stone from their pocket and put it on the table, and then either speak or not.

Conclude with the closing hymn, "Jesus, Rock of ages," *HWB* 515. Bless each person individually, for example, "Daniel, may God-our-Rock bless you and keep you," or "Kathy, may you, like a living stone, be built together with Christ Jesus."

Sifting through Associations with Rock
Psalm 61:1-4

For reflection in silence:
Do your own word association with "rock."

If God is like a rock, what does that say to you about God?

Turn to Psalm 61. What do you hear? What makes you nervous? What is good news? What is this Psalm asking of you?

Take a walk to find a stone, one that seems to draw you. Pocket it for the day.

Sifting through the Decades
Isaiah 51:1-8

For reflection in silence
Create a personal time line beginning with birth. Note significant world events alongside family and spiritual happenings.

What do you know about the rock of your own ancestry?

Reflect on your perceptions of God's presence and absence through the time line memories.

Read Genesis 28:10-22, the story of Jacob with a stone for a pillow. What are the hard realities of your life found in the past and present? Are you ready to lay precious grudges, thoughts, and refusals on an altar of stone?

Looking for Rest
Exodus 33:12-23

For reflection in silence
Ponder God's protection and guidance through the decades. Let your mind fill with wonder.

How has God offered rest through the decades?

How and where do you find the cleft of the rock?

Rest, walk, or nap. Rest in God.

Look at 1 Corinthians 10:4 and reflect on Christ as spiritual rock.

Pondering Rock and Stone
1 Peter 2:4-10

For reflection in silence
After further pondering, write your thoughts about the use of "stone" rather than "rock" in the 1 Peter 2:4-10 text.

What would you say is a LIVING stone? A CORNERstone?

Hold the stone in your pocket. What does it remind you of? How does it represent living stones?

A Day of Rest: Meeting Jesus in a Gospel Story

Contributed by Ron and Judy Zook

PURPOSE

Many of us live busy lives filled with demands and responsibilities that are sometimes overwhelming. During this retreat, participants are invited by Jesus to come away to a quiet place and find rest.

MATERIALS NEEDED

- Room arrangement: Large open space for individuals to sit or walk in solitude; indoor area for participants to sit in a circle; indoor space with a few tables to eat lunch. All areas should be handicapped accessible.
- Copies: Schedule and Handouts 1-3
- Worship center: Cloths and candles
- Food: Drinks and light snacks after first session and throughout the day; a simple lunch with baskets of dinner rolls, cold vegetables, and sandwich meats and cheeses
- Music: A CD player and recorded music to play as people arrive at each session

SCHEDULE

8:45 a.m.	Arrive and settle in
9:00	Gathering activity
9:30	Session 1 – Rest for the Tired and Weary
9:45	Time of being with God in solitude
10:45	Session 2 – Rest when Facing the Impossible
11:00	Time of being with God in solitude
12:00	Lunch in silence or in small groups
1:00	Session 3 – Rest for the Journey
1:15	Time of being with God in solitude
2:30	Closing worship
3:30	Close of retreat

GATHERING ACTIVITY

Light the candles and play worshipful music as people arrive. Invite them to have a cup of coffee, tea, or juice and then be seated in a circle. Welcome everyone to this day of rest, a day set apart to be with God. Affirm God's presence in this place. This is a holy place because God is here among us. Intentionally make space for God and invite others to do the same. Recognize the many voices and feelings that arise when one becomes silent, and the intense struggle that can emerge. Acknowledge God's presence in the midst of the struggle. Consider how the struggle is an open door for a new encounter with God.

Affirm the joyous and spontaneous surprises of God. Invite the group to pay attention to how God may be present in unexpected ways throughout the day. Introduce journaling as a way to write a two-way dialogue with God.

Invite retreatants to introduce themselves, giving their name, where they are from, and their work or ministry. Review the schedule for the day and lead the group in a prayer, thanking God for being present and inviting God to move and work among us as we enter this holy time and space together.

RETREAT ACTIVITIES
Session 1—Rest for the Tired and Weary

Briefly introduce the background to Mark 6:30-34. The disciples had just returned from their first mission assignment of being sent out two by two. When they returned, they gathered around Jesus and began telling him everything. But so many were coming and going that they didn't even have time to eat. Jesus noticed the busyness and all the activity. Having compassion, he invited them to a quiet, deserted place to get some rest. But when the exhausted disciples reached the quiet place, they discovered that the crowds had run on ahead of them.

When we go away to a quiet place to get some rest, we often face the same surprise. The demands and stresses of our busy lives run on ahead and meet us there. Tell the story in your own words, inviting the participants to enter into the story with their hearts and minds.

Distribute Handout 1 and note the questions for reflection. Invite the group to leave and return in silence. Demonstrate the music cue that you will give to signal that it is time to return.

Session 2—Rest when Facing the Impossible

Continue to live into the experience of the disciples through telling the story of Mark 6:35-44.

> The disciples request that Jesus send the crowds away. If prayed today it might be, "Dear Jesus, send the crowds away. We are so tired. Please send them away. Thank you. Amen."
>
> But Jesus responds, "Give them something to eat." The disciples face the overwhelming task of feeding thousands of people in a remote area. And yet Jesus invites them to investigate, "How many loaves are here? Go and see."
>
> The disciples returned saying, "What we've got Lord is just not enough!"
>
> And Jesus says, "Don't wait until you have enough.

All I'm asking for is what you've got. No more. No less. Give me what you currently have and are. And get ready to be surprised. Watch what I can do with a willing heart!"

Jesus blessed the loaves and fishes. Then he broke the loaves, divided the fish, and gave the food back to the disciples. And the disciples gave it to the crowd until they were satisfied. It was enough with lots to spare.

Invite participants to reflect on one or more of the questions on Handout 2. These questions are a guide. Assure people that they need not be limited to these nor feel obligated to answer.

Lunch

To continue to experience the disciple's journey, have several baskets of rolls or small loaves available for persons to make their own sandwiches. Invite the participants to eat their fill. Give the option to join with others around the tables or to find a place outside to eat in silence.

Session 3—Rest for the Journey

Invite the participants back into the story by reflecting on how it would feel to have lived all the surprises the disciples had encountered so far. But the day was far from over. It was time for the disciples to leave the quiet place, the place of retreat, and go back to the familiar. Tell the story from Mark 6:45-52.

The disciples are still tired, still waiting to be by themselves in a quiet place with Jesus. Surely Jesus will now send the crowds away so they can finally be with him by themselves. But instead, Jesus makes the disciples get into a boat and go on ahead of him.

Now wait a minute! Jesus should have sent the crowds away, not the disciples! But instead he sends the disciples away by themselves while he goes off to the mountainside by himself to pray.

So now the disciples find themselves in the middle

of a lake, in the midst of fierce storm. "Jesus, why did you send us off by ourselves? Why didn't you come with us? This whole idea of going away for a quiet retreat is going from bad to worse!"

And, it was about to get much worse. Suddenly they see something that looks like a ghost walking on the lake toward them. Scared to death, one of them screams. Jesus is about to pass them by, but when he hears the scream, he turns and begins walking toward them.

Imagine being in the boat with the disciples, rowing as hard as you can, making little progress. And here comes Jesus, walking on top of the water, walking along toward the other side as though there is no wind. As he walks by, Jesus sees your faces filled with terror.

Jesus could have chosen to continue on to the other side of the lake. Walking on top of the water appears to be a whole lot faster than rowing. But instead Jesus stops. He notices the terror. He sees your fear. He speaks to you. "Take heart! It is I. Don't be afraid."

Jesus comes to you, climbs into the boat, and the wind dies down. You are amazed. This is more than just a miracle worker, more than a teacher with amazing wisdom.

It is easy to get so caught up with the winds and the storms that we miss the fact that Jesus is with us. This afternoon we will be leaving this place, but as we leave, God will be leaving with us. God longs to journey with us. God longs to return with us to our ordinary lives.

Distribute Handout 3. Invite retreatants to reflect on the questions and return promptly by 2:30 for a time of sharing, blessing, and sending. Invite persons to bring an object that symbolizes what they would like to share with the group. Remind everyone that they are free to remain silent during this time as well.

CLOSING WORSHIP

As the participants reassemble for the sharing time, play quiet music on a tape or CD. When everyone has gathered, begin the sharing time with a brief prayer acknowledging God's presence among us in this holy space. Invite persons to share any of their experiences during this day of retreat. How have you experienced or not experienced God today? What has spoken to you today? Again remind the group that answering is voluntary.

Conclude with a blessing. Throughout the day, pay attention to how God may want to bless this group. You may want to use one of the blessings of Jesus or Paul. Or use the priestly blessing from Numbers 6:24-26: "The Lord bless you and keep you; the Lord make his face to shine upon you, and be gracious to you; the Lord lift up his countenance upon you, and give you peace."

Rest for the Tired and Weary
Mark 6:30-34

"Come away to a deserted place all by yourselves and rest a while." Mark 6:31

The Lord is my shepherd, I shall not want. He makes me lie down in green pastures; he leads me beside still waters; he restores my soul. Psalm 23:1-3

What is it that needs restoring in my life? In my prayer life, in my ministry, in my relationships?

Identify what makes you feel weary and tired. What has run on ahead and keeps you from finding rest?

What are the green pastures and quiet waters Jesus is inviting you to?

"Come to me, all you that are weary and are carrying heavy burdens, and I will give you rest." Matthew 11:28

Rest when Faced with the Impossible
Mark 6:37-44

"How many loaves have you? Go and see." Mark 6:38

You prepare a table before me in the presence of my enemies; you anoint my head with oil; my cup overflows. Psalm 23:5

Name any impossible situations you face. What might God want to do in these situations? What is Jesus inviting you to "go and see"?

Name any voices that hinder you from bringing your "five loaves and two fish." How might God want to surprise you? What might the situation look like if you did not listen to the voices?

Perhaps, your situation causes you to cry out, "It's impossible, God!" Write out Psalm 13 and personalize it. For what are you crying out?

Now to him who by the power at work within us is able to accomplish abundantly far more than all we can ask or imagine, to him be glory in the church and in Christ Jesus to all generations, forever and ever. Amen. Ephesians 3:20-21

Rest for the Journey
Mark 6:45-52

But immediately he spoke to them and said, "Take heart, it is I; do not be afraid." Then he got into the boat with them and the wind ceased. And they were utterly astounded. Mark 6:50b-51

I fear no evil; for you are with me; your rod and your staff—they comfort me. Psalm 23:4b

How might Jesus be saying to you, "It is I! Take heart! Don't be afraid!"? What creates a storm around you? What stormy part of your life would you have Jesus quiet?

As you prepare to return to the activities of your ordinary life, how is Jesus inviting you to make space for rest and Sabbath? How is God calling you to create places and times of rest? What reminds you to look for Jesus?

For God alone my soul waits in silence, for my hope is from him. Psalm 62:5

Encountering the "I Am": A Spiritual Formation Retreat

Contributed by Sherill Hostetter

PURPOSE

This overnight retreat based in the book of John is designed to call us to Jesus' invitation to make our home in him. During this retreat we will be invited to allow Jesus' healing presence to bring light and to open ourselves to the resurrection power living within.

This retreat requires a setting where people can spread out if they desire solitude.

MATERIALS NEEDED

- Music: Hymnals (suggested songs are from *Hymnal: A Worship Book*), CD player with earphones and recorded music
- Resources: *The Message: The Bible in Contemporary Language* by Eugene H. Peterson (NavPress, 2002)
- Copies: Schedule, Handouts 1-3, map of the retreat center and walking paths
- Visuals for worship table: Grapevine wreath, ivy plants, grapes (session 1), variety of oil lamps and candles (session 2), bread and wine/juice for communion (session 3)

•Other: Oil for anointing, symbolic pins for those desiring silence, alternative to wheat bread if anyone is allergic to wheat

SCHEDULE
Day One

1:00 p.m.	Arrive and settle into rooms
1:30	Gathering
2:00	Session 1 – I Am the Vine
3:00	Individual exercise – Walk, sit outdoors
5:00	Supper
7:00	Session 2 – I Am the Light
8:00	Group guided reflection

Day Two

8:00	Breakfast
9:00	Session 3 – I Am the Resurrection
10:30	Small groups to share communion
12:00	Lunch

GATHERING ACTIVITY

As persons arrive, welcome them and give them their room number and key, as well as a schedule and map of where meetings will be held.

As participants gather back at the meeting area, explain what the retreat will include. Describe it as a time for Sabbath and rest. There will be time for prayer and reflection on Scripture, time for exercise and being out in nature, time to be alone in solitude with God and also time to be with others in community. Describe what the options are for exercise, such as taking hikes.

Talk about respecting each other's need for silence. In order for all to be aware of those who want to remain in silence, request that persons desiring silence wear a symbolic pin or badge so others will know to honor silence in their presence. Explain how and where participants may use music as a part of their retreat if desired.

Invite persons to introduce themselves and state at least one thing they left behind in order to come to the retreat.

Lead in prayer, inviting participants to open themselves to God's presence and voice, let their weariness fall away, and center their hearts and minds in Jesus, the great I Am. Offer up to God anything that was shared by participants that would tend to distract them from being in Sabbath during the retreat.

RETREAT ACTIVITIES
Session 1—I Am the Vine

Begin the session with worshipful songs that center on Jesus being our place of refuge. You may want to include "Thou true Vine, that heals," *HWB* 373.

Read John 15:1-17 from *The Message*. Read it slowly. Verse 4 says, "Make your home in me, as I make mine in you." Ask the group what it means to be at home; home is where _____. Jesus, in whom the fullness of God dwells, has become our home. He offers us the opportunity to enter into intimacy with God. We can be truly ourselves when we are at home in God. But, there's always a choice. Ask the group what little word is used over and over again in this passage. "If" is a powerful word. We have a choice to keep opening ourselves to the intimacy offered us at home in the vine. We remain in his love by choosing to receive the life-giving, whirling, nourishing sap from the vine.

Ask the group to describe what they think it would be like to be homeless. Probably no one has had this experience, but we have seen people who are homeless and we can try to use our imaginations. Describe a time in your own journey when you felt homeless in your walk with God, and how you reconnected in finding yourself at home again.

John 15:5 says, "Those who remain in me with me in them, bear in plenty." Jesus never commands us to be fruitful in this passage. He wants us to be fruitful, but fruit only results from fullness. Fruit is the overflow of life-giving sap. Fruit makes the invisible visible. To be fruitful requires a winter season. A branch is never meant to live in continual harvest. A deeper invisible work is going on beneath the surface in winter before new buds are able to form on the branch. It's a time of vulnerability, nakedness, nothing to hide behind. It's the season for the gardener to gently prune the vine. He cuts away worldly passions and distractions. He cuts some of the little buds off because he knows the branch cannot carry all the forming buds to harvest. God is interested in fruitfulness, not busyness. Fear often causes us to withdraw from the vine or get involved in productivity to produce fruit on our own efforts.

Invite participants to reflect on this passage while on a walk or sitting outdoors. We can open ourselves to being "at home" with Jesus. Distribute questions for reflection, Handout 1. Leave in silence.

Session 2—I Am the Light of the World

You may want to start this session with group worship and/or play recorded music while persons gather.

Introduce this session by explaining that in Hellenism and Judaism, light was a common symbol for the Law. Jesus challenges the meaning that symbol held in his own time by stating that he, himself, is the light of the world (see John 1:4-5; 8:12; 9:5).

Distribute Handout 3, which has John 9:1-41 arranged in dialogue form. Ask for volunteers to read the parts of the characters: Jesus, man born blind, disciples, neighbors, parents, Pharisees.

Suggest that many of the characters in this story were stuck in some kind of blindness. Ask the participants to name the blindness with which each of the characters struggled.

> Disciples—Blinded by their preconceived perspectives on the traditional view of illness and sin. They saw suffering as an occasion for discussing the "why" of it all, while Jesus was concerned about relieving the suffering and pain.
>
> Neighbors—Blinded by what they had always known; they questioned the work of healing because it didn't fit into their experience of God.

Parents—Blinded by their fears. The fear of their reputation
in the synagogue blinded them from truth. They threw
questions back to their son, even though it meant he
would suffer the rejection they were unwilling to face.

Pharisees—Blinded by their own pride. Even when Jesus
pointed it out, no one admitted to blindness and asked
to be healed.

Invite the group to spend a couple of minutes in silence
reflecting on what feels like blindness in their life. It may be the
unknown of the future, a broken relationship, or other situation.
Suggest that there is a part of us that identifies with every character spoken of in this story.

Invite participants to name where they need light and healing from various kinds of blindness. Ask questions from
Handout 2 during the guided reflection time. Allow time for
silent reflection at the end of each section.

The healing of the man born blind was not only physical.
Sight also becomes insight. It means understanding who Jesus is
and having a willingness to believe. First the man saw Jesus as
a man, then as a prophet, then someone from God, and finally
as the Son of man. He then worships him as Lord. Psalm 18:28
says, "My God turns my darkness into light." Invite participants
to sit in the silence and open themselves to Jesus, the Light. Give
them time to be still and attentive to Jesus, the Light.

End this session with an invitation to be anointed with oil
during group singing. Sing "Holy Spirit, come with power,"
HWB 26, and "Healer of our every ill," *HWB* 377. Close with a
night blessing.

> Jesus, light of the world,
> because you are our light and our life
> we welcome the darkness of this night.
> Give us rest and your protection.
> Give us early morning insight
> as we wake to the light of tomorrow. Amen.

Session 3—I Am the Resurrection and the Life

Open with a prayer of thanksgiving for insights that have come in the night, for the light of the new day. Sing "Jesus, stand among us," *HWB* 25, and verse one of "Here in this place," *HWB* 6.

Read John 11:17-27. We lament with Martha at the devastation of tragic and unexpected death. As we see injustice and violence around us we ask, "Where were you Jesus? Why didn't you prevent this from happening?" Jesus' answer is, "I am the resurrection and the life." As we wait for Christ's return, we face problems and suffering in this life. But the resurrection of Jesus offers us hope. The resurrection of Christ demonstrates to us that God is not absent from us, but is most profoundly present and revealed in situations permeated by suffering and despair. Christ's resurrection power is available to us in ways beyond all comprehension!

How does Christ come and stand among us today? Have the group turn to John 20 to examine how the resurrected Christ came to stand with different persons.

Mary was grieving and feeling hopeless. Christ came to stand with Mary in her grief though she did not immediately recognize him. In our losses and grief, we often don't recognize Christ's presence. But the risen Christ comes and stands among us, waiting for our moment of recognition.

The disciples lived in constant fear. Would they be arrested and killed as well? Jesus came and stood among them saying, "Peace be with you!" He gave the Holy Spirit to live within them to give them strength and resurrection hope that conquers fear. That same power is available to us today as God's Spirit permeates our lives.

Thomas had not yet seen evidence of the resurrection. Could he believe? Jesus cared for him in his doubting. Jesus came on a special visit just for Thomas, and Thomas was transformed. Jesus knows when we have difficulty believing and trust grows weak. The risen Christ stands among us and says, "Peace be with you! Blessed are you that believe in me and accept me even though you don't understand everything about me. Blessed are you who can't see the future, but yet you trust in me!"

Ask participants to form in groups of four or five to share communion together. Invite people to share with each other an area in which they need Christ's risen power in their own lives as they break the bread and remember Jesus' broken body. After sharing the bread together, pray for one another. Then instruct them to share together the symbol of Christ's shed blood in the grape juice, remembering that wine comes from the crushing of grapes. Drink the cup with God's promise of resurrection power being available to transform any situation or person.

CLOSING WORSHIP

Sing "Jesus, stand among us," *HWB* 25, or another song as you gather for lunch. At the end of the lunch, gather around the tables with hands uplifted for this benediction:

Now may you find your home, your hope, your life in Jesus.

Abide in Christ. Walk in the light of Christ. Live in his resurrection power.

Amen.

I Am the Vine

I am the true vine, and my Father is the vinegrower.
Abide in me as I abide in you.
Just as the branch cannot bear fruit by itself unless it abides in the vine,
neither can you unless you abide in me.
I am the vine, you are the branches. *John 15:1, 4, 5a*

Questions for prayerful reflection:

O God, what are the distractions in my life that cause me to resist the
flow of God's nourishing sap?

What are the buds of opportunity that God may want to prune in my
life in order to bring more focus and greater fruitfulness?

I Am the Light

How am I like the disciples in being consumed with figuring out how
and why my darkness has come about? Did God cause it? Is it my fault?
Others' fault? Who is to blame? Ask Jesus what he is concerned about.

How am I like the neighbors? Have I become so used to my darkness
that I cannot see glimmers of light entering in? Does God need to stay
within the framework of past experience or can I invite God to do
something new within me?

How am I like the parents, blinded by my fear? Am I fearful of opening
myself to God in this or any area of my life? Am I afraid of the consequences of taking a risk? On the other hand, is this a time to seek God's
protection and care in the midst of great risk?

How am I like the Pharisees who were blinded by their pride? Am I
willing to be vulnerable? Willing to admit where I need the light of
Christ?

John 9:1-41

Characters: Jesus, Disciples, Man Born Blind, Neighbors, Parents, Pharisees

As he walked along, he saw a man blind from birth. His disciples asked him, "Rabbi, who sinned, this man or his parents, that he was born blind?"

Jesus answered, "Neither this man nor his parents sinned; he was born blind so that God's works might be revealed in him. We must work the works of him who sent me while it is day; night is coming when no one can work. As long as I am in the world, I am the light of the world." When he had said this, he spat on the ground and made mud with the saliva and spread the mud on the man's eyes, saying to him, "Go, wash in the pool of Siloam" (which means Sent). Then he went and washed and came back able to see.

The neighbors and those who had seen him before as a beggar began to ask, "Is this not the man who used to sit and beg?" Some were saying, "It is he." Others were saying, "No, but it is someone like him."

He kept saying, "I am the man."

But they kept asking him, "Then how were your eyes opened?"

He answered, "The man called Jesus made mud, spread it on my eyes, and said to me, 'Go to Siloam and wash.' Then I went and washed and received my sight."

They said to him, "Where is he?"

He said, "I do not know."

They brought to the Pharisees the man who had formerly been blind. Now it was a Sabbath day when Jesus made the mud and opened his eyes. Then the Pharisees also began to ask him how he had received his sight.

He said to them, "He put mud on my eyes. Then I washed, and now I see."

Some of the Pharisees said, "This man is not from God, for he does not observe the sabbath." But others said, "How can a man who is a sinner perform such signs?" And they were divided. So they said again to the blind man, "What do you say about him? It was your eyes he opened."

He said, "He is a prophet."

The Jews did not believe that he had been blind and had received his sight until they called the parents of the man who had received his sight and asked them, "Is this your son, who you say was born blind? How then does he now see?"

His parents answered, "We know that this is our son, and that he was born blind; but we do not know how it is that now he sees, nor do we know who opened his eyes. Ask him; he is of age. He will speak for himself." His parents said this because they were afraid of the Jews; for the Jews had already agreed that anyone who confessed Jesus to be the Messiah would be put out of the synagogue. Therefore his parents said, "He is of age; ask him."

So for the second time they called the man who had been blind, and they said to him, "Give glory to God! We know that this man is a sinner."

He answered, "I do not know whether he is a sinner. One thing

I do know, that though I was blind, now I see."

They said to him, "What did he do to you? How did he open your eyes?"

He answered them, "I have told you already, and you would not listen. Why do you want to hear it again? Do you also want to become his disciples?"

Then they reviled him, saying, "You are his disciple, but we are disciples of Moses. We know that God has spoken to Moses, but as for this man, we do not know where he comes from."

The man answered, "Here is an astonishing thing! You do not know where he comes from, and yet he opened my eyes. We know that God does not listen to sinners, but he does listen to one who worships him and obeys his will. Never since the world began has it been heard that anyone opened the eyes of a person born blind. If this man were not from God, he could do nothing."

They answered him, "You were born entirely in sin, and are you trying to teach us?" And they drove him out.

Jesus heard that they had driven him out, and when he found him, he said, "Do you believe in the Son of Man?"

He answered, "And who is he, sir? Tell me, so that I may believe in him."

Jesus said to him, "You have seen him, and the one speaking with you is he."

He said, "Lord, I believe." And he worshiped him.

Jesus said, "I came into this world for judgment so that those who do not see may see, and those who do see may become blind."

Some of the Pharisees near him heard this and said to him, "Surely we are not blind, are we?"

Jesus said to them, "If you were blind, you would not have sin. But now that you say, 'We see,' your sin remains."

Appendix A

Praying the Scriptures: Lectio Divina

by Marlene Kropf

From the Benedictines of the fifth century comes a way of praying the Scriptures known as *Lectio Divina* or sacred reading. The Benedictines were people of God who lived a life of prayer and manual labor. They developed an approach to prayer that encouraged restful silence, waiting, listening, and thoughtful response.

Their idea was a simple but potent one, as revolutionary as the yeast kneaded by the woman in the Gospel parable. If we devote ourselves to meditation on God's word for a few minutes a day, we will gradually be changed; a new person will emerge who looks at life and humanity with a transformed attitude, a person who sees with the heart of Christ.

1. *Lectio* (Reading) Under the eye of God

Begin by placing yourself in God's loving presence. You may want to spend a few minutes in silence, pray a prayer of openness, or listen to a piece of meditative music. Then read through a selected Scripture in a slow, thoughtful way, listening to God's word for you. It is best to read the text out loud very slowly, perhaps several times.

2. *Meditatio* (Meditation) When your heart is touched

Read the text until you come to a word, a phrase, or a sentence that attracts you or touches your heart. Stop to reread the phrase, savoring its goodness and sweetness in much the same way that you would delight in a well-seasoned meal. Let your thoughts and imagination become part of the meditation.

3. *Oratio* (Personal prayer) Expressing to God what is in your heart

Respond to God in prayer, silently, aloud, or by writing. You may be prompted to give thanks or make a confession, to respond to an invitation or warning, to note some connection to your life or need, to pour out your heart to God or to intercede for others. This is the prayer of the heart.

4. *Contemplatio* (Contemplation) Giving yourself up to love

Rest in God's presence. Wait silently. Thank God for being with you and loving you. You are being held by God. Trust the Spirit to pray within you.

Appendix B

Spiritual Friendship

by Marlene Kropf

Spiritual friendships take place when two people agree to give their full attention to what God is doing in their lives and seek to respond in faith. It offers a way for us to be intentional about building up the body of Christ and provides a practical handle for us to carry each other's burdens (Gal. 6:2).

Some guiding questions for conversation between spiritual friends:

1. Where was God at work in my life this week? What were the signs of God's grace to me? What images of God from Scripture, prayer, or worship were helpful to me?

2. What may have blocked God's voice to me this week? Where might I have failed to experience God's grace? What brokenness or failure have I known? What sin do I need to confess?

3. What decision(s) do I want to make regarding the week to come? What changes am I being called to make? What do I want to be held accountable for next week?

ADDITIONAL RESOURCES

Thomas N. Hart. *The Art of Christian Listening*. Paulist Press, 1980.

Timothy Jones. *Finding a Spiritual Friend: How Friends and Mentors Can Make Your Faith Grow*. Upper Room Books, 1998.

Marlene Kropf. "How can we be more accountable to each other?" *Gospel Herald*, April 16, 1991.

Wendy Miller. *Learning to Listen: A Guide for Spiritual Friends*. The Upper Room, 1993.

Barry A. Woodbridge. *A Guidebook for Spiritual Friends*. The Upper Room, 1985.

Appendix C

The Consciousness Examen: A Traditional Evening Prayer

by Marlene Kropf

This short evening prayer exercise is a discipline by which we discover how God has been present throughout the day. It helps us take account of how we have responded to God's love and call. Practiced daily, the examen brings healing and integration, which are essential for deepening faith.

1. Prayer of openness to the Spirit

   Begin by asking the Spirit of God to illuminate your reflections as you think about the events of the day just past. Ask for wisdom to discern God's voice and guidance in your life.

2. Prayer of thanksgiving

   Look back over the day and become aware of God's gifts to you. Don't choose what you think you should be thankful for. Instead, simply let the events and people of the day pass before your mind's eye and give thanks for all you have been given.

3. Prayer of confession

   Look over the events of the day again. This time ask for grace to recognize your sin. Wait quietly until the Spirit reveals what needs attention. Where did you fail to respond to God's gifts? When did you ignore or turn away from God's love? What happened in your relationships with other people? Were you faithful in carrying out your vocation in the world? How are you being called to transformation?

4. Prayer for guidance

Look ahead to the next day. Offer your hopes and concerns to God. Ask God to supply your needs. Give yourself into God's care, and rest in the comfort of God's everlasting love.

Appendix D

Spiritual Check-In

by Thomas D. Harries

Several years ago I read an article in *Action Information* in which a pastor described inviting the entire parish in, one by one, for a spiritual checkup. The rationale behind the meetings was that people regularly visit dentists and doctors for preventive checkups that provide a baseline for later care. Why not a similar visit with their pastor to examine their spiritual health?

After reading the article, I discussed the idea with several colleagues. To a person we thought it sounded wonderful, and also to a person we were convinced we couldn't possibly find the time to do such a thing. But the idea stuck in my head.

When I entered formal spiritual direction and then a spiritual direction training program, I received another nudge toward trying the checkup idea. My director had a profound influence on my life and faith. He also impressed upon me the value of articulating and reflecting upon my own encounters with God. The average parishioner does not benefit from anything like this experience, yet it was transforming my faith. The checkups would give people at least one chance to articulate their faith and have it affirmed. Perhaps, I thought, they would be worth the effort.

Finally, last April I gathered up my courage and approached the wardens with the idea of setting aside most other work during June in order to invite each person in the parish for an individual spiritual check-in. They loved the idea! The senior warden undertook to organize the calling and scheduling of appointments. I wrote articles, made pitches on Sundays, and nearly every adult in the parish was called on the phone and offered an appointment. In the end, sixty-nine people out of perhaps 150 active adult members came.

The people who came, also loved it. A number said they had never before in their lives in the church had half an hour of private time with the rector. Everyone was most appreciative of the opportunity, if somewhat amazed that I would take the time to do it. Most people, I suppose, seldom find occasion to talk of their faith experiences. Certainly few have had the chance to share them with their priest and have them confirmed.

But faith experiences they do have! I can't think of a single person who did not demonstrate a meaningful relationship with God, the Spirit, or Jesus Christ. Different people related most easily to different persons of the Trinity. Many spoke of Jesus as a personal friend who walks with them. Others saw the Spirit of God at work in the myriad details of daily life, and to them this seemed more than mere chance. A few had one or more pivotal numinous experiences, while quite a number found God easily in the beauty and rhythms of nature.

I went home from these days of visits walking on air. People expected me to be exhausted, but instead I was energized and inspired. This is undoubtedly the most fulfilling single "program" I've undertaken in ministry. Imagine, if you can, listening all day to stories about God's presence in your parish. Imagine lay people telling clergy how central faith is in their lives. I came away with a rich sense of how God meets with and dwells in the people of St. Nicholas Parish.

For those who might wish to try this check-in idea, I include a few notes on the process, which may be helpful:

1. Someone else handled the logistics, which was a great relief to me.

2. I drew up about a page of questions, beginning with family health and well-being, moving to images/experiences of God, then to times and styles of prayer, and finally to areas of Christian service. These I regarded as discussion starters. I never worried about getting to the end. Finding that people didn't always understand the questions on the first try, I

also found several ways to phrase each question.

3. We scheduled the meetings every half hour for twenty-five minutes. Generally this was too short a time, but better that than too long. Plenty of value was accomplished in twenty-five minutes.

4. What with time out for sermons and essential meetings, I seldom saw as many as twelve in a day or twenty in a week.

—Originally published in *Action Information* (Sept/Oct 1991), reprinted with permission from The Alban Institute, Inc., 7315 Wisconsin Ave., Suite 1250W, Bethesda, MD 20814. Copyright 1991. All rights reserved.

Appendix E

A Liturgist for Presbytery Meetings?

How can worship and prayer become a more lively part of the work of church boards and committees? The following account of what happened at a presbytery meeting can serve as a model for other meetings. Chuck Olsen, the director of Worshipful-Work: Center for Transforming Religious Leadership, describes what happened when he was invited at the last minute to use the concepts of Worshipful-Work at a Presbytery Meeting. (Worshipful-Work integrates spirituality and administration in church governance.)

> "We first considered the text of the sermon, which was taken from Ezekiel 47, and which offered a rich metaphor—the trickle, then flood of waters from the temple which flowed into an ever-rising, productive river. I suggested that this image could be used to picture the waters from the worship service flowing through the remaining four hours of the meeting. The waters of the text and worship could wash over the docket of the meeting when we inserted brief liturgical elements or practices along the way.
>
> The moderator graciously granted me ten minutes as the meeting was being convened to explain "worshipful-work" and how that might be applied in this meeting. I indicated that I would attempt to respond to what was happening in the meeting and make continuing connections with the inspiring worship which we had

just experienced. Moderator Wigger, who was conducting the meeting from the pulpit side of the chancel, announced that she would turn to me from time to time to invite a response. She also invited me—while working from the lectern side—to stand at any time to make a liturgical offering.

This was a risky move for all of us, for none of us "had ever done it this way before." She would function as moderator and I as liturgist—both working together as a team.

I made a few notes on my copy of the agenda about some possibilities, but as the meeting progressed, none of these were actually used! During the course of the meeting seven liturgical elements were inserted as I was either called upon or was "moved" to respond. The Bible and hymnbooks were used (without instrumental accompaniment). The total time taken for these would not have exceeded ten minutes, thus not prolonging the meeting. Here is a record of what we did:

- Following the interpretation and stewardship report on the "Joy Gift," we stood to sing one verse of a hymn: "Were the whole realm of nature mine...."
- In response to three autobiographical introductions by new ministers in the presbytery, we prayed for them via the third verse of "God of our life through all the circling years."
- With the nomination and election of the moderator and vice-moderator, we affirmed with them our "yes" to leadership and ministry via a repeating sung refrain, "Now thank we all our God."
- In gathering after lunch, we called out the blessings we were seeking in the remainder of the meeting, singing the refrain, "We gather together to ask the Lord's blessing," after each.

- After words of affirmation and appreciation for the faithful service of a departing office secretary, voices were raised together in "Blest be the tie that binds."
- In introducing a process for the consideration of a difficult issue before the church, the body entered an extended period of silence, broken every minute or so with the singing of "Silently now we wait for Thee, ready my/our God Thy will to see. Open our eyes, illumine me/us. Spirit Divine."
- In response to the peacemaking report, Psalm 46, which was sung in the earlier worship service, was revisited and one verse was read/prayed in unison. Then sisters and brothers were invited to pass the peace to one another.
- I made closing theological and liturgical reflections at the conclusion of the meeting to "tie a bow" on the experience. Throughout the meeting I kept calling the rising waters of worship to wash over the presbytery and tried to name where we were—ankle deep, knee deep, waist deep, and over our heads!

Following the meeting, a planning committee observed, "We could do that! Why don't you come back and work with us so that an individual or a team of two or three could serve as liturgists for future meetings!"

—From *Gracious Space of Worshipful-Work*, March 1997. Used by permission.

Appendix F

Seeking Spiritual Direction: A Practical Guide

by Joan Yoder Miller

"To 'listen' another's soul into a condition of disclosure and discovery may be almost the greatest service that any human being ever performs for another."—Douglas Steere

We need places where we can be heard by another who is attentive with us. We need someone who can help us tap into the deeper roots and springs that encourage and inspire us. We need someone who can help us sort things through and make choices.

Originally associated with the Catholic Church, spiritual direction is an ancient resource that now reaches across denominational lines to seekers wanting to articulate the movement of God in their lives.

Spiritual direction is not therapy, doctrinal teaching, advice, or figuring out the answers. It is companionship. Awareness. Listening. Searching. Questioning. Surrender. It is of mystery, of prayer, of obedience, of abandonment to God.

The term "spiritual direction" is woefully wanting, for its concern is not simply with the spiritual but with the whole person, not simply with the life of prayer but with the whole life. Neither is it "direction" in the sense that the director knows the way and instructs another in what to do and how to do it. To the extent there is a director, the director is always the Holy Spirit.

Yet the spiritual direction hour is "spiritual" in that one looks at the Spirit at work in the deepest dimensions of human experience. It is "direction" as it facilitates the finding of one's own path in response to the Spirit's movement. Spiritual guidance, then, is the process of bringing to awareness this deepest level of reality in which one lives, watching for and attending to the presence of God.

A spiritual director encourages the hearing of God's Word, observes the movement of the Spirit, hears confession, encourages prayer, and offers a place of accountability. The relationship is not that of parent to child, teacher to student, or guru to disciple. It's more like the South African proverb that says, "The reason two antelopes walk together is so that one can blow the dust from the other's eyes."

Perhaps the director has a bit more understanding and objectivity, but the Way is a precious mystery to both, informed by Scripture, the life of Christ, prayer, dreams, spiritual reading, creation, and life itself.

Why or when might one seek out spiritual companionship? When lost. When found. When Scriptures seem alive. When Scriptures seem dead. To connect with the inner language of dreams. To sort out God's absence or presence. For accountability. For honesty.

It is perfectly acceptable to shop for a director in order to find a person to whom we can show our less-than-perfect selves and who will speak the truth in love. Beware of a director who has all the answers, who knows with certainty what God's will is for you, or who is in problem-solving mode.

Look for someone who listens, responds, laughs, probes, wonders, prompts, confronts. Look for someone who feels safe to you. Look for someone whose connection to the Gospel you trust. Look for someone who continues to do their own work with their own spiritual director. Ask yourself what matters most to you: Gender? Age? Distance? Faith tradition? Training?

In the first meeting, a seeker might be prepared to ponder a few questions: What matters to you now? What do you know about what you are seeking? What is your experience of God? This would also be a time to ask a few questions of the director.

An agreed-upon evaluation several months down the road can be useful. Generally, a directee can expect a one-hour session monthly.

Monetary compensation for the work of spiritual direction varies. For some, it is always offered as a spiritual gift. For others, it is the means of livelihood. Certainly, it is a costly exchange for both persons. In the U.S., when something is taken seriously, usually a monetary value is put upon it. It is best to ask a director what is desired around money.

Both the offering and the receiving of spiritual direction are a wonderful privilege. Listening and being listened to are precious gifts we can offer one another.

Or in the words of the psalmist: "We took sweet counsel together, and walked unto the house of God in company" (Ps. 55:14, KJV).

—This article first appeared in *Timbrel,* September/October 2000, and is reprinted with permission from the author.

Finding a Spiritual Director

Spiritual directors rarely hang out a shingle, so how are they found?

The Executive Board Office of Congregational Life lists Mennonite spiritual directors on the web at www.mennonite-usa.org/executive/congregational_life. A pastor of friend may be able to make a recommendation. Retreat centers may offer direction or can point the way to finding it. You can also check with a nearby training center listed on the Spiritual Directors International site at www.sdiworld.org.

Or it may be as simple as asking someone if he or she would become a spiritual companion to you. As Henri Nouwen once said, "Many would become wise and holy for our sake if we'd invite them to assist us in our search for the prayer of the heart."

Appendix G

Centering Prayer: Be Still and Know that I Am God

by Marlene Kropf

Rooted in the prayer tradition of the Psalms where we are reminded, "Be still and know that I am God" (Ps. 46:10), centering prayer is a simple, wordless way of praying that makes space for simply being with God and becoming more deeply aware of God's presence. Just as two people who are truly close friends do not need to spend all their time talking when they are together, so the soul and God can enjoy a quiet, deep communion that goes beyond words.

Not meant to replace other forms of prayer, centering prayer is practiced not only for the intimacy with God it nourishes but also for the fruits of love and joy it produces. As those who practice centering prayer reach a place of interior silence and peace, they are more and more able to turn away from practicing violence and aggression in the world. They become "blessed peacemakers" who radiate God's love and peace.

TO GET STARTED

1. Find a place to pray that is quiet and relaxed. Sit in silence, breathing deeply and setting aside the concerns of the day. If your body is tense, spend some moments consciously relaxing each part of the body.

2. Focus your attention on God. Become aware of God's presence surrounding you and allow yourself to be present to God.

3. Choose a word for God as a focus for your prayer. A one-syllable word works best—Love, Peace, Joy, Christ, Friend, etc. Slowly and effortlessly, repeat the word until you become more and more deeply aware of God's presence at the center of your being.

4. Continue to wait in God's presence. If you find yourself straying from your awareness of God or if other thoughts intrude, gently return to the word you have chosen. Let God draw you into wordless communion of adoration, love, and praise.

5. When your prayer feels complete, slowly leave the silence at the center and return to words—perhaps offering the Lord's Prayer as a conclusion, savoring the words and meaning of the prayer.

ADDITIONAL GUIDANCE

Because many people have little practice with sustained silence, centering prayer can begin with as short a time as 5-10 minutes. Later, it can expand to 20-30 minutes a day (some prefer to spend time both morning and evening in centering prayer).

Many people have difficulty dealing with stray thoughts in the beginning. Thomas Keating, in his guide to centering prayer, offers helpful guidance with two images. One is that of tuning a radio from long wave to short wave. "If you want to hear stations from far away, you have to turn to the other wave length." The second image is of our thoughts as boats packed on a river so tightly that we forget the river on which they float. "The prayer of centering is a method of directing our attention from the boats to the river on which they are resting." In centering prayer we practice an "intimate kind of self-denial" and let go of our own thoughts and feelings (*Finding Grace at the Center*, St. Bede's Publications, 1978, pp. 24-34).

When practiced regularly, centering prayer becomes a place of integration and peace. It is the source from which a faithful life of worship and obedience can grow, and it prepares us to enjoy God's presence as we "dwell in the house of the Lord" (Ps. 23:6) forever.

Appendix H

Spiritual Resources for Retreat Leaders

by Marlene Kropf

Bohler, Carolyn Stahl. *Opening to God: Guided Imagery Meditation on Scripture.* Upper Room Books, 1996. Scripture-based meditations with step-by-step instructions for leading individuals and groups in praying Scripture. Includes guidelines for the use of imagery.

Foster, Richard J. *Prayer: Finding the Heart's True Home.* Harper-SanFrancisco, 1992. Includes 21 chapters, each describing a different type of prayer, with examples and prayer exercises.

Guenther, Margaret. *Holy Listening: The Art of Spiritual Direction.* Cambridge, Mass.: Cowley Publications, 1992. Warm, untechnical guide to the ministry of spiritual direction. Good background reading for anyone who leads spiritual retreats.

Hall, Thelma. *Too Deep for Words: Rediscovering Lectio Divina.* Paulist Press, 1988. Introduces Lectio Divina and includes 500 suggested Scripture texts for prayer.

Halverson, Delia. *Teaching Prayer in the Classroom: Experiences for Children and Youth.* Rev. ed. Abingdon Press, 2003. Contains practical, step-by-step activities to engage children in many different prayer experiences. Presents sound theological, theoretical, and educational principles.

Keating, Abbot Thomas. *Finding Grace at the Center.* St. Bede's Publications, 1978. Simple guide to the ancient practice of centering prayer.

Kropf, Marlene, and Eddy Hall. *Praying with the Anabaptists: The Secret of Bearing Fruit.* Faith & Life Press, 1994. Using John 15-17 as a biblical foundation, this guide to prayer includes fifteen meditations with Scripture, stories from the early Anabaptists, hymns, and prayer exercises. Exercises for "Lectio Divina" (praying Scripture) and the "consciousness examen" (prayer of reflection) are included.

Linn, Dennis, Sheila Fabricant Linn, and Matthew Linn. *Sleeping with Bread: Holding What Gives You Life.* Paulist Press, 1995. Delightful presentation of the "consciousness examen," with suggestions for personal, family, and group use.

Miller, Wendy. *Invitation to Presence: A Guide to Spiritual Disciplines.* Upper Room Books, 1995. Combines reflections on Scripture, contemporary anecdotes, and simple exercises to introduce the spiritual disciplines. Provides challenge for both beginners and experienced folk.

Mulholland, M. Robert, Jr. *Shaped by the Word: The Power of Scripture in Spiritual Formation.* Rev. ed. Upper Room Books, 2002. The best guide for understanding both the formative and informative use of Scripture in spiritual formation. Emphasizes listening for the voice of God in Scripture.

Newell, J. Philip. *Celtic Prayers from Iona.* Paulist Press, 1997. *Celtic Benediction: Morning and Night Prayer.* Eerdmans, 2000. *Sounds of the Eternal: A Celtic Psalter.* Eerdmans, 2002. Three collections of simple, beautifully poetic Celtic prayers for use in morning and evening prayer settings.

Thompson, Marjorie J. *Soul Feast: An Invitation to the Christian Spiritual Life.* Westminster John Knox Press, 1995. Clearly written guide for exploring the riches of spiritual disciplines, as well as instruction in developing and nurturing those practices. Includes discussions of prayer, spiritual reading, worship, fasting, self-examination, and hospitality.

Vennard, Jane E. *Be Still: Designing and Leading Contemplative Retreats*. Alban Institue, 2000. How-to guide for designing and leading contemplative retreats. Includes reflections on the nature and use of silence, prayer, spiritual friendship, home retreats, and guided meditations.

———. *Praying with Body and Soul: A Way to Intimacy with God*. Augsburg, 1998. A biblically-grounded resource with simple and imaginative suggestions for ways to pray through our bodies, through our emotions and relationships, and through our work in the world.

Wiederkehr, Macrina. *The Song of the Seed: A Monastic Way of Tending the Soul*. HarperSanFrancisco, 1995. An at-home retreat guide with meditations to nurture spiritual retreat leaders.

The Editor

Rose Mary Stutzman is an educator, writer, and editor. She is currently living in Nairobi, Kenya, where she and her husband Mervin are completing a three-year Mennonite Central Committee service assignment. Prior to that she served as children's editor and director of Faith & Life Resources at Mennonite Publishing House.